The Rise and Fall of Air Force Cambridge Research Laboratories

Edward E. Altshuler

Table of Contents

Table of Figures

Preface

This monograph provides a chronological account of a fledgling research laboratory, which evolved from the MIT Radiation Laboratory and the Harvard Radio Research Laboratory after World War II, rose to become one of the premier research laboratories in the world as evidenced by its major accomplishments throughout its 66 year history. After many years of outstanding productivity the laboratory was slowly downsized. Even though the downsizing began in1974, the Hanscom Research Site continued to be very productive until its final days. In 2005 it was placed on the Base Realignment And Closure (BRAC) list and in August 2011 it was closed. Many of the major events that led to this decline were politically motivated. I had the privilege of collaborating with outstanding scientists from May 1960 to May 2011 and was blessed with a very rewarding career. However, as a supervisor and as a bench scientist, I never liked to be subjected to situations that consumed an unnecessary amount of my time or that of the employees under me. Fortunately, these events did not occur very often, but I have discussed some of my "pet peeves". One of the most ironic outcomes of the AFCRL history was the fact that when the laboratory was first established, the original plan was to move the new laboratory to Wright Field in Dayton, Ohio in 1946; this move actually occurred 65 years later. Also, over the years, there were numerous attempts to move the Geophysics Research Directorate (GRD) to Kirtland AFB, New Mexico. This also occurred in 2011.

Acknowledgements

First I wish to thank Dr. Ruth Liebowitz, former historian of the Air Force Geophysics Laboratory who published two Chronologies on the AFRL Hanscom Field Site and its predecessor laboratories covering the periods from its inception in 1945 to 1985 and then from 1985 to 1995. These Chronologies documented most of the major events that took place over that 50-year period and I was able to use this information, as a starting point, to prepare many of the more detailed accounts that are provided in this book. I also wish to thank my wife, Dr. Ruth Altshuler and my sons Dr. David Altshuler and Bob Altshuler for taking the time to review and edit this manuscript. Finally, I wish to thank members of the SAVE Committee for their effort in successfully fending off previous closures and moves and for the battle that they waged in trying to rescind BRAC 2005.

Chapter 1: Introduction

It was the worst of times. World War II had begun in September 1939 with the German invasion of Poland. Realizing that the United States may be eventually drawn into the War, it was decided that the government should establish a research and development laboratory to study technologies that would be applicable for the war effort. Shortly before the onset of World War II, it was realized by the UK and US that radar systems would play an important role in the war effort. One of the key components of the radar system was the cavity magnetron, which was being developed by the British at the University of Birmingham. The plan was to export this technology to the United States for further development and production. Other areas of interest were microwave physics, electromagnetics, communications and properties of matter. In October 1940, the government established a new laboratory at the Massachusetts Institute of Technology; it was named the Radiation Laboratory and became more commonly known as the MIT Rad Lab. The Rad Lab eventually grew in size to employ about 4,000 scientists, engineers, technicians and support personnel. Another laboratory, which conducted research and development in the general area of radar countermeasures, was later established at Harvard University in 1942. It was named the Harvard Radio Research Laboratory. It reached a peak employment of close to 900 employees.

The end of World War II resulted in the closure of the MIT and Harvard laboratories. Since these labs had proved very valuable during the War years, the Army Air Forces decided to continue to support electronics research during peacetime. At the time, the Army Air Forces had electronics laboratories located at Wright Field, Dayton, Ohio and the Watson Laboratories at Red Bank, New Jersey. An interim laboratory would be established in Cambridge, Massachusetts. The Army proceeded to send a team of Officers from Watson Laboratories in New Jersey to recruit the highly skilled workforce from MIT and Harvard to work in a new Army Air Forces laboratory. It would be initially supervised by the Watson Laboratories and the plan was to later transfer it to a permanent location at Wright Field. This laboratory was named the Watson Laboratories Cambridge Field Station (CFS).

As the years went by the Laboratory underwent many reorganizations and name changes. The Cambridge Field Station, (September 1945-July 1949) was later designated the Air Force Cambridge Research Laboratories (July 1949-July 1951) and then named Air Force Cambridge Research Center (July 1951-May 1960). In May 1960, it was for a very short period of time called Detachment 2 of the Air Force Research Division, however, it was renamed Air Force Cambridge Research Laboratories (AFCRL) in August 1960 and it kept that name until it was closed in

January 1976. Throughout its first 21 years AFCRL had developed into one of the finest research laboratories in the world.

However, the following events, which will be described in detail, would eventually lead to the demise of AFCRL and its successor Laboratories at the Hanscom Research Site

- 1969 - The Mansfield Amendment
- 1970 - The closure of the Office of Aerospace Research
- 1974 - The Chapman Report
- 1976 - The splitting of the Air Force Cambridge Research Laboratories into the Air Force Geophysics Laboratory (AFGL) and the merging of the former Electronics Research Directorate into the Rome Air Development Center (RADC)
- 1990 - Air Force Space Technology Center study to move AFGL to Kirtland AFB, NM
- 1990 - The further reorganization of RADC into Rome Laboratory and AFGL into Phillips Laboratory along with other Air Force research laboratories to form four "Superlabs"
- 1996 - Program Objective Memorandum (POM) that would zero fund the Geophysics Directorate Exploratory Development (6.2) and Advanced Development (6.3) funding
- 1997 - The consolidation of the "Superlabs" into one Air Force Research Laboratory (AFRL)
- 1999 - The attempted closure of the Electromagnetics Technology Division
- 2005 - Finally, the announcement of the Base Realignment and Closure (BRAC) of the Air Force Hanscom Research Site that led to its close in the summer of 2011

I arrived at AFCRL in May 1960 to work in the Electromagnetic Radiation Laboratory. I was familiar with the Lab, since they had supported both my Master's thesis on "Microwave Strip Transmission Lines" in 1954 at Tufts College and my doctoral thesis on "The Travelling Wave Linear Antenna" in 1960 at Harvard University. I considered it an excellent opportunity to work with this outstanding group of scientists and engineers. As part of the Office of Aerospace Research (OAR), the emphasis was on conducting quality basic research and most important, publishing the results. Relevance to Air Force applications was not mandatory, so we had a research atmosphere similar to that of a university, but without the need to solicit research funds. Throughout the course of its history, AFCRL had many significant accomplishments. I tried to focus on those accomplishments, which were both most noteworthy and for which I also had sufficient information to document their details.

Chapter 2: The Recruitment Process

The end of World War II brought about the closure of the Office of Scientific Research and Development (OSRD) and the National Defense Research Council (NDRC). These two organizations, which were created by Executive Order to mobilize scientific manpower and facilities and to coordinate research and development on weapons and devices of warfare had performed admirably during the war years. The MIT Rad Lab and the Harvard Radio Research Lab had been conducting electronics research for the Army Air Forces under OSRD. Personnel at these laboratories were among the country's most capable scientists and engineers. On 13 August 1945, interviewing of personnel for positions at a new Army Air Forces (AAF) research laboratory, which would be called the Cambridge Field Station (CFS) would commence. As of 3 September 1945, 852 people had been interviewed and 563 had tentatively agreed to work for the Laboratory. On 18 September 1945, it was requested by Colonel Oscar C. Maier, Commanding Officer of Watson Laboratories, that the Cambridge Field Station be established by Headquarters, Air Technical Services Command (ATSC), as a Class III installation, under the provisions of ATSC Regulation 55-6 and 55-6a. The organizational structure of the station would closely follow that of the Watson Laboratories and on 20 September 1945 the Cambridge Field Station of Watson Laboratories was officially established with the following mission.

> "The mission of the Cambridge Field Station is to assume and execute the functions of research and development of radio and radar equipment peculiar to the AAF, transferred to the ATSC from the National Defense Research Committee. The Cambridge Field Station will serve as an agency for the assimilation of facilities, personnel and projects during the transition period prior to physical transfer of its facilities to Headquarters, Watson Laboratories and to other activities of the ATSC."

It was decided that the main location of the Cambridge Field Station would be 224-230 Albany Street, Cambridge, MA. A photo of the entrance is shown in Fig. 1 and a photo of the research laboratory buildings are shown in Fig. 2. While the building at 224 Albany Street was government owned, the building at 230 Albany Street was owned by Remington Rand Corporation and leased to OSRD. A problem arose in CFS taking over the building in that Remington Rand wanted to sell the building, while the Government wanted to lease it. A lease was finally signed on 14 December 1945. In addition to the Albany Street location, outlying facilities at the Ipswich Antenna Station and the Bedford Army Air Field would be utilized.

Figure 1 Entrance to AFCRL at 230 Albany St

Figure 2 224-230 Albany Street

The following memo from Gen H.H. (Hap) Arnold, Army Air Forces was forwarded by Dr. L. A. DuBridge, Director of the MIT Radiation Laboratory, for the staff members.

RADIATION LABORATORY
Massachusetts Institute of Technology
Cambridge, Massachusetts
October 26, 1945
Memorandum to: All Staff Members
From: L. A. DuBridge, Director

The following is a copy of a telegram addressed to the Director and the Staff Members of the Radiation Laboratory from General of the Army H. H. Arnold, Commanding General, Army Air Forces. This is being circulated to all Staff Members for their information.

Radiation Laboratory
Massachusetts Institute of Technology
Cambridge, Massachusetts
Attention: Director and Staff Members

I have been informed of the attempt now being made by the Air Technical Service Command, Wright Field, Dayton, Ohio to interest many of the senior Staff Members of the Radiation Laboratory, Massachusetts Institute of Technology, in accepting high-level positions with the Army Air Forces at Cambridge Field Station. This is to facilitate the absorption of research and development functions and personnel in order to carry on the work being terminated at Radiation Laboratory, which I consider to be of vital interest. I cannot overemphasize the importance of our future Air Force of research and development work in the electronic field, which I feel your senior Staff Members are capable of carrying out. To this end I would appreciate your giving serious consideration to the proposals of Air Technical Service Command for post-war employment. I would deem it a privilege to have you continue to work for the Army Air Forces to carry on the work you have so ably participated in during the war just ended.
(signed)
H. H. Arnold
General, Army Air Forces

Scientists and engineers were concerned that employment by a government laboratory might have the strict Civil Service rules and procedures that would be contrary for a research establishment. This was due partially to the fact that during the war, in some service laboratories, these situations had existed, which made them undesirable places to conduct research. Some of the basic grievances were the administration of scientific establishments by managers who were not qualified for such tasks and a concern of government "red tape." However, one of the attractions was that the laboratory would be located, at least temporarily, in the Boston area and many employees would be able to continue to live in their current homes. Also, Boston was considered to be an up and coming electronics area and had the advantage of being able to utilize the resources of Harvard, MIT and other top notch universities. Finally, the people being interviewed were given the overall picture of what to expect while employed by the Army Air Forces and this frank handling of the situation served to dispel a number of their previous concerns.

On 6 November 1945, a letter from personnel of the MIT Rad Lab and Harvard Radio Research Lab was sent to Dr. E.L. Bowles, Expert Consultant of the Office of the Secretary of War concerning future employment with the Army Air Forces. Their main concern was that the information provided to them had been too vague and that they would like clarification regarding a number of the following issues.

- "How long will the Cambridge Field Station (CFS) remain in Cambridge, MA and is it possible that it could remain there for at least 18 months? (It was stated that if the CFS were to remain in Boston for only a few months, then it would hardly be worthwhile to move equipment to a location in Cambridge for this short period of time.)
- What will be the permanent location of the personnel hired by the Cambridge Field Station? (The consensus of the personnel would be to preferably be relocated well north of Washington, DC or on the Pacific coast but not in the south.)
- Can the laboratory be located near a university?
- Will adequate housing and good schools be available?
- Will the personnel of the CFS become a research group of the Army Air Forces that will be kept as a unit?
- Is there a strong directive that this organization will exist whether sufficient people are enrolled from the CFS or not?
- Will the personnel of the CFS have the freedom to conduct research and development and also help determine the policy regarding research?
- Will the "red tape" that often accompanies a government organization be held to a minimum?
- What procedures are being contemplated to permit top research civilians to be heard at a high level?

- What would be the final form of such a research group organizationally and who would provide the control and supervision of the lab?"

On 19 November 1945, a letter was sent to Dr. Bowles from BGen Tom C. Rives, Chief of the Electronic Engineering Subdivision of Watson Laboratory regarding the questions that had been raised by the potential employees for the CFS. He prefaced his remarks by stating "the plan must be approved by Congress and the War Department in the final analysis."

- "It is planned to move the CFS to Wright Field at the earliest date that facilities, both working and housing can be made available. It is estimated that this move may start as early as January 1946 and be completed by June 1946. However, realizing that there is currently no space available at Wright Field to accommodate personnel nor is there sufficient housing available in the Dayton area, this move could be delayed.
- The Electronic Subdivision currently has a contract with Ohio State University (OSU) and arrangements are being made to accredit engineering personnel as instructors of OSU. Consideration is also being given to detailing certain engineering personnel to OSU with the intent of having them work on government contracts with the university.
- The local schools, both grammar and high school are believed to be on a par with schools of like size in the United States and in many instances superior.
- There will be a strong electronic research and development laboratory regardless of the number of people obtained from the CFS. While it is desired that as many as possible of the high caliber personnel from the CFS transfer to Wright Field, the Army Air Forces will still have the responsibility for continuing a research and development program.
- High caliber civilian and officer personnel have been on committees and boards that consider plans and policies for electronics research and there is no intention of changing this policy.
- It is anticipated that the personnel recruited will eventually be integrated into the proposed post-war Electronic Subdivision. Normally, it is not contemplated that pure research will be performed at Wright Field but will be procured by contract from colleges, universities and industrial laboratories. However, some research for which the facilities are available at Wright Field, but not available at other locations, will be performed at Wright Field."

This response proved to be satisfactory to the new employees of the Cambridge Field Station.

Chapter 3: The Early Years of the Cambridge Field Station (1945-1949)

On 20 September 1945, Major John W. Marchetti, on temporary duty at CFS, was named Acting Commanding Officer of the new Cambridge Field Station. In July 1946, under the leadership of Col Francis H. Richardson and his assistant chief, Wilfred Champlain, the technical portion of CFS was organized as a Radio Physics Research Division, which would initially consist of four components laboratories and six systems laboratories. The Components Laboratories were
- Antenna
- RF Components
- Mechanical and Electrical Engineering
- Electronic Components.

The Systems Laboratories were
- Ground Radar
- Navigation
- Communications
- Relay Systems
- Countermeasures
- Special Studies

Fifteen projects from MIT and Harvard would be transferred to these Laboratories. Laboratory Chiefs were Dr. Sherrard B. Welles, Dr. Marcus D. O'Day, Dr. Edward W. Samson, Dr. Donald D. Foster, Dr. Lowell M. Hollingsworth, Mr. Charles Davis, Dr. Robert F. Nicholson, Mr. Horace MacKechnie and Dr. Harry Stockman.

By June 1946, the Station had grown to 770 personnel, 350 scientists, engineers and technicians and 420 support and administrative personnel. In June 1947, the Commonwealth of Massachusetts and the Army Air Corps signed a 5-year lease for joint use of Hanscom Field until 30 June 1952.

On 26 March 1947, the Air Staff for Research and Development at Army Air Forces Headquarters directed through the following letters that the responsibility for research and development in meteorology and related geophysical fields be transferred from the Air Weather Service (AWS) to the Air Materiel Command (AMC). A group of four expert AWS personnel were transferred to AMC to form the nucleus of a staff for its new functions.

WAR DEPARTMENT
HEADQUARTERS ARMY AIR FORCES
Washington, D. C.
AFDRE-2A 26 March 1947
SUBJECT: Meteorological Research and Development Responsibilities
in the Air Forces
TO: Commanding General
Air Materiel Command
Wright Field, Dayton, Ohio
Attention: Chief of Administration

1. Responsibilities for research and development in meteorology and related geophysical fields as assigned to the Army Air Forces and referred to in AR 95-150, dated 19 May 1945, and delegated to the Air Weather Service by AAF Regulation 20-58, dated 1 July 1945, are hereby redelegated to your Command. Appropriate charges to existing AAF regulations pertaining to these responsibilities will be issued at a later date.

2. Army Air Forces and War Department requirements for atmospheric research and development go far beyond the problems of forecasting weather in the troposphere and for the purposes of this directive are defined to encompass, among other elements, the following theoretical researches:

a. Theoretical Researches: Researches relating to atmospheric radiation, ozone measurements, meteorological aspects of terrestrial magnetism, ionospheric weather relationships, radar-weather propagation relationships, atmospheric acoustics, atmospheric electricity, diffusion, turbulence, meteorological optics, atmospheric composition, meteorological application of electronic computers, meteorological aspects of biological problems, meteorological ballistics, all phases of statistical and mathematical forecasting, seismic weather problems, theoretical aspects of optimum-flight techniques, theoretical aspects of artificial control of weather, meteorological problems relating to hydrodynamics, thermodynamics and hydrostatics, verification of forecast methods and forecaster abilities, theoretical aspects and development of special diagrams, computers, wind scales, and other devices leading to increased efficiency and accuracy of special meteorological work.

b. Applied Researches: Researches relating to weather analysis and forecasting, station and observational techniques, soil trafficability, long-range forecasting, upper air and constant pressure analysis techniques, weather accident analysis, display and presentation of weather charts and data, the practical application of flight techniques; practical applications of the artificial control of weather; forecasting, measurement and analysis relating to micro- and hydro-meteorology; climatological aids to forecasting; use of radiation measurements and ozone observations in forecasting; observational aspects of meteorological acoustics, optics, and high-atmosphere parameters; and specialized arctic and tropic techniques.

3. The Air Weather Service of Air Transport Command will be responsible for providing observational and forecast information, advice, and intelligence for all War Department agencies as outlined in AR-95-150. In addition, the Air Weather Service will be responsible for the submission of requirements for research and development of techniques and equipment in the meteorological and allied geophysical fields, as outlined in Par 2, which will permit the Air Weather Service to perform its mission.

4. In order to assist in the performance of the functions herewith assigned, a total of twenty (20) civilian position vacancies will be transferred to your Command from the Commanding General, Air Transport Command on or before 30 April 1947. In addition, sixty-one (61) military personnel allotments will be similarly transferred and your manning increased accordingly. Two (2) civilians and two (2) military incumbents, the Air Weather Service competent in performing subject functions will be transferred to your Command on or about 30 April 1947 as a nucleus for establishing an activity to perform subject responsibilities. Subsequently, as they become available, ten (10) additional Air Weather Service military personnel will be similarly transferred upon completion of present temporary duty field assignments. At a later date, additional Air Weather Service military personnel will be made available for training to meet qualifications for laboratory assignments and transfer to your Command.

5. All Air Transport Command functions, facilities, records, reference material and contracts, relating to subject responsibilities, will also be transferred to your Command for carrying out these responsibilities. Funds under Budget Project 630 in the approximate amount of $300,000 have been allocated to your Command for research and development projects in this field.

6. Appropriate rotation procedures for military personnel will be set up between the Air Weather Service and your Command to provide for career development opportunity in these technical and specialized fields of endeavor.

7. Close cooperation and active liaison will be maintained between the Headquarters, Air Weather Service and your command in carrying out the intent of this directive.

Brig Gen A R Crawford
Written 24 March 1947

Ltr to CG, AMC, Wright Field, Dayton, Ohio: Sub: Meteorological Research and Development Responsibilities in the Air Forces.

It is desired that immediate and aggressive action be taken to implement this directive. Information and comments are requested regarding the manner in which your Command will discharge these responsibilities with the personnel made available by this section or already assigned to Air Materiel Command projects, which meet the definition of Paragraph 2 above and with the funds now in your Command.

BY COMMAND OF GENERAL SPAATZ:
CURTIS E. LeMAY,
Major General, USA
Deputy Chief of the
Air Staff for Research
and Development.

In September 1947, the Air Force was established as a separate service and in the following December, the CFS was removed from Watson Laboratories and reported directly to the Air Material Command (AMC) Headquarters. On 25 February 1948, the Atmospheric Laboratory of Watson Laboratories in New Jersey was redesignated the Geophysical Research Division and in July of that year the Air Material Command issued orders for this new Division to move and become part of the Cambridge Field Station. In July 1949, the Cambridge Field Station was renamed the Air Force Cambridge Research Laboratories (AFCRL), a name that it would keep through most of its history; it would consist of two Directorates, the Electronics Research Directorate (ERD) and the Geophysics Research Directorate (GRD). ERD had the following six laboratories:
- Radar Systems
- Antenna
- Electro-mechanical
- Communications
- RF Components
- Special Studies.

GRD had the following:
- Atmospheric Physics
- Atmospheric Analysis
- Ionospheric
- Upper Air
- Terrestrial.
- Also part of GRD was the Upper Air Research Observatory located on Sacramento Peak in Sunspot, New Mexico.

3.1 State of the Art of Research in the Early Years

It should be emphasized that research in the late 1940's and early 1950's was conducted completely different from today; there were no computers. Calculations were generally made with a slide rule, a mechanical analog computer. The slide rule was used primarily for multiplication and division, and also for functions such as roots, exponentials, logarithms and trigonometry, but was not normally used for addition or subtraction. Also available were Marchant and Friden calculators. These were used to add, subtract, multiply, divide, and obtain square roots, and exponentials, much more accurately than those from a slide rule.

To digress briefly, these calculators had an interesting history. The Marchant Calculating Machine Co. was founded in 1911 by Rodney and Alfred Marchant in Oakland, California. The company built mechanical, and then electromechanical calculators, which had a reputation for reliability. First models were similar to the Odhner arithmometer. In 1918, Marchant employee Carl Friden designed a new model in response to patent challenges. It was a great success, and Friden became the chief designer until he left in 1934 to found the Friden Company. I was not aware that Friden had worked for Marchant. In 1958, Marchant was acquired by the Smith Corona typewriter company in a diversification move that proved unsound; the company, which was now known as SCM, tried to stay competitive by introducing the SCM Cogito 240SR electronic calculator (designed by Manhattan Project veteran Stan Frankel) in 1965. However, within a few years a tidal wave of cheaper electronic calculators had devastated their business, and by the mid 1980s, SCM's typewriter business, too, had been ruined by the advent of inexpensive personal computers used as word processors.

Communications with other scientists was usually done through the mail. The telephone was used for local calls, but long distance calls were often limited because of the cost. Overseas calls were made using a government Wide Area Telephone Service (WATS) line wherein one would call an operator who would in turn call you when a line was available and then dial the number for you.

All documents were typed on standard government 8 by 10 1/2 inch paper with carbon copies. Almost all of the typing was done by secretaries with the rare exception of some scientists who were able to do their own typing. With the advent of the ozalid machine and later on, the photocopier, the need for carbon copies disappeared; also, the government finally relented and changed over to standard 8 1/2 by 11 inch paper.

My first exposure to a computer occurred when I took a course in Numerical Analysis as a graduate student at Harvard in 1958. One of our assignments was to write a computer program for the Univac computer. My partner and I decided to write a program to compute the first twenty prime numbers. The procedure for writing the program was as follows: Each step of the computation was written as a line of zeros and ones in machine language. The final program was given to the computer operator who in turn typed these numbers into the computer. He then attempted to run the program but in our case, within milliseconds, there was a buzz, which indicated that the program had to be debugged. So we reviewed the program and found the errors and ran it again. After several failures, we finally succeeded in obtaining the prime numbers. However, I never forgot this frustrating experience and later on, when my colleagues were learning how to program in Fortran and other languages, I shied away from programming; I was fortunate to have someone else, usually an Air Force officer, do my computations. However, I eventually reached a point where I had to "bite the bullet" and do my own computations. Fortunately, by that time, computers had become more "user friendly" and I became more proficient.

One of my next exposures to computers was in 1964 with the IBM 360, which was used primarily to control the 29-Foot Millimeter Wave Antenna that we operated at Prospect Hill, Waltham, MA. Our experiments consisted of
- mapping the sun to see if there was an active region that may be a pre-curser for a solar event,
- using the sun as a source to make atmospheric absorption measurements
- using the limb of the sun to make refractive bending measurements at low elevation angles.
- We also conducted lunar and troposcatter measurements.

In order to conduct these measurements, a tracking program was prepared on a deck of punched cards, each card providing an instruction to the antenna. It was very important to run a magic marker along the side of the deck, in the event that if the cards fell, they could be replaced in the correct order. Also in the 1960's Hewlett-Packard came out with their first hand calculator, the HP35. We bought one for $395. Later on, a group of us were able to purchase a TI-30 for a bargain price of about $95. Better hand calculators are now available today for a few dollars.

If one were presenting a paper at a conference, figures such as graphs would often be prepared using a pencil with a French curve and straight edge. The figure was then given to a draftsman who would in turn reproduce it in ink. One would then bring the drawing to the photo lab where they would make a glass 3 1/4 by 4 inch lantern slide that could be shown with a slide projector. Later on, the figures could be prepared for a 35 mm slide projector. The next advance was the ability to make 8 1/2 x 11 inch viewgraphs using a copying machine. These were shown using an overhead projector.

The measurement of the input impedance of an antenna or other microwave components was usually done with a Hewlett-Packard slotted line. These measurements were very time consuming in that each frequency required a separate measurement. The data were often transferred to a Smith Chart for analysis. Radiation patterns were measured with the antenna under test placed on a turntable and each cut of frequency or polarization required a separate measurement, also time consuming.

Overseas travel was handled using the Military Airlift Command (MAC). To go to Hawaii or Asia, one would go to Travis AFB in California. To go to Europe, one would take a flight to Philadelphia. An Army shuttle would then take you to McGuire AFB in New Jersey where you would board a plane with soldiers, their dependents and other civilians to your destination. All flights were full. I recall a flight where I had a NATO meeting and had to fly into Rhein-Mein AFB in Frankfurt Germany. I had a tight connection to Philadelphia and the shuttle had not arrived. We were supposed to be at McGuire four hours in advance of the flight and I realized that I was not going to be able to get there on time so I called the desk to tell them that I may be a little bit late but to hold my seat.

Their response was that they would cancel my reservation and the Air Force would not receive a demerit for a no-show. I explained that I had to be on that flight or I would miss my meeting, but it appeared to be of no avail. In any case the shuttle finally came and six recruits with all of their paraphernalia were to go to Fort Dix and three of us to McGuire AFB. I sat behind the driver and I asked him who he was going to drop off first. He said that he would drop off the recruits and then take us to McGuire. I asked him if it would be worth five bucks to drop us off first, since I was running late. He did not answer me but he did go to McGuire first and I happily gave him five dollars. When I entered the terminal, the people at the desk knew it was me who had called and sort of chuckled. Needless to say I was not a happy camper.

Although there was not an official dress code, men wore jackets and ties and woman wore dresses. Those who did not wish to dirty their clothes used lab coats. In the summer, dress was more casual with men not wearing ties. As the years went by, most men started to wear jeans and sneakers and women started to wear slacks.

3.2 The Second Threat of a Move - 1948

The first threat was the plan to move the Cambridge Field Station to Wright Field as soon as possible. That proposed move faded away and for the most part, in spite of the many changes of command, the Cambridge Field Station had developed into a fairly stable organization. However, in 1948, it was announced that the Cambridge Field Station would be moved to Griffiss AFB, Rome, NY. This was one of the many threats that Air Force Cambridge Research Laboratories and its predecessor and successor laboratories would encounter through subsequent years. Fortunately, with the support of Congressmen John F. Kennedy and John W. McCormack and Assistant Secretary of the Air Force, Eugene Zuckert, this move was averted. In July 1950, the Secretary of the Air Force announced that the research activities of AFCRL would remain in the Boston Area; thus, the original plan to relocate the station to Wright Field would no longer be considered.

3.3 Outstanding Accomplishments

In spite of the limitations described above, significant breakthroughs were occurring at the Cambridge Field Station.

3.3.1 Project Blossom - 1946

The United States began launching its reconstructed V-2's at the White Sands Missile Range in New Mexico on May 10, 1946. In November 1946, the first successful Army Air Forces firing of a V-2 rocket was supervised by Dr. Marcus O'Day, Chief of the Navigation Laboratory of the Cambridge Field Station. For this study, photoelectric methods for measuring radiation were preferred to others because of requirements imposed by the telemeter system. Seven photoelectric cells and their associated circuits were used. For the initial measurements, cells were selected with light responses in the ultraviolet, visible and infrared regions. Two cells of each wavelength region were placed 180 degrees apart in the pressurized warhead of the rocket. The seventh cell employed a filter that passed only a narrow band of sky blue light. To avoid direct sunlight, each cell was recessed in the warhead. Previously, the sky brightness radiation from the sun and sky had been measured on a horizontal surface near the earth, with pyroheliometers and photometers, up to four miles. Using photoelectric cells and filters with special characteristics, sky brightness could be measured at various heights for selected wavelengths, a major improvement.

Project Blossom continued under the guidance of an NYU team and with support from the newly created Balloon Operations Unit at Holloman Air Force Base, New Mexico. The first launch lifted off on February 20, 1947. It was intended to test methods of recovering payloads from the fringes of space. At its farthest distance from earth, it ejected its nose cone, containing an 8-foot ribbon-like parachute. As the payload lowered to an altitude of 30 miles, it deployed another parachute that was 14 feet in diameter. After falling for 50 minutes it came to rest on the ground. It broke the record for the highest altitude of a parachute drop.

Ten flights were planned in which V-2 payloads would be recovered by parachute. The experimenters then acquired a larger V-2 rocket and added a bigger payload capsule to it. The instruments were supposed to gather information on high-energy particles, X-rays, upper atmospheric weather and air composition. However, several neoprene balloons failed soon after launch and the Blossom recovery system continued to fail on later launches so the experimenters finally concluded that parachutes could not be recovered from extremely high altitudes. By 1948 the launches started to be performed by Air Force personnel, and the next year the Balloon Branch was officially organized as a subdivision within the Electronic and Atmospheric Projects section at Holloman AFB and was operated by the Cambridge Field Station. On July 21, 1950, the launch of the first polyethylene balloon devoted to perform atmospheric sampling took place. This series of experiments was considered one of the major accomplishments of the newly formed Cambridge Field Station

3.3.2 Project Mogul - 1947

US authorities were aware of the fact that the Soviets were probably pursuing their own atomic bomb, so the Central Intelligence Agency (CIA) started a study on long range detection of nuclear detonations, through the so called "Atmospheric Sound Channel." For this purpose they initially used large trains of neoprene balloons and then switched to the innovative polyethylene balloons developed by General Mills Inc. of Minneapolis that carried low frequency acoustic detectors to the stratosphere, which would "hear" the compression waves generated by such a test. The codename of the program was Project Mogul, a top-secret project by the Army Air Forces. The project was carried out from 1947 until early 1949. The project was moderately successful, but was very expensive, so it was superseded by a network of seismic detectors and air sampling for fallout which were cheaper, more reliable, and easier to deploy and operate.

During June and July of 1947 there were numerous UFO reports, many of ships flying in formation, which were obviously generated by MOGUL flights. On 4 June Prof. Moore and his team launched MOGUL flight #4, and on 14 June rancher Mark Brazel found paper, foil, and rubber debris, on his grounds, which he initially ignored. However, on 24 June, private pilot Kenneth Arnold sighted something he couldn't explain on a flight over Oregon and Washington. His report caused a flurry of press reports about "flying saucers." (Sometimes "flying disks.") The saucer craze peaked on 4 July and on the 5th Brazel drove into town and heard about the saucers for the first time. Weather balloons had descended on his property before, but now he became uncertain of this new debris. Returning to the "crash site," he studied it some more. Then, on the 7th, he informed the Roswell (NM) Sheriff "kinda confidential like," that he just might have the remains of a genuine flying saucer. This became known as the "Roswell Incident" which would surface almost 30 years later.

3.3.3 The Roswell Incident - 1947

Reports of flying saucers and alien bodies allegedly sighted in the Roswell area in 1947 were the subject of intense domestic and international media attention. This attention had resulted in countless pictures, and even a film purported to be a U.S. government "alien autopsy." Finally, in July 1994, the Office of the Secretary of the Air Force concluded an exhaustive search for records in response to a General Accounting Office (GAO) inquiry of an event popularly known as the "Roswell Incident." The focus of the GAO probe, initiated at the request of New Mexico Congressman Steven Schiff, was to determine if the U.S. Air Force, or any other U.S. government agency, possessed information on the alleged crash and recovery of an extraterrestrial vehicle and its alien occupants near Roswell, N.M. in June 1947. The July 1994 Air Force report concluded that the predecessor to the U.S. Air Force, the U.S. Army Air Forces, did indeed recover material near Roswell in June 1947. This 1000-page report methodically explained that what was recovered by the Army Air Forces was not the remnants of an extraterrestrial spacecraft and its alien crew, but debris from an Army Air Forces balloon-borne, Project Mogul. Records located describing research carried out under that project, most of which were never classified (and publicly available) were collected, provided to the GAO, and published in one volume for ease of access for the general public. Although Mogul components clearly accounted for the claims of 'flying saucer' debris recovered in 1947, lingering questions remained concerning anecdotal accounts that included descriptions of "alien" bodies. The issue of "bodies" was not discussed extensively in the 1994 report because there were not any bodies connected with events that occurred in 1947. The extensive Secretary of the Air Force-directed search of Army Air Forces and U.S. Air Force records from 1947 did not yield information that even suggested the 1947 "Roswell" events were anything related to a "flying saucer."

3.3.4 Project Volscan - 1947

In December 1947, plans were outlined for Project Volscan, an experimental volume scanning air traffic control system and for Project VOLIR, a volume indicating automated scanning radar. When a large number of military aircraft return to a base within a short time, a serious air traffic control problem arises. The problem became greater when we consider that more and more jets were being used. They have to be landed as quickly as possible because the lower they fly, the more fuel they use. Therefore, if the landing operation takes too long, the jets can very easily run out of fuel and crash. No human being can control more than 40 planes an hour. The problem was how to land 120 planes or more an hour. It was solved with the Volscan Air Traffic Control System, developed under Ben F. Green, of the Cambridge Field Station.

Volscan worked in the following way. In order to control 120 aircraft an hour Volscan used two identical Traffic Operator Consoles and one Monitor Console. The Traffic Operators used a common radio channel to answer incoming aircraft. Each console had a Plan Position Indicator (PPI) scope, a panel controlling seven Antrac-Datac channels, and a Volscan Light Gun for assigning Antracs (Automatic tracking-while-scanning). The Monitor's PPI permitted him to watch the progress of all controlled aircraft. His time-situation panel showed the type and scheduled arrival time of each aircraft. Push buttons permitted him to change their automatically assigned schedules or to reserve time in the future for take-offs. The control for setting in the wind direction and velocity and entry gate locations was also on his panel. Although very successful for many years, Project VOLIR was phased out in July 1953. However, another significant accomplishment!

3.3.5 Modem - 1949

Jack Harrington and Paul Rosen created the first telephone-based modem (modulation and demodulation). While at the Cambridge Field Station, they were developing techniques for digital signal processing and digital transmission. They initially tried using atmospheric microwave links but found them too slow for data transmission so they switched over to using telephone lines. They had many troubles with radar data transmission, most of which could not be foreseen without trying the equipment out in the real world. Sending digits over telephone lines sounds easy, and it is, but sending them reliably was not. The telephone system had been elegantly designed for sending analog voice, but suffered a number of distortions and noise interferences that only digits could notice -- and notice them they did. At first the telephone company was dubious about what they were doing. When the first telephone line for radar data eventually came into the Whirlwind building to be wired into one of Jack's modems, the telephone installer insisted on wiring it into a handset. Harrington told him that he didn't want the handset, but he was told that it was a regulation and that was that. When the telephone installer left, Harrington connected the telephone line to the modem with success; later the telephone company became interested in digital transmission and designed and built the modems for the Semi-Automatic Ground Environment (SAGE), an automated control system for tracking and intercepting enemy bomber aircraft used by the North American Air Defense (NORAD) from the late 1950s into the 1980s. An improved version of this modem was patented by Jack Harrington and Paul Rosen and later became the basis of Bell Telephone's A-1 Data Service. Another significant breakthrough!

3.3.6 Printed Circuit Transmission Line - 1949

Robert Barrett, of the Cambridge Field Station, invented the microwave printed circuit (MPC) transmission line. Barrett was trying to devise a new method for feeding a microwave "Wullenweber" antenna. It occurred to him that a flattened coaxial line, in which the center conductor became a metal strip could be fabricated as a printed circuit, and the outer conductor, which would become a pair of ground planes, could be used for this application. Furthermore, he realized that this technique could not only be used as a transmission line, but could also be used for a variety of microwave components. Shortly after reporting on this new technique at an IRE Meeting in 1951, engineers from the Federal Communications Research Laboratories announced that they had developed a variation of Barrett's MPC where the center conductor was placed over a single ground plane and named "Micro-strip". In 1955, Prof. Donald D. King of Johns Hopkins University placed a dielectric in between the center conductor and the ground plane and he called it the "dielectric image line". Barrett later used dielectric spacers to support the outer conductors. A commercial form of this configuration was later developed by Sanders Associates under an AFCRL contract and called "Tri-Plate". Barrett received the 1992 IEEE Microwave Pioneer Award for "Pioneering the development of the strip transmission line." In summary, Barrett's invention had spawned many companies and found numerous applications in both military and commercial systems.

Chapter 4: The Golden Years (1950-1975)

Throughout the 1950's, 60's and mid 70's, AFCRL continued to grow and prosper and became recognized as one of the leading research laboratories in the world as evidenced by numerous significant accomplishments. In June 1951, AFCRL underwent another name change to Air Force Cambridge Research Center (AFCRC) and with the retirement of Col Hugh Mitchell, Col Harvey Davidson assumed command. Shortly after, Major General James F. Phillips replaced Colonel Harvey D. Davidson as AFCRC Commander. On the same date, John W. Marchetti became Technical Deputy to the Commander, however this position would be abolished in December 1953. In August 1951, the Geophysics Research Directorate received its first civilian director, Dr. Helmut E. Landsberg, and ERD received Dr. Edwin G. Schneider as its director.

4.1 The Move to Hanscom Field

AFCRC would now begin the planning that would lead to its relocation from Cambridge to Hanscom Field. In April 1954, Buildings "A" and "B" of the AFCRC complex were occupied by ERD and the new Research Services Division (which was discontinued in June 1956). The official address for AFCRC became Laurence G. Hanscom Field, Bedford, MA. In January 1957, the Atmospheric Devices Laboratory of GRD moved into the newly constructed Building "F" of the Hanscom complex, later to be joined by most of the other laboratories of GRD. By March 1959, the remaining GRD personnel moved into the new Building "C" along with two ERD sections that had stayed at Albany Street in Cambridge. Now essentially all AFCRC personnel were located a Hanscom Field with the exception of those at off-base sites.

Extensive reorganizations followed and in the beginning of 1960 the Air Force Research Division (AFRD) was established as part of the Air Research and Development Command (ARDC). The AFRD mission was to plan, program and manage the ARDC basic and applied research programs. Shortly afterwards, in April of that year, the Air Force Command and Control Development Division (AFCCDD), was activated at Hanscom Field and was assigned control over the following units: the Air Force Cambridge Research Center, the Electronic Support System Project Offices, the 3245th Air Base Wing, and the ARDC portion of ADSID. AFCRC's Lincoln Project Office became the Lincoln Laboratory Liaison Office under the Director of Technology, AFCCDD. In May, the Air Force Cambridge Research Center (AFCRC) was dissolved. Its Geophysics and Electronics Directorates (GRD and ERD) were reassigned to the new Air Force Research Division and designated Detachment 2, Headquarters AFRD. For administrative and logistic support,

Detachment 2, AFRD, was attached to AFCCDD, in effect becoming a tenant at Hanscom Field.

Fortunately, this reorganization was short lived and in August it was renamed the Air Force Cambridge Research Laboratories (AFCRL). At this point in time, AFCRL consisted of the Electronics and Geophysics Research Directorates and the Commander's staff. In March 1961, the Secretary of the Air Force announced that, effective 1 April, the Air Materiel Command (AMC) would be redesignated as the Air Force Logistics Command (AFLC), and the Air Research and Development Command (ARDC) as the Air Force Systems Command (AFSC); and that ARDC's Air Force Research Division (AFRD) would become the Office of Aerospace Research (OAR), assigned directly to the Air Force Chief of Staff.

Figure 3 Air Force Cambridge Research Laboratories – Hanscom Air Force Base

4.2 Office of Aerospace Research (OAR) 1961-1970

The Office of Aerospace Research (OAR), a new command under Major General Daniel E. Hooks, in Washington, DC, was designated as a separate operating agency under Headquarters, United States Air Force, with the functions and responsibilities of a major air command and with the autonomy to focus on quality research without interference from a systems command. OAR consisted of four research organizations; our own Air Force Cambridge Research Laboratories (AFCRL) at Hanscom AFB, the Aeronautical Research Laboratory (ARL) at Wright Field, the Frank J. Seiler Laboratory at the Air Force Academy and the Air Force Office of Scientific Research (AFOSR). OAR was not organizationally coupled to the Air Force's developmental program for reasons that were clear to all those who have witnessed the consequences of the dual management of research and development programs. When the two are closely coupled, research with its long range goals falls victim to the urgent demands of development with its schedules and priorities; manpower and funds for meeting urgent schedules can often be drawn without apparent effect from research activities. The two activities are inherently different and it has been increasingly realized that the overly tight linking of research and development is unwise.

Unfortunately, in February 1970, as a result of the Mansfield Amendment, the Secretary of the Air Force, Robert Seamans, approved the reorganization that would dissolve OAR and once again place AFCRL under the Air Force Systems Command (AFSC). The reason for this merger was to bring about a closer coupling between research and development to assure that research results would be more quickly transitioned into Air Force applications. In actuality, this all came about because of a change in attitude of the DOD toward the role of science.

Also, the military budget was shrinking and it was expected that by having a single headquarters staff, there would be a savings. However, this consolidation creates a two-edged sword in that although there is a financial savings, the pressure to transfer basic research to development as quickly as possible, impedes the creativity that is often needed to conduct truly basic research. For example, when one is engaged in basic research, it happens more often than not, that a more interesting application arises during the course of the research. If one is too closely coupled to a particular development program, one may not have the option to pursue this different and possibly more important application. Two of the best examples of this were the invention of the transistor by William Shockley, Walter Brattain and John Bardeen at AT&T's Bell Labs and the invention of the maser by Charles Townes when he was at Bell Labs and later at Columbia University. The initial application of the transistor was for radio and communications. Yet the application that benefited most from the transistor was the computer, which was in its infancy at the time of the invention and was probably of little interest to Bell Labs. The initial goal of the maser was to create a precise and stable frequency source. Who would have known that this research would lead to the laser, which now has a multitude of military and commercial applications.

4.3 Major Reorganization of AFCRL

Upon reviewing AFCRL's management structure, Brigadier General Bernard G. Holzman, Commander of AFCRL, became increasingly concerned over the two-headed administration of the laboratories. He noted that while the classical separation between electronics and geophysics had considerably narrowed and in some cases overlapped, the Directorates continued to function in near-isolation from one another. Each had developed different methods of preparing and submitting annual budget requests; each had dissimilar procedures for seeking logistic support; and each had differing publication programs.

The Commander became convinced that in the programming area in particular, the time had come for centralized management. As a result of this organizational review, which was discussed with officials in Washington, the Office of Aerospace Research on 1 September 1961 directed General Holzman "to consolidate administrative, logistics and programming functions" within his headquarters. Subsequently, the Commander appointed a task force of key personnel to work up a detailed plan. General Holzman then addressed a meeting of laboratory and staff personnel to explain the reasons for the impending consolidation, and dispel any concern that might have arisen over the changes. He reviewed several of the administrative problems he had encountered, and the weaknesses flowing from the two-sided organizational structure. In late September the special task force drew a consolidation plan, which was adopted with some modifications,. Effective 9 October 1961 five major staff and support elements were established under Headquarters AFCRL for plans and programs, logistics, administrative management, technical services and research information. Personnel to man these offices were drawn largely from the separate Directorate programming and management divisions, which were eliminated. The heads of the Directorates continued to serve in those positions, being responsible for providing scientific advice on all research matters to the Commander and to the AFCRL scientists. The heart of the organization, the 14 research laboratories, continued to function with only minor changes and consolidations. The new AFCRL Organizational Chart is shown below.

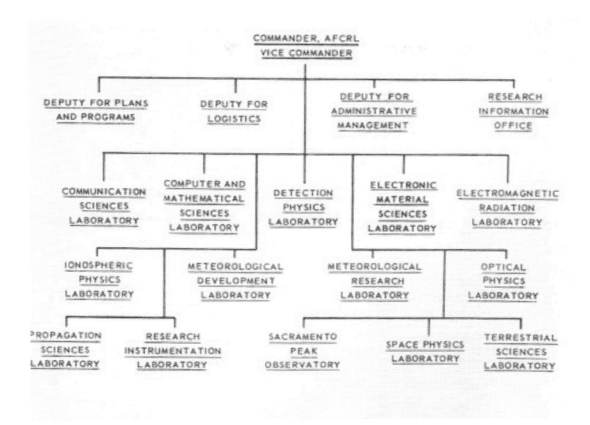

Figure 4 AFCRL Organization 1961

By 1962, AFCRL had almost 1,100 employees, 680 professional personnel with the remainder support personnel. Of the professional workers, over 100 held Ph.D.'s and 205 held Masters degrees. This workforce would remain essentially constant until June 1970, at which time an increase of over 100 personnel was approved. This increase was somewhat artificial in that most of the workers who were hired had previously been on-site, "arms and legs" contractors, which the Air Force frowned upon. Thus the total workforce did not really increase; it just had fewer contractors.

In April 1963, there was another full-scale internal reorganization of AFCRL, eliminating the Geophysics and Electronics Research Directorates (GRD and ERD) and consolidating their fourteen laboratory elements into nine major laboratories. In March 1968, several changes in Laboratory structure became effective. The Sacramento Peak Observatory was removed from the Space Physics Laboratory to become a separate entity. Elements related to ionospheric research were drawn from the Space Physics and Upper Atmosphere Physics Laboratories to create a new Ionospheric Physics Laboratory. The reduced Upper Atmosphere Physics Laboratory was renamed the Aeronomy Laboratory. In June 1972, the Data Sciences Laboratory was abolished in response to a large reduction in manpower authorizations. The

Laboratory had been created from other units in the 1963 reorganization. Its research on speech patterns dated back to the late 1940's. In June 1974, further reductions in civilian manpower authorizations resulted in a cut of more than fourteen percent in civilian staffing from that in 1970. As a result of these cuts, the Energy Conversion, Plasma Physics, Solar Plasma Dynamics, and Space Forecasting Branches of the Space Physics Laboratory were terminated. The Vertical Sounding Techniques Branch of the Meteorology Laboratory was also abolished.

4.4 The Mansfield Amendment – November 1969

Research at AFCRL had focused on basic physical mechanisms and environmental phenomena. The correspondence between these basic research studies and Air Force operational requirements did not have to be direct. Up until this time the Laboratories for the most part had not suffered many serious setbacks beyond those mentioned above. However in November 1969 the Mansfield Amendment was passed into law as part of the fiscal year 1970 Military Authorization Act (Public Law 91-121). The Department of Defense (DOD) funded research primarily to in-house government laboratories and universities; since most of it was basic research, it was not always directly related to military activities. In the late 1960s there were protests on college campuses against the war in Viet Nam and against military research being done on campus. In an effort to calm the anti-war protests on college campuses Senate Majority Leader Mike Mansfield, a liberal Democrat from Montana, proposed the Mansfield Amendment. This amendment required that DOD only support basic research "with a direct and apparent relationship to a specific military function or operation." Apparently the intent was to diminish the DOD presence and perceived influence on college campuses. When faced with this dilemma, people doing research on borderline areas had to become creative. They imagined a variety of futuristic devices on battlefields. However, the net result was that although some scientists and engineers were able to use their ingenuity to continue to conduct basic research, many others lost their DOD support. These cuts resulted in a decrease of about 14% of the lab personnel from its high of over 1200 employees in 1970. A plot of the lab manpower is shown in Fig. 5. It is seen that there is a continual downsizing-taking place.

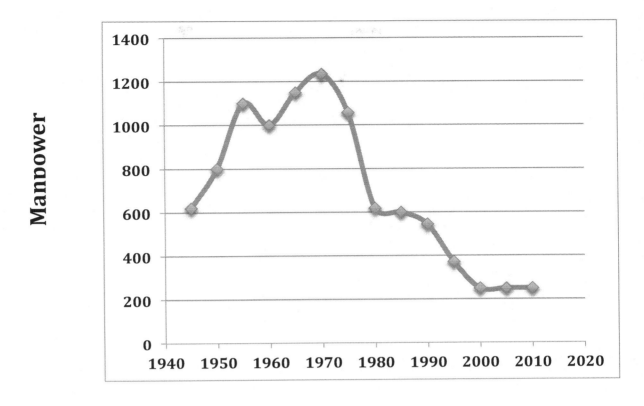

Figure 5 Manpower History

4.5 The Chapman Report – August 1974

In the summer of 1974, a laboratory utilization study was commissioned by the Air Force to look at how the Air Force could best spend its research resources. It emphasized the need to ensure the transfer of technology from the laboratories to the product divisions. Maj Gen Kenneth R. Chapman, Assistant Deputy Chief of Staff for R & D, headed the study panel. The committee was critical of Air Force management for failing to clearly define the role of the research laboratories and the criteria by which their performance was judged. The committee, which had no understanding of the importance of basic research, emphasized the need to tie research to product development. For example, they emphasized the importance of command, control and communications (C3) and suggested that a C3 center be located at Hanscom AFB. The center would use relevant personnel from AFCRL and RADC. The existing non-C3 geophysics and environmental sciences would be relocated to Kirtland AFB.

Finally, the panel concluded that the Air Force did not need in-house research and that basic research should be eliminated wherever possible.

4.6 Realignment and Reduction Actions – November 1974

As a result of the Chapman Report, the Air Force announced in November 1974 Realignment and Reduction Actions. As part of these Actions, the Air Force directed that geophysics research, then being conducted at AFCRL, be transferred to Kirtland Air Force Base, New Mexico. The space left open by this move was to be filled by the transfer to Hanscom the major activities of the Rome Air Development Center (RADC), which would concentrate Command, Control, Communications, and Intelligence activities at Hanscom Air Force Base. It was also announced that civilian staffing at AFCRL would be reduced by 200 positions.

In January 1975, Program Action Directive (AFSC75-6) set out a plan for implementing the 22 November 1974 decisions regarding AFCRL and RADC and in April 1975, the Ad Hoc Committee on Relocation of the Air Force's laboratories made its report to move the geophysics research to Kirtland Air Force Base, New Mexico.

As a response to this plan, a number of AFCRL scientists formed a SAVE (Scientists Allied to Veto Extinction) committee, and began a process for lobbying support from Senators Ted Kennedy and Edward Brooke and Representative Paul Tsongas. In November 1974, senior representatives of AFCRL sent the following memorandum to the Air Force.

A RESPONSE TO PROPOSED AIR FORCE RESEARCH POLICY

This letter is to apprise you of developments and proposed plans which affect the status of USAF military technology. Secretary of the Air Force McLucas has written a policy letter dated 10 Oct 1974 that will have significant impact on the future of Air Force in-house research. He states that "the emphasis of Air Force basic research be shifted at a reasonable pace from predominantly support of in-house activities to predominantly outside University support."

Air Force Cambridge Research Laboratories (AFCRL) is the leading in-house research laboratory within the Air Force and is supported almost entirely with basic research funds. We are deeply concerned with the policy being established by Secretary McLucas since we believe it to be a significant step toward the elimination of AFCRL. Other events presently taking place support this belief. We understand there is a proposal to divide AFCRL into two separate agencies; this will definitely weaken the organization. We also understand there is a proposed Air Force plan to impose a 22% manpower cut on AFCRL. This would be in addition to a 15% manpower reduction that has already taken place within the past 2 1/2 years. Finally we understand that there is a proposed Air Force plan to take all basic research funds from AFCRL. If these plans are effected, AFCRL surely faces extinction.

We are hard pressed to understand the rationale behind the McLucas policy. Can the Air Force rely entirely on Universities for research support? What responsibility or obligation do the universities really have for Air Force research requirements? The objective of the University is education and training, not a dedication to defense research needs. We clearly remember when many Universities refused DOD support in socially or politically controversial areas, for example, the unpopular war in Southeast Asia. Fortunately because of the competence of DOD in-house laboratories such as Air Force Cambridge Research Laboratories, Naval Research Laboratory and the Army Ballistic Research Laboratory, continuity in DOD research was maintained. Under the McLucas policy Air Force research could be seriously disrupted. Can the United States and the Air Force afford this risk?

AFCRL in its 30 years of existence has developed into one of the outstanding research centers in the world. With a strong scientific base and an appreciation of Air Force problems, AFCRL has provided technical support, that could not have been obtained elsewhere, to numerous Air Force, DOD and other federal agencies. The McLucas policy would deplete the Air Force of its technically capable people who are critically needed to assess and improve present and future complex DOD systems.

As Senior Scientists and Engineers at AFCRL, we ask that you investigate this matter before the McLucas policy is implemented.

Senator Brooke met with Secretary of the Air Force McLucas on 6 February 1975 and Representative Tsongas met with him on 18 February to discuss the recommendation of the Chapman Report. McLucas assured Tsongas that before the plans for the AFCRL reorganization were implemented, the Air Force would have to demonstrate that there would be a significant cost savings and would have to assess and take into account the impact on the local area. Fortunately, on 31 July 1975, the Secretary of the Air Force, John L. McLucas, decided not to relocate the geophysics portion of AFCRL to Kirtland Air Force Base, New Mexico or have the electronics personnel from AFCRL and RADC fall under a new C3.

4.7 New Facilities

4.7.1 The Computation Center - 1950

In November 1950, AFCRL operated its first computer, a Remington Rand with circular card punches. As a side note, this company got its start into computers by buying the Eckert Mauchly Computer Corporation in 1950. Eckert and Mauchly developed the ENIAC and this led to the foundation of the Univac Division that produced some of the earliest commercially available machines ahead of the more famous firms such as IBM. The large management structure of the company often frustrated their engineers, many of whom left to found very influential computer firms (e.g. Control Data Corporation). This bureaucracy was thought by many (including their Vice President, J. Presper Eckert) to have eventually limited their ability to take advantage of rapidly changing technology and to give the lead to others such as IBM. In January 1952, a CADAC computer was installed at AFCRC. The CADAC was used for general-purpose computation, not requiring large storage. It measured 3.5 feet by 2.5 feet, utilized Magnetic Drum technology, a 100 Kc clock rate, 195 tubes, 2,500 crystal rectifiers and 10 relays.

Remington Rand and several other companies conducted research on magnetic amplifiers in the years after World War II. The UNIVAC Solid State Computer had its genesis in the Air Force Cambridge Research Center (AFCRC) computer, which the Philadelphia division of Remington Rand developed from 1952 to 1955. Aside from fifteen vacuum tubes, all the CPU circuitry used magnetic amplifiers, which Remington Rand named FERRACTORs. For long-term storage, the AFCRC computer had a magnetic drum.

Several types of memory were used in first generation computers: mercury delay lines, electrostatic tubes, magnetic drums, and magnetic cores. Core memory was superior to the other three types, and, as we know, eventually prevailed. It was initially very expensive, so that for some time the drum continued to be the memory device for small-scale, low-cost systems. The Remington Rand product line needed such a system. Both the UNIVAC I, from the Philadelphia division and the 1103 from St. Paul were large systems, selling for about $1 million. IBM's drum memory 650 computer, announced in 1953, sold for $200,000 to $400,000 and was a great success: over 1800 were sold or leased. However, the drum memory of the AFCRC computer was faster (16,500 rpm versus 12,500) and bigger (4000 8-bit words versus 2000) than that of the original IBM 650. The AFCRC computer was completed in June 1955 and shipped to Hanscom Field, where it passed its acceptance test in April 1956. The total project cost was $800,000. The Air Force used it for various scientific computation problems, and Air Force engineers added a large three-color display scope for a plotting output.

Although there were a number of types of small, highly specialized data processing equipment and a small-scale UNIVAC M460/1004 within the laboratory, a need existed for a large-scale general-purpose computer, since AFCRL was forced to rely on contractors for computer services. Hq USAF recognized the need for a state of the art computer and in late 1964 approved the purchase of a new IBM 7044-1460. With the rapid advance in computer technology, in 1966, the Computation Center acquired a dual computer system consisting of an IBM 7094-II and an IBM 7044, which were coupled together with common input and output equipment. With the Computation Center expanding, a permanent two-story building consisting of 43,000 square feet of space was occupied in November 1970. This $2 million dollar addition linked wings "A" and "B" with wings "C" and "F". The first of two CDC 6600 systems was installed upon completion of the building and the second was installed in 1972. These systems consisted of modular designed multiprocessor operation with extensive input-output devices and peripheral and communications equipment. They provided mathematical analysis, scientific programmer services and a large-scale analog/hybrid facility for simulation studies. The systems also provided remote batch, interactive graphics and conversational capabilities through a network of about 50 remote stations throughout the laboratory and offsite locations. In addition, there was a decommutation facility that processed data from satellites, rockets, aircraft and balloons using two special purpose Honeywell computers.

The next major change in the Computation Center occurred in August 1983, when a Cyber 170-750 replaced the two CDC 660's, which had been in operation since the early 1970's. This was later upgraded to a Cyber 850 in October 1985. In January 1987, the new VAX 8650 computer went on line. This was followed in December 1991 by the installation of mainline computers; a VAX 9000 and a CONVEX. However, with the advent of the personal computer in the1990's, the need for mainframe computers began to diminish. In September 1992, the Center closed the Cyber mainframe marking the end of a 22-year era during which the laboratory had relied on Control Data Corporation mainframes for computer capability. In mid 1993, the Computation Center essentially retired the rest of its mainframe computers.

4.7.2 Lincoln Laboratory- 1951

In February 1951, MIT initiated Project Charles, which would later be renamed Project Lincoln and finally Lincoln Laboratory. In May 1951, the legal transfer of Hanscom Field from the Commonwealth of Massachusetts to the Air Force became effective. The first building on the Hanscom Field complex was occupied by Project Lincoln personnel. ARDC would initially assume responsibility for the administration of Lincoln Laboratory. However, in 1953, the Air Force announced its decision to place full reliance on the Lincoln Transition System for air defense with AFCRC responsible for systems engineering of the ground electronics equipment. The Lincoln Lab Project Office was later established as a subdivision of the Electronics Research Division of AFCRC. However, the precise role of AFCRC in relation to Project Lincoln, which was a contractor operated by MIT, underwent various changes and never amounted to full technical management. In January 1955 the Lincoln Project Office was established as a subdivision of ERD but in July 1956, the Lincoln Project Office was withdrawn from the Electronics Research Directorate and established as a separate office.

4.7.3 Geophysics Corporation of America (GCA) -1957

Another interesting event that took place in the late 1950's was the mass exodus of senior GRD managers.   About 1955, Milton Greenberg, Director of the Geophysics Research Directorate, and others, realized that they had worked up to positions where they were near the top of the government ladder. They thought, "Why don't we start our own company?" In the summer of 1957 Greenberg and six others worked all summer long, every weekend, and prepared a business plan to start a small company, take a lot of their colleagues with their Ph.Ds. and get government contracts; then they would work towards the industrial applications. In October 1958, Greenberg proposed to the Air Force that GRD become a private corporation. When this was informally disapproved by Air Force Headquarters, Greenberg, together with the Chiefs of GRD's Management Requirements Division, Programs Division, Thermal Radiation Laboratory and Photochemistry Laboratory, resigned from AFCRC and founded the Geophysics Corporation of America (GCA). GCA made many acquisitions and prospered for close to thirty years. However, by 1984 GCA was experiencing hard times and by 1990, GCA would eventually close its doors.

4.7.4 The AFCRL Research Library - 1961

In February 1958, AFCRC's Technical Library, had moved from the Boston Army Base to new quarters in Building "A" of the AFCRC complex. This space proved to be insufficient so in December 1961, the research library was moved into a newly constructed building. This new Research Library would become one of the "crown jewels" of AFCRL and grow into one of the finest research libraries in the world. It would contain 200,000 technical documents, 95,000 serials and 75,000 monographs. It had subscriptions to all of the major scientific electronic and geophysical journals and magazines. In addition, it would obtain complete collections of the Philosophical Transactions of the Royal Society dating back to 1665, the Histoire of the Paris Academie, dating back to 1699 and the Commentari of the Russian Academy of Science dating back to 1726.

The acquisition of these collections deserves special commentary. It seems that at the end of World War II, these collections were found in a boxcar on a German railroad siding. A librarian at MIT, Oliver Groos, was brought over by the military to evaluate this collection. He immediately realized its unbelievable value and arranged to have the contents sent to Cambridge for further evaluation. Ultimately, Ollie Groos became the AFCRL librarian and he brought the collection with him. The fact that this valuable collection resided in an Air Force library was never publicized for fear that the collection might later be repossessed by a more legitimate claimer. Fortunately this never came to pass.

Also of particular interest was the large collection of the original notebooks of the third and fourth Lords Rayleigh as well as nearly all of their manuscript material. The acquisition of this collection was also a very interesting story published in Applied Optics in 1964 and as "The Rayleigh Archives Dedication" in AFCRL Report 67-0266 in April 1967. Dr. John Howard, the AFCRL Chief Scientist, describes how through the diligence of two AFCRL scientists, this rare collection was obtained. Drs. Sam Silverman and Gonzalo Hernandez of the Upper Atmosphere Physics Laboratory were endeavoring to publish a manuscript on the earth's aurora and airglow in the Journal of Geophysical Research. The only data believed to be available before 1950 were obtained by Robert Strout, the fourth Lord Rayleigh, starting around 1920 and continuing to his death in 1947. He had published monthly mean averages but had not bothered to include data on minor variations, which could possibly be correlated with an entire 22-year sunspot cycle. Dr. Hernandez started out by calling the Boston British Consulate. He was referred to several British agencies until he finally learned that the collection had been auctioned off to a book dealer named Dawson. AFCRL agreed to purchase the whole collection from Dawson. When the box was opened in the fall of 1963, there were not only the 22 notebooks of the fourth Lord Rayleigh but 12 additional notebooks, 11 of which were those of the third Lord Rayleigh. Dr. Howard visited the home of Rayleigh's son at a later time and learned that there were additional documents that could be purchased. These arrived in early 1965 with much more material than had been in the notebooks. It is remarkable that AFCRL was able to find a way to purchase this historical material for a military library. I question whether this would be possible today.

4.7.5 <u>Solid State Physics Building -1962</u>

In February 1962, AFCRL built a new Solid State Sciences Building as is seen in Fig. 6. It provided the Air Force with the finest facility in the free world for research into the basic mechanisms of crystal growth and growth of electronically-active materials. The program covered what was originally called the ultra purification of electronic and optical materials, advanced analytical techniques for measuring levels of purity, the growth of a great variety of single crystals, measurement of material properties and phenomena, and the fabrication of electronic devices. Behind this research were Air Force operational needs for equipments for detection, surveillance, computation, communication, display, weaponry, and control operations. With respect to these equipments, AFCRL improved radiation and temperature resistance, greater sensitivity, higher power operations, improved speed, enhanced reliability, and decreased size and weight. For the study of the effects of radiation on materials and devices, AFCRL operated a I Mev Dynamitron, a 3 Mev Van de Graaff generator, and a nominal 12 Mev linear accelerator.

Figure 6 The Solid State Sciences Complex

4.8 Observatories and Field Sites

4.8.1 Sacramento Peak Observatory- 1952

It is a solar observatory at an altitude of 2810 m in the Sacramento Mountains, 20 km southeast of Alamogordo, New Mexico. It was founded in 1952 by the Air Force Cambridge Research Laboratories, which operated it until 1976 when it was taken over by the Association of Universities for Research in Astronomy (AURA). It became part of the National Solar Observatory when that body was founded in 1984. Its main instruments were a 0.4-micron coronagraph (the John W. Evans facility), opened in 1953; the Hilltop Dome, opened in 1963, containing solar patrol cameras; and in 1966, the Richard B. Dunn Solar Telescope, a vacuum tower telescope with a 0.76-micron entrance window atop a tower. The Sacramento Peak Observatory was one of the most productive solar observatories in the world. With its powerful observational equipment, Sacramento Peak conducted a variety of research programs ranging from routine, continuous monitoring of the sun to theoretical studies of the various phenomena that occur on the sun's visible surface and in its atmosphere.

4.8.2 Geopole Observatory at Thule – 1958

AFCRC established an observatory at Thule, Greenland in order to participate in the International Geophysical Year studies. The site was used by AFCRC scientists, along with many other scientists to observe magnetic activity, aurora phenomena, and ionospheric variations. Simultaneous measurements of solar electrons and protons in interplanetary space and in the magneto-tail were made during the onset of a solar particle event. These particle measurements, when compared with continuous transpolar very low frequency (VLF) measurements on three propagation paths, indicated the solar electrons had access to the magnetotail and north polar cap. In addition, the phase of the signal was also monitored.

4.8.3 Sagamore Hill Radio Observatory at Hamilton - 1958

The 84-foot radio telescope was used for Air Force research related to communications and detection. It was also used to determine the electromagnetic reflection and emission properties of planetary atmospheres; investigations of the modulation processes of solar bursts; and hydrogen line research on radiation processes from extra galactic sources. Utilizing signals from radio stars and the sun, AFCRL scientists conducted multi-frequency studies of both ionospheric and tropospheric absorption, refraction and scintillation. During periods of intense magnetic disturbances, special effects were recorded. It was also shown that the scintillation index varied directly with some power of the frequency in the radio spectrum below instead of the normal inverse frequency law and that this inversion effect was strongly localized and temporal.

This 150-foot telescope was primarily used for studying scintillation and refraction observed from a radio star. These studies led to a better understanding of irregularities in the structure of the ionosphere's F region. Lunar reflection work was done using the 150-ft antenna and 84-foot antenna together as an interferometer. Also, daily measurements of the scintillation rate of Cassiopeia were made with the 150-foot antenna.

Figure 7 Sagamore Hill Radio Observatory - 1962

4.8.4 Prospect Hill Millimeter Wave Observatory – 1964

This 29-foot diameter antenna was used primarily for communications and radar research at millimeter wavelengths. Atmospheric attenuation and low elevation angle refraction measurements were conducted. The attenuation was measured using the sun as a source. The brightness temperature of the sun was measured at high elevation angles at which the attenuation was minimal and then at lower elevation angles at which the attenuation was much greater. This was done for clear sky, partial clouds, cloudy conditions and rain. These results would prove very helpful in the design of the Milstar Satellite Communications System, a joint service satellite communications system that provided secure, jam resistant, worldwide communications to meet essential wartime requirements for high priority military users.

Low angle refractive bending measurements were made using the limb of the sun as a source. It was shown that there was a high correlation of the bending with the surface absolute humidity and the elevation angle. These results would later be applied to tropospheric refraction corrections for the Global Positioning System (GPS).

The antenna was also used for solar activity studies. With its high resolution of about 0.07 degrees at a frequency of 35 GHz, it could map the sun and search for active regions, which were often a precursor of solar events. Finally the antenna was used at a frequency of 15 GHz to conduct troposcatter experiments with the Canadian Communications Center in Ottawa, Canada. This was the highest frequency at which troposcatter measurements had been conducted. By measuring the Doppler shift of the transmitted signal, it was possible to infer the wind velocity in the common volume in which the transmitted and received beams intersected. The 29-foot antenna was torn down in 2000, after over 30 years of research.

Figure 8 Prospect Hill Millimeter Wave Observatory - 1964

4.8.5 Ipswich Field Site

The Ipswich Antenna Test Range was used during WWII. It was turned over to the Cambridge Field Station when it was established.

Figure 9 Ipswich Field Site

4.8.6 Sudbury Field Site

In 1954, the Weather Radar Branch moved their Blue Hills Site to the Sudbury Field Site. Many significant meteorological accomplishments were achieved. Later on, the site was used to conduct experiments to detect tanks and other military vehicles hidden in foliage.

Figure 10 Sudbury Field Site

4.9 Scientific Research Society of America - 1952

In 1947, a group of Sigma Xi members formed the Scientific Research Society of America (RESA) to encourage research in government and industrial laboratories, in the same way that Sigma Xi encouraged research in the academic community. In 1952 the Hanscom Chapter of RESA, the first in New England, was formed. Throughout the 1950s and 1960s, Sigma Xi's growth continued unabated until it had more than doubled in size. Its influence also grew. In 1974, RESA merged with Sigma Xi, under the name of Sigma Xi, The Scientific Research Society of North America. A few years later, the present name was adopted: Hanscom Chapter of Sigma Xi. The Hanscom Chapter remained active until July 2011, when the AFRL Hanscom Field Site was closed. A plague, shown In Fig. 11 was donated by the Chapter and is located at the Sigma Xi Headquarters.

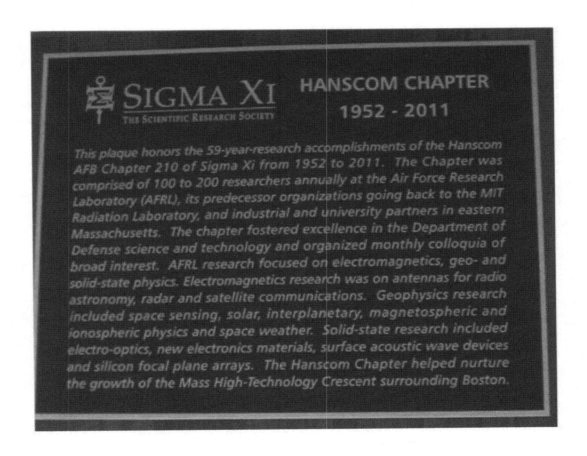

Figure 11 Sigma Xi Plaque

4.10 Guenter Loesser Award – 1955

In July 1953, an Air Force helicopter crashed in Nebraska while pre-testing new methods of wind measurements during the Great Plains Turbulence Field Program. Dr. Guenter Loesser of the Atmospheric Analysis Laboratory died in the crash. In June 1954, the first Guenter Loesser Memorial Lecture was delivered as part of an annual award established in his memory.

4.11 Marcus O'Day Award – 1962

The first Marcus O'Day Award was established in honor of one of AFCRL's most distinguished scientists who died in November 1961. During World War II, he was employed at the MIT Radiation Laboratory where he worked on the radar IFF system. In 1945 he joined the Air Force Cambridge Field Station. In 1946 and in1947 he guided a team named the Project Blossom research group that worked to launch scientific payloads into the ionosphere using V-2 rockets which had been brought to the United States from Germany following the war. Marcus O'Day was also a member of the Rocket and Satellite Research Panel until it ceased operating in 1960. He would theorize in 1958 that solar power could be used to sustain a colony on the Moon, and hypothesized that there may be water under the lunar surface. The crater O'Day on the Moon is named after him, as is this award.

4.12 The National Federation of Federal Employees Union - 1962

In November 1962, The National Federation of Federal Employees granted a charter for Laboratory staff members to form Professional Local No. 1384, Bedford, Massachusetts. I did not see the need for a Union at that time since I felt that the scientists, engineers and support personnel had the best of all worlds and the need to have a Union was unnecessary. However when AFCRL was threatened with a closure or relocation, the Union had a very important role, in that we were able to get the attention of politicians more easily, than if we had not had a Union.

A Partnership Council, consisting of management and union representatives, was established to provide communication channels between rank and file S&E's and management, as well as to settle disputes and worker grievances.

4.13 Major Accomplishments

During these "golden years " the thousands of research accomplishments of AFCRL were truly phenomenal. Scientists and engineers published annually an average of 200 papers in scientific journals, presented 300 papers at scientific conferences, published 250 technical reports and obtained hundreds of patents. AFCRL scientists lectured at Harvard, Yale, Brandeis, MIT, Northeastern and other Universities. Also they were invited to be visiting professors at West German and Israeli universities. In addition, they hosted many international conferences, served as editors and associate editors of major scientific journals and chaired and participated in many NATO Research Study Groups. They received numerous awards and worldwide recognition for their achievements. It is not possible to summarize all of these accomplishments, since many were not sufficiently documented to be included. However, I have attempted to mention those programs that deserve special recognition. Also, I have separated out the balloon, rocket, aircraft and satellite experiments from the others since they tended to overlap with one another.

4.13.1 The Experimental (Semi Automatic Ground Environment) (SAGE) Air Defense System – July 1950

The air-defense capability of the U.S. military was of great concern, so in July 1950, John Marchetti, Technical Deputy to the Commander of AFCRL and George E. Valley, a former Rad Lab scientist who had joined the MIT physics faculty, established the Air Defense Systems Engineering Committee. Based on the recommendations of this committee, the Air Defense Project was officially formed at AFCRL. It was soon recognized that information from multiple radars would need to be handled by a central, high-performing, real-time computer; Marchetti proposed that the Whirlwind digital computer, under development by Prof. Jay W. Forrester at MIT, fit the requirements and should be used for aircraft detection. The system would use the SCR-584 (Signal Corps Radio # 584), which was extremely advanced for its era. In service, it proved to be an outstanding system, much more advanced than any other battlefield radar system deployed during the war. To achieve high accuracy it used a conical scanning system, in which the beam was rotated around the antenna's axis to find the maximum signal point, thus indicating which direction the antenna should move in order to point directly at the target. Once the target had been detected and was within range, the system would keep the radar pointed at the target automatically, driven by motors mounted in the antenna's base. Coupled with the related developments from AFCRL (modems for transmitting radar signals and the light gun for handling displays), this eventually became the SAGE (Semi Automatic Ground Environment) air defense system for North America; it was under the cognizance of AFCRL and the integration of the project's radars became a major activity. In March 1952, radar data were sent from Bedford to the Whirlwind computer at MIT over an 8-digit telephone link developed by AFCRL, allowing the first fully automated aircraft interception, using SAGE. By the end of 1952, there were 12 radars operating at Cape Cod in the experimental SAGE system.

4.13.2 Fletcher's Island -1952

In March 1952, the first AFCRC scientist, Lt. Col (Dr.) Joseph Fletcher, arrived at Ice Island T-3. It was later named Fletcher's Island in his honor. He retired from the US Air Force in 1963 after 23 years of flying in Polar environments. In fact, he was the first person to fly and land an airplane on both North and South Poles. Dr. Fletcher provided a uniquely cogent review of present climate insights, and provided a projection into the next century. His hypothesis was based on the likelihood that past processes are cyclic, and would repeat themselves with a period of 170-180 years

4.13.3 Ellesmere Ice Shelf -1954

Dr. Albert P. Crary of the Geophysics Research Directorate conducted seismic measurements of the Ellesmere ice shelf. The climatic history of the area during the past periods of ice shelf formation could be deduced from these studies. Ice cores, 3 inches in diameter, were obtained with a manually operated hand corer at selected sites on the ice shelf. Four ice types, iced firn, glacier ice, lake ice, and sea ice, were identified as components of the ice shelf by means of their characteristic textures seen in the sections and by field observations during the period of bare ice. These investigations indicated that the thick primary portion of the Ellesmere ice shelf was composed stratigraphically of three major ice units. Two of these units were observed, the third was postulated, and was not encountered at the surface or in cores down to the depth of 80 feet. A. P. Crary, concluded that the ice had a total thickness of approximately 150 feet. The upper unit of the ice shelf was a sedimentary section of granular iced firn with a grain diameter averaging about 1 cm. Interstratified lenses of lake ice of typical columnar structure, represented local, and in some cases widespread ponding of meltwater during the latest period of ice shelf formation. The annual accumulation of this iced firn section was found to be approximately 3 inches per year, on the basis of vertical changes in grain size, together with the stratigraphic position of dust layers. These structural and stratigraphic studies of the Ellesmere ice shelf have provided information on the structure of areas of potential ice islands. The Albert P. Crary Science and Engineering Center at McMurdo Station was dedicated in November 1991. As the first person to set foot on both the North and South Poles, the laboratory was named in his honor.

4.13.4 The Clam Shell Furnace for Growing Crystals – 1956

AFCRC conceived and designed its first image furnace, the Clam Shell Furnace, for growing crystals. Image furnaces are highly suitable for high-temperature experimentation and measurements. For successful operation, however, it was important to consider the unusual heating conditions, which existed at the focal area. In most cases, conventional instruments and techniques could not be used because of the small size and uneven flux distribution of the image. Another restriction of operating conditions was the fact that heating takes place only at the front surface of the specimen. In order to overcome these difficulties, completely new methods and instruments had to be devised in many cases to accommodate the unusual space and radiation conditions in the image furnace. Thus, AFCRL recognized the need of requirements for a precision solar imager and for the development of thermal imaging techniques to be used in high-temperature refractory-materials research.

4.13.5 Sputnik - October 1957

On 4 October 1957, the Russian Sputnik I satellite was launched. On 5 October, AFCRC began taping Sputnik transmissions and on 7 October, the Labs utilized four interferometers together with Doppler radar to obtain Sputnik orbital data.

4.13.6 System 433L Weather System – 1957

AFCRC completed the first development model of an Air Force semiautomatic weather system for System 433L. The AN/GGC-52 ASR terminal represented the first noiseless, non-impact, electronic ASR terminal meeting full military requirements of operation in a tactical environment. The unit consisted of a console containing a keyboard send/receive unit. It had the capabilities of preparing and editing off-line teletype messages as well as performing normal send/receive teletype functions. Printing was accomplished by the contact of a 5 X 7 dot matrix printing head with thermal paper. The unit met the high and low temperature, humidity, barometric pressure, and shock requirements of MIL-STD-BIOB, vibration requirements of M114-S-52059 and the EMI requirements of MIL-STD-4~6IA. In December 1958, the system was taken over by the ARDC Electronic System Project Office.

4.13.7 Multiplate Antenna - 1962

A test model of the AFCRL large aperture multiplate antenna was constructed at the AFCRL Strawberry Hill site in 1962. Each of the 220 plates of the antenna measured 5 feet square. The plates were adjusted manually with respect to the feed, which was mounted atop a 100 ft tower. This new multiple plate technique provided an effective aperture diameter of 2400 feet, yielding a beamwidth of one minute of arc at L band. The proposed new antenna would consist of 7,000 flat reflecting plates, each about 20 feet square, which when viewed from above would appear as a giant cloverleaf pattern. Located in the center of the array of plates would be an 800-foot tower for the antenna feed. This novel approach would be capable of: (a) providing the greatest coherent aperture and consequently communication or radar range at a minimum loss per square foot of aperture; (b) allowing extreme angular resolution on satellites and missiles near the earth; (c) control the antenna beam patterns for target acquisition at near ranges; and (d) providing rapid beam-scanning on a 90' cone.

4.13.8 The Rotman Lens - 1963

The Rotman lens, named after its inventor, Walter Rotman of AFCRL, was a bidirectional electrical lens, which together with an array antenna, was capable of generating a discrete number of radiated beams simultaneously, each having a predefined direction in space. The lens consisted of a parallel plate cavity region with coupling ports surrounding the cavity. There were a specified number of beam and antenna ports. Each of the antenna ports was connected to one of the elements of an array antenna by a cable of a specified length. Each beam could be formed by exciting the beam port corresponding to the desired beam. A beam was generated using the full aperture of the array and was radiated with a (sin x)/x form, with a direction proportional to the magnitude of the incremental time delay between the antenna ports, and the antenna port separation. Any combination of the available beams could be generated simultaneously by the concurrent excitation of the respective beam ports for the desired beams. The Rotman lens was what is called a "true time delay" device. A different time delay was established between each beam port and each of the antenna ports. When any of the beam ports was excited, a signal of uniform amplitude was produced at each of the antenna ports. There was a progressively increasing delay between the excitation signal and the antenna port signals, depending on which beam port was being excited. The delay increment between antenna ports was a different constant for each different beam port being excited; for this reason, the beam that resulted from the excitation of each of the beam ports was oriented in a different direction. This ingenious device was used in hundreds of radar systems.

4.13.9 Arecibo Observatory - 1963

In 1958, Prof. William Gordon of Cornell University proposed to the Advanced Research Projects Agency (ARPA) that they support the construction of a very large radio telescope to study the ionosphere at a frequency of 430 MHz. At the time, two locations were being considered, Puerto Rico and Cuba. Fortunately, Arecibo, Puerto Rico was selected, since it had a natural depression in the terrain that would be suitable for a very large reflector. Originally, a fixed parabolic reflector was envisioned, pointing in a fixed direction with a 150 m (500 ft) tower to hold equipment at the antenna focal point. This design would have limited its use in other areas of research, such as planetary science and radio astronomy, which required the ability to point at different positions in the sky and to track those positions for an extended period as the Earth rotated. Ward Low of ARPA pointed out this flaw, and put Gordon in touch with antenna experts at AFCRL. The idea of using a fixed spherical reflector set in the ground evolved from a report written in 1950 by R.C.Spencer, C J. Sletten and J. E. Walsh of AFCRL, entitled "Correction of Spherical Aberration by a Phased Line Source." They showed that if the focal point feed of a parabolic reflector were replaced by a line source feed for a hemispherical reflector, the aberration could be corrected. The spherical reflector also had the advantage of providing limited scanning, at the cost of not using the entire reflector. A contract was signed between AFCRL and Cornell University in November 1959 and the 1000-foot hemispherical reflector, the largest reflector in the world, was built between the summer of 1960 and November 1963. The reflector was fed from a 96-foot tapered slotted square waveguide that was perpendicular to its surface and provided circular polarization.

Many significant scientific discoveries were made using the Arecibo telescope. On 7 April 1964, shortly after it began operations, Gordon Pettengill's team used it to determine that the rotation rate of Mercury was not 88 days, as previously thought, but only 59 days. The significance of 88 days was that the same face of Mercury would always face the sun, just as one face of the moon faces the earth. The discovery that Mercury didn't keep one face to the Sun surprised and interested planetary scientists. In 1968, the discovery of the periodicity of the Crab Pulsar (33 milliseconds) by Lovelace and others provided the first solid evidence that neutron stars existed. In 1974, Hulse and Taylor discovered the first binary pulsar PSR B1913+16, an accomplishment for which they later received the Nobel Prize in Physics. In 1982, the first millisecond pulsar, PSR B1937+21, was discovered by Donald C. Backer, Shrinivas Kulkarni, Carl Heiles, Michael Davis, and Miller Goss. This object spun at 642 times per second, and until the discovery of PSR J1748-2446ad in 2005, it was the fastest-spinning pulsar known. In August 1989, the observatory directly imaged an asteroid for the first time in history: 4769 Castalia. The following year, Polish astronomer Aleksander Wolszczan made the discovery of pulsar PSR B1257+12, which later led him to discover its three orbiting planets and a possible comet. These were the first extra-solar planets discovered. In 1994, John Harmon used the Arecibo radio telescope to map the distribution of ice in the poles of Mercury. In January 2008, detection of prebiotic molecules methanimine and hydrogen cyanide were reported from Arecibo Observatory radio spectroscopy measurements of the distant starburst galaxy Arp 220.

The telescope was upgraded several times. Initially, when the maximum expected operating frequency was about 500 MHz, the surface consisted of half-inch galvanized wire mesh laid directly on the support cables. In 1974, a high-precision surface consisting of thousands of individually adjustable aluminum panels replaced the old wire mesh, and the highest usable frequency was raised to about 5,000 MHz. A Gregorian reflector feed system was installed in 1997, incorporating secondary and tertiary reflectors to focus radio waves at a single point. This allowed the installation of a suite of receivers, covering the whole 1–10 GHz range, that could be easily moved onto the focal point, giving Arecibo a new flexibility. At the same time, a ground screen was installed around the perimeter to block the ground's thermal radiation from reaching the feed antennas, and a more powerful 2,400 MHz transmitter was installed. New discoveries have continued to be made using this very large and unique antenna.

4.13.10 Physical Properties of the Solar Wind – 1965

Theoretical studies at AFCRL were directed toward an understanding of the basic physical processes of the solar wind, its hydromagnetic interactions with the magnetopause and the propagation of hydromagnetic waves in the plasmasphere that surrounded the earth. Using a linearized hydromagnetic theory, it was shown that the time dependent solutions were spatially unstable at the zero-order transonic point unless a unique relationship among the flow variables persisted in each harmonic mode and that the solar wind was responsible for a variety of geomagnetic phenomena. Finally, a generalized formulation was developed for analyzing the propagation of linearized hydromagnetic waves in an infinitely conducting plasma of radially varying density, the plasma being permeated by a pure multipole field. Another series of fundamental studies related to auroral phenomena was able to reproduce the observed spectrum of C2 and predicted the existence and location of more than ten additional band systems.

4.13.11 Sporadic E-Layer Altitudes -1965

A program to investigate the interaction between neutral and ionized components of the E-layer was conducted at AFCRL. They showed that since the positive ion gyrofrequency was of the order of the collision frequency, the geomagnetic field had a strong influence on the ion motion. Thus, the neutral wind drove the ion motion through the high collision frequency, while the ion motion was constrained by the geomagnetic field since the gyrofrequency was comparable to the collision frequency. AFCRL scientists proceeded to construct a simple macroscopic hydrodynamic theory, which predicted a number of characteristics of the ion motions from knowledge of the variation of the neutral wind with altitude. The agreement between theory and experiment was shown in the prediction of sporadic E-layer altitudes. Of 17 layers observed, 13 fell within 3 km of the predicted altitude, with a strong peak in the 0-1 km separation interval.

4.13.12 Lunar Geodesy-1965

AFCRL conducted two programs in lunar geodesy, cartography and the measurement of earth to moon distances. Using lunar photographs acquired from long focal-length terrestrial telescopes, features as small as +/- 5 microns were measured with a linear comparator. AFCRL also developed experiments in which a pulsed laser, operated from a terrestrial site, was used to bounce signals off of a corner reflector on the moon's surface to obtain precise distances. These measurements yielded refined values of lunar moment-of-inertia ratios and improved lunar ephemeris, thus allowing an improvement of existing mapping control networks which were based on inadequate physical libration constants. AFCRL also conducted mid-infrared spectral observations of selected features on the lunar surface with a 60 cm ground-based telescope and showed that the differences were compositional rather than due to the average grain size, thus confirming compositional heterogeneity. The optical properties of lunar surface materials were investigated by comparing their infrared emission spectra with those of a wide selection of minerals and rocks. Experiments concerned with the physical properties of lunar material were conducted using three lunar simulation chambers. In particular, two ion pumped vacuum chambers were used to study the high-vacuum adhesion of silicates and its influence on the angle of repose, the density and the bearing strength of silicate powders. These results substantiated previous findings of the significant adhesion effects that take place.

4.13.13 Short Backfire Antenna – November 1969

The short backfire antenna, invented by Dr. Hermann Ehrenspeck, was a type of directional antenna, characterized by high gain, relatively small size, and narrow band. It had a shape of a disc with a straight edge, with a vertical pillar with a dipole acting as the driven element in roughly the middle and a conductive disc at the top acting as a sub-reflector. The bottom disc had the diameter of two wavelengths, and its collar (edge) was a quarter wavelength tall. The center pillar consisted of two coaxial tubes (their diameter had to be carefully chosen to give the desired impedance), with a quarter-wavelength slot cut into the outer tube. This structure behaved like a resonant cavity, resulting in a substantial gain in small space. Short backfire antennas were used in some satellites, and in high-frequency (short-wavelength) communication equipment (often for communication with satellites) on ships and other applications where rugged construction was an advantage. They were also used to provide Tactical Satellite Communications for U.S. Army ground forces due to its portability and gain. The bandwidth of the antenna could also be increased by using a conical main reflector instead of a flat one.

4.13.14 Crystal Growth Experiment – December 1969

The Crystal Growth Experiment produced a novel process for growing single crystals of insoluble substances by allowing two or more reactant solutions to diffuse toward each other through a region of pure solvent in zero-g. The experiment was entirely successful and yielded crystals of about the expected size, quality, and number. Gel methods were particularly applicable to the growth of crystals that had very small solubility in the solvent (usually water) that was used. In these methods, two or more reactant solutions, separated by a gel, diffused slowly together and reacted according to a chemical equation.

4.13.15 A High Performance Injection-Locked Magnetron – January 1973

A coherent echo-detection system utilizing an acoustic delay medium to simulate a radar pulse return was employed to study phase coherence of injection-locked positive-pulsed magnetrons. Pulse-to-pulse coherence at 9 GHz was observed for extremely low input power. Injection locking had had only limited application to microwave magnetron oscillators because of the relatively large amount of input power required. This technique consisted of injecting output power from a low power oscillator into the interaction circuit of a second higher power oscillator. When the two output frequencies became sufficiently close, the higher power device locked or synchronized to the lower power device and a single output frequency resulted. A nearly perfect textbook example of this asymmetric spectrum containing simultaneous amplitude and frequency modulation was obtained. Further development led to a renewed interest in magnetrons in the field of coherent radar; for example, pulse doppler radar and moving target indication (MTI). At the higher microwave frequencies, where the amplifier device made up the larger portion of the weight and volume of the coherent radar system, the existence of a small, lightweight, efficient magnetron capable of being injection-locked represented an advance in the coherent radar state-of-the-art.

4.14 Major Balloons, Rockets, Satellites and Aircraft Accomplishments

At AFCRL, complete in-house facilities were available to design and fabricate most sounding rocket, satellite, and balloon payloads as well as to perform most pre-launch tests and to decommutate and computer-process telemetry data. The number of programs in which AFCRL had been involved was overwhelming.

4.14.1 Balloons

AFCRL was the largest developer and user of research balloons in the country. The Balloon Group conducted thousands of experiments from launch sites at Holloman AFB, NM and Chico, CA, since the late 1940's for the DoD and NASA. In 1954, AFCRC was given full responsibility by the Air Force for the development of new balloon systems. It had achieved the following world records:
- the maximum balloon size of 47.8 million cubic feet,
- a maximum altitude of 170,000 feet
- a maximum payload of 7 tons.

In 1962, they successfully demonstrated that super pressure balloons could be designed to maintain a constant volume with internal gas pressure varying diurnally and also maintain a constant altitude without the use of ballast. They further showed that these balloons could be kept aloft for months and even years, thus enabling scientists to make long duration observations at high altitudes.

4.14.2 Rockets

Since AFCRL launched its first rocket in 1946, the laboratories have launched about 50 rockets per year, not including an even larger number of smaller meteorological sounding rockets, probably larger than any other group in the world. These rockets were used to examine almost every aspect of the earth's upper and near space environment, including atmospheric winds, temperatures and densities, the electrical structure of the ionosphere, solar ultraviolet radiation, atmospheric composition, radiation belts, cosmic ray activity, airglow and the aurora. These experiments provided the scientific community with a detailed picture of the earth's dynamic environment.

4.14.3 Research Aircraft

AFCRL used a fleet of six aircraft to conduct space research. These aircraft included
- one KC-135 principally instrumented with a Granger sounder, gamma ray monitor, visible photometer, and infrared spectrometer;
- one KC-135 equipped with a variety of advanced optical and infrared instruments, including radiometers, interferometers, spectrometers, photometers, cameras, and other associated equipment;
- one C-130 with an infrared scanner, multiband camera, various types of gravity meters, and associated instrumentation;
- one C-130 with a refractometer, APNI-144 Doppler radar, vortex thermometer, and water-content measuring device;
- one C-130 with an aerosol spectrometer, microwave refractometer, spectroradiometer, magnetic recording equipment, and a horizontal path-function meter
- one C-131 equipped for balloon and meteorological sensing research.

These were considered the most completely equipped flying laboratories in the world.

4.14.4 Satellites

The first US satellite, 1958 Alpha, launched in January1958, carried an AFCRL experiment, a microphone type micrometeorite detector. Since then, AFCRL scientists have had one or more experiments aboard scores of Air Force, DoD and NASA satellites. Experiments have measured electromagnetic radiation and high-energy particles coming in from the sun, the characteristics of near-Earth space, and phenomena at lower altitudes or at the Earth's surface that are accessible from a space platform, to mention just some of the major program areas. In the late 1940s and early 1950s the original Geophysics Research Directorate built expertise in probe instrumentation. This expertise was transferred to satellites in the late1950s. AFCRL managed a series of research orbiting vehicles in the mid-1960s and built two of them (OV 3-5 and OV 3-6) completely in-house. However, most of its space experiments have "piggybacked" rides on a variety of satellites flown by DOD and also by NASA.

4.15 Major Balloons, Rockets, Satellites and Aircraft Experiments

During these "Golden Years", hundreds of experiments were conducted by AFCRL. I have attempted to describe those that had documented details. There were many other significant experiments that I was not able to include due to a lack of information.

4.15.1 Operation BUSTER-JANGLE -1951

In November 1951 the Geophysics Research Division participated in Operation BUSTER-JANGLE, the second series of atmospheric nuclear weapon tests conducted at the Nevada Proving Ground (NPG). It consisted of seven nuclear detonations. Four of the detonations were airdrops. The other three shots consisted of one tower, one surface, and one underground detonation. The surface and underground detonations were the first of either type at the NPG. Operation BUSTER-JANGLE lasted from 22 October to 29 November 1951 and involved an estimated 9,000 Department of Defense personnel in observer programs, tactical maneuvers, damage effects tests, scientific and diagnostic studies, and support activities. The series was intended to test nuclear devices for possible inclusion in the weapons arsenal and to improve military tactics, equipment, and training.

4.15.2 Project Moby Dick -1952

In February 1952, Project Moby Dick was launched from Holloman Air Force Base, New Mexico. It flew for 92 hours at 52,000 feet, setting a new record for sustained constant high altitude balloon flight. Moby Dick was a Cold War reconnaissance operation by the U.S. Military in which large balloons floated cameras over the Soviet Union. The spy balloons would photograph sensitive Soviet sites and hang in the air until a crew flying the C-119 Flying Boxcar came by to collect them. The project caused a row between the U.S. and Soviet forces when the Soviets discovered what they (accurately) believed to be the remnants of a U.S. spy camera in February 1952. The final weather balloons were launched in August 1954. Other reconnaissance balloon projects from the era included Project Skyhook, Project Mogul, Project Grandson, and Project Genetrix.

4.15.3 Project Gopher -1953

In May 1953, Project Gopher was assigned to the Geophysics Research Directorate of AFCRC. The design goal for Project Gopher was a balloon, which could carry a 225 kg (500 lb) payload gondola to 21000 m (70000 ft), and remain there at constant altitude for at least 16 days. Originally it had been hoped that Gopher could conduct the first operational missions by the end of 1951, but this proved to be far too optimistic. A series of test flights in 1952 was only partially successful, mainly because of continuing problems during balloon launch and with payload reliability. Project Gopher was a top-secret project, but the balloon test flights could obviously not be hidden from the public. Therefore all test flights were officially part of Project Moby Dick (MX-1498), the USAF's unclassified research balloon project. Moby Dick had been started around the same time as Gopher, and used Skyhook balloons to measure global high-altitude wind patterns. Gopher's camera gondolas, which could parachute to earth anywhere after a test flight, were accordingly labeled as Air Force property (together with a fire hazard warning to discourage potential souvenir hunters).

4.15.4 Project Space Track -1957

Project Space Track was a research and development project of the US Air Force, to create a system for tracking all artificial earth satellites and space probes, domestic and foreign. On 29 November 1957, shortly after the launch of Sputnik I on 4 October, two German expatriates, Dr. G. R. Miczaika (from Prussia) and Dr. Eberhart W. Wahl (from Berlin) formed Project Space Track (originally called Project Harvest Moon). It was established in Building 1535 of the Geophysics Research Directorate (GRD). Both scientists had backgrounds in astronomy, although Dr. Wahl's Ph.D. was in meteorology. Observations were obtained from some 150 sensors worldwide by 1960 and regular orbital predictions were issued to the sensors and interested parties. Space Track was the only organization that used observations from all types of sources: radar, optical, radio, and visual.

In late August 1958, Space Track obtained its first computer, an IBM 610, used in conjunction with the AFCRC IBM 650. The IBM 610 was a very primitive machine, the programming of which was done with a plug board (similar to the ones used for IBM accounting machines in the early 1950s) and a punched paper tape. Drs. Miczaika and Wahl had assembled a list of facilities that could track satellites, either by monitoring telemetry or by using radar. Some sites could record the Doppler shift of satellite transmission or, in a few cases, the Doppler shift from their own transmissions reflected from the orbiting object. One Doppler site was the Space Track Doppler Field Site at Billerica, Massachusetts. The observations obtained by this technique were the time of closest approach to the station.

4.15.5 Explorer I -1958

Explorer 1 (1958 Alpha 1) was the first Earth satellite of the United States, launched as part of its participation in the International Geophysical Year. The mission followed the first two Earth satellites the previous year, the Soviet Union's Sputnik 1 and 2, beginning the Cold War Space Race between the two nations. Explorer 1 was launched on January 31, 1958. It was the first spacecraft to detect the Van Allen radiation belt, returning data until its batteries were exhausted after nearly four months. It remained in orbit until 1970, and has been followed by more than 90 scientific spacecraft in the Explorer series. The principal investigator of one of the direct measurements of micrometeorites was Dr. E. Manning of the AFCRC Geophysics Research Directorate. Explorer 1 used two separate detectors: a wire grid detector and a crystal transducer. The parameters determined were the influx rates of each size interval, the impinging velocity, the composition, and the density of the micrometeorite. The wire grid detector consisted of 12 cards (connected in parallel) mounted in a fiberglass-supporting ring, which in turn was mounted on the satellite's cylindrical surface. Each card was wound with enameled 17-micron-diameter nickel alloy wire. Two layers of wire were wound on each card to ensure that a total area of 1 cm by 1 cm was completely covered. A micrometeorite of about 10 microns would fracture the wire upon impact, destroy the electrical connection, and thus record the event. The acoustic detector (transducer and solid-state amplifier) was placed in acoustical contact with the middle section skin where it could respond to meteorite impacts on the spacecraft skin such that each recorded event would be a function of mass and velocity. The effective area of this section was 0.075 sq m, and the average threshold sensitivity was 0.0025 g-cm/s.

4.15.6 Operation Argus -1958

Operation Argus was a series of nuclear weapons tests and missile tests secretly conducted during August and September 1958 over the South Atlantic Ocean by the Defense Nuclear Agency, in conjunction with the Explorer 4 space mission. Operation Argus was conducted between the nuclear test series Operation Hardtack I and Operation Hardtack II. Contractors from Lockheed Aircraft Corporation as well as a few personnel and contractors from the U.S. Atomic Energy Commission were on hand as well. The time frame for Argus was substantially expedited due to the instability of the political environment, i.e., forthcoming bans on atmospheric and exoatmospheric testing. Consequently, the tests were conducted within a mere half-year of conception (whereas "normal" testing took one to two years). The ship, Norton Sound, carried a 27-MHz COZI radar, which was operated by AFCRC and was used to monitor effects of the shots.
  Original mission objectives were the following:
- Two missiles, with warheads 136–227 kg to be launched within one month of each other, originating from a single site.

- The missiles were to be detonated at altitudes of 200–1,000 mi, and also at 2,000–4,000 miles. Both detonations would occur near the geomagnetic equator.
- Satellites were to be placed in equatorial (up to 30°) and polar (up to 70°) orbits, with perigees of roughly 322 km and apogees of roughly 2,900 km or greater. These satellites were to be used to measure electron density over time, and included a magnetometer, as well as a means for measuring ambient radio noise. Measurements were to be taken before the shots to determine a baseline, as well as during and after the events.
- Sounding rockets, fired from appropriate ground locations, were to carry the same instrumentation as the satellites, except for radio noise. Ground stations were to be used to study effects on radio astronomy and radar probing as well as auroral measurement.

4.15.7 Project Firefly - 1960

In July 1960, under the direction of Dr. N.W.Rosenberg, Project Firefly, which dealt with chemical releases in the upper atmosphere showed that Brode's solution for blast waves from a spherical charge could be adapted to high-altitude releases despite a value of 104 to 107 for the ratio of released gas to ambient density. Above 115 km, diffusion constants measured from radial growth of Firefly releases agreed with molecular diffusion constants. In the region 75 to 110 km, however, the growth of certain clouds was faster than expected by molecular diffusion, and more in line with turbulent growth. It was suggested that the energy imparted from shear to large-scale eddies was dissipated not only by viscous forces but also by gravity forces. It was concluded that at the present state of the theory of multiple scattering, the radar cross sections from turbulent clouds had no direct physical meaning in terms of cloud size and electron densities.

4.15.8 The BANSHEE Program - 1961

BANSHEE (Balloon and Nike Scaled High Explosives Experiment) investigated non-nuclear blast effects at high altitudes. It was a program that consisted of a series of experiments to provide data at altitudes of 38,000, 80,000, 100,000 and 115,000 feet. AFCRL was responsible for:
- developing and field testing flight systems including special deployment and launch techniques;
- developing and testing a suitable ground and airborne control system; providing instrumental balloon flights for testing other agencies' equipment;
- selecting and establishing suitable launch sites;
- providing forecast analysis and balloon flight trajectory forecasts for all flights;

- preparing balloons and airborne control equipment and launching balloon systems for all flights.

The system was also designed to deploy and launch a balloon borne instrumented train, 200 feet in length. Of particular significance was using a M-48-42 Army tank as the launch vehicle. By the end of June 1961, a total of 22 development test flights had been made.

4.15.9 The Earth's Main Magnetic Field - 1961

Work on spherical harmonic analysis of the earth's main magnetic field was conducted at AFCRL using a new method that initially proved to be very successful for a limited set of data so it was tried on a much larger data set. These new results compared favorably with the best available results. AFCRL also extended the open tail model of the magnetosphere to describe the spatial configuration of auroral radiation in space by defining the auroral zone as the locus of field lines leaving the polar cap that form the outer surface of the magnetospheric tail and the remainder of the outer surface of the magnetosphere. This model agreed with the magnetic configuration that was measured by the IMP 1 satellite.

4.15.10 Project Fishbowl - 1962

Project Fishbowl consisted of a highly classified series of high altitude nuclear tests that were conducted in the Pacific to study the effects of nuclear detonations on radio propagation and optical systems. It was by far the largest logistics operation that had been conducted by AFCRL scientists and its contractors, numbering 247 personnel. Four KC-135 aircraft were used for these tests, three for studying thermal and optical emissions and one for measuring atmospheric and ionospheric effects. It also marked the first time that a Michelson interferometer was successfully operated on an aircraft.

4.15.11 Trapped Proton Flux - 1962

AFCRL scientists measured the trapped proton flux of about 55 MeV over the period of 1961 to 1965 at altitudes of several hundred kilometers by exposing photographic nuclear emulsions. From directional dependence determinations, it was shown that the majority of the protons was trapped in the earth's magnetic field and entered the emulsion during the passage through a small region of the South Atlantic where radiation dips occurred at low altitudes. These results led to the conclusions that the flux was relatively constant from August 1961 to June 1962. A significant increase in altitude dependent proton flux was observed following the July 1962 high-altitude thermonuclear test (Starfish) with the largest increase occurring at 275 km which was consistent with the equatorial pitch angle distribution caused by a magnetic perturbation associated with Starfish. After 1963, the decay at 400 km appeared to be arrested, most likely because of the decreases in atmospheric densities caused by solar cycle changes in exospheric heating.

4.15.12 Terrestrial Aeronomy and Meteorology - 1962

AFCRL conducted a program of stratospheric humidity research from monthly balloon launches at Chico, CA to altitudes of 30 km and found that there may well be transport of tropospheric water vapor to higher altitudes to explain its wetness. AFCRL also obtained useful data on atmospheric scattering parameters as a function of altitude up to 70 km through the use of intersecting searchlight beams. These measurements were also used to determine atmospheric density. The transmission through the atmosphere at 2.7 microns was measured from a balloon using the sun as a source.

AFCRL has correlated the intensities of airglow emissions with other geophysical parameters and showed that data from tropical regions had a diurnal variation that was appreciably different from that in the temperate latitudes. They also measured the day-sky light intensity from 20 to 90 km using rocket-borne instrumentation, thus covering the entire altitude interval to the region where the airglow intensity became predominant. Since scattered sunlight acted as a background when using navigational instruments, this information was essential for the design of these systems.

4.15.13 Project Cat Feet -1964

An instrument for determining the size distribution of fog droplets 4 microns in diameter and larger using a collimated beam film record was obtained as they passed relatively undisturbed through the beam of light from a Q-switched pulsed ruby laser. Diffraction patterns associated with the individual droplets were observed and recorded. Measurement of the characteristic dimensions in the diffraction patterns allowed the droplet diameters to be accurately calculated from well-established diffraction relationships. This laser disdrometer was capable of sampling volumes up to five cubic centimeters on each frame of 35 mm film at a rate of 10 frames per minute. The short pulse length of the laser, as short as 1.0 microsecond, enabled measurements to be made in moderately high winds without loss of accuracy. The measured distribution was relatively unaffected by the measuring technique, since no sample collection or dilution was involved.

4.15.14 Project Stormy Spring -1965

Precipitation systems within a mature extratropical cyclone were related to the mesoscale thermal and circulation fields aloft using data from Project Stormy Spring conducted by AFCRL. Precipitation systems were analyzed using radars and recording raingages, including a special mesoscale array; upper-air structures were deduced from a 10-site mesoscale rawinsonde network including serial soundings at 90-min intervals. Results showed that most of the widespread precipitation, in conjunction with the cyclonic-scale vertical motions in frontal baroclinic zones, occurred in bands and groups of showers. A sub-synoptic core of cold dry air in the middle troposphere ahead of the surface occlusion was found to be subsiding and surpressing wide-spread cloudiness, while it was furnishing a large amount of potential instability. The cyclone-scale ascending motions then released the potential instability around this cold core and also above the warm frontal stable layer. The convection became aligned in bands roughly parallel to the wind shear in the convective layer. These bands included clusters of cells of more intense precipitation. The cyclonic-scale baroclinic zone associated with the synoptic fronts was made up of multiple mesoscale hyper-baroclinic zones which were shown to be related to the existence and production of potential instability and to precipitation bands and groups of cells.

4.15.15 Aerobee Rocket Probes -1965

Six Aerobee rocket probes were successfully launched by AFCRL during 1965, each equipped with an extreme ultraviolet monochromator (spectrophotometer) for the measurements of EUV fluxes, a retarding potential analyzer for the determination of ion and electron densities, and a solar pointing control for accurate optical pointing of the instruments at the sun. One payload also carried an X-ray proportional counter for the measurement of soft X-rays.

4.15.16 Physical Quantities in the Aurora - 1965

AFCRL scientists equipped two Aerobee rockets with instrumentation to measure physical quantities in the aurora. In each payload, about 15 different experiments were incorporated in an attempt to gain a thorough understanding of the processes involved. The rockets were flown in March 1965 at Fort Churchill, one into a diffuse aurora and the other into rapidly moving discrete forms. The results of the first rocket indicated a relatively soft electron-energy spectrum that could be approximated by an e-folding energy of about 5 keV while the second had a greater energy of about 8 keV but did not vary as much as would have been expected.

4.15.17 OGO-2 Scanning Spectrophotometer - 1965

An AFCRL scanning spectrophotometer was orbited successfully on the OGO-2 satellite. A plane grating spectrophotometer developed by AFCRL to examine the solar spectrum in the range from 170 to 1700 Angstroms was launched into orbit with the OGO-2 satellite in October 1965. This instrument was the equivalent of six monochromators and was mounted on one of the solar arrays of the OGO spacecraft.

4.15.18 Structure of the Ionosphere - 1965

A series of measurements at 40 and 41 MHz from beacon transmissions from OGO-1 were measured at Arecibo, Sagamore Hill and Thule. Individual passes were studied to obtain a picture of the irregularity structure of the ionosphere. The Thule data showed that irregularities exist over the polar cap at all times. Although sunset measurements from all three stations could only be made at sunset for a two-week period in April 1965, it was found that a low scintillation index prevailed at low and mid latitudes whereas at higher latitudes the indices rapidly moved into a completely scintillating mode. However, for an early morning time period prior to sunset, medium amplitude scintillations did exist from low to subauroral latitudes.

4.15.19 Nike-Apache Rockets -1965

This AFCRL rocket program investigated the modes of vibration in the magnetosphere, the current systems in the ionosphere and the excitation mechanisms for the aurora. AFCRL Nike Apache rockets were launched in March 1965 in the South Pacific, near the geomagnetic equator. The payloads were designed to measure the total intensity of the Earth's magnetic field as a function of altitude and thereby investigate the effects of the equatorial electrojet. The four experiments were successfully completed and produced valuable insight into the above- mentioned areas of interest.

4.15.20 EXOS Rocket Flights -1965

In another area of interest, AFCRL studied the mechanisms by which very low frequency waves penetrated the ionosphere and the relation of these fields to the electron density and other parameters. In May 1965, two successful EXOS rocket flights were launched, one during daytime and the other at night. These flights provided, for the first time, continuous records of the VLF field variation from the ground to the rocket's peak altitude of 500 km. The results showed that below about 100 km, the field structure could be closely approximated using one or two modes during the day, but at night, the structure was considerably more complicated. Above 100 km, group delays consistent with high electron concentrations were observed.

4.15.21 Effects of Magnetic Storm -1967

Data from OV1-9 (1966-111A) obtained before, during and after the magnetic storm of May 25, 1967 were used by AFCRL to study the effects of the storm on the outer belt particle population. Severe depletion of the outer belt electrons coincident with the onset of the magnetic storm, subsequent growth of the peak flux and spectral hardening were observed. The proton fluxes also showed severe depletion. Radial diffusion theory was not able to explain these observations, thus the data were interpreted within the framework of radial bimodal diffusion. Both proton and electron data were later observed from June 7- 26 1968 from OV1-13 (1968-26A). The observed proton fluxes during this storm were consistent with radial diffusion conserving the first two adiabatic varients, however the electron fluxes showed a preferential hardening consistent with a weak acceleration mechanism.

4.15.22 Orbiting Radio Beacon Ionospheric Satellite (ORBIS) - 1969

In this AFCRL experiment, ionospheric ducting of satellite beacon signals was performed in March 1969. Propagation ranges of 20,000 kilometers were recorded frequently at day and night hours at Thule, Greenland and at Sagamore Hill, Massachusetts. The results of this experiment were compared with those of earlier ORBIS attempts, and the probable propagation mechanisms were investigated. Rough path-loss calculations indicated that received levels exceeded those of free-space propagation by about 5 decibels.

4.15.23 ALADDIN I – November 1970

The ALADDIN (Atmospheric Layering and Density Distribution of Ions and Neutrals) Program was conceived to study atmospheric mass transport processes and their influence on the distributions of ions and minor neutral species. The program was organized and directed by AFCRL and included a total of nine rocket payloads from AFCRL, NASA Goddard and the Army. The rocket payloads were launched at sunset from Eglin AFB. Results were obtained on Sporadic E, positive ion mass spectra, neutral mass spectra, drastic changes in D-region ion composition and water cluster ion concentrations.

4.15.24 Project HAVEN HOP-1972

Data from Project HAVEN HOP, an AFCRL clear-air turbulence program, were collected. Clear Air Turbulence (CAT) encounters and associated meteorological data were shown for several individual cases. Analyses of these data showed the stronger CAT was associated with strong static stability. This was in agreement with theoretical considerations in which K-H instability may form in stable layers associated with strong vertical wind shear. The analyses also suggested an association between CAT and the horizontal shear regions of the jet flow.

4.15.25 Trailblazer II -1973

AFCRL used the Trailblazer II rocket from Wallops Island to study re-entry communications. The first three flights were used to determine the effects of the ionization on antenna performance. At low-power levels, the ionization caused antenna impedance mismatch, signal attenuation and antenna pattern distortion. The antennas placed at various positions on the vehicle experienced a variety of conditions and the levels of signal degradation changed as a function of altitude. At high-power transmission levels, additional effects were found. For example, the ionization reduced the antenna breakdown threshold and this placed considerable constraint on the useful power.

In the second phase of the program (Flights 4 and 5), the emphasis was on eliminating or greatly reducing the effects of the shock-induced ionization. The problem was caused by the presence of' unattached electrons in the medium through which the signal propagated. The electrons were free to oscillate with the signal and produced distorting effects when their number became sufficiently large. The method selected to overcome this problem was to reduce the free electron concentration by introducing chemical additives into the flow, particularly substances that had a strong affinity for attaching electrons. This alleviation technique was much more efficient than simply cooling the flow which would require the addition of much larger amounts of material. Two quite different additive techniques were tested in the rocket flights. One technique was the localized injection of a liquid; the other was use of electrophilic material in the vehicle heat shield. On the fifth flight, a Teflon coating was effective in its dual role of providing heat protection to the vehicle and of reducing the electron density levels around the surface of the nose cone. Both methods were shown to be effective and viable approaches for reducing electron concentrations in the shock layer. On these last two test flights, signal attenuation levels for the test antennas were improved by about 30 dB through the use of the alleviants. The valuation of the flight data indicated that both types of alleviation techniques (liquid injection and electrophilic heat shields) could be applied successfully and that differences in weight, penetration, and distribution would decide which approach would be most applicable for a given mission requirement.

4.15.26 Satellite Geodesy - 1974

AFCRL used stroboscopic lights on the ANNA 1-B satellite as a photographic target for long-range triangulation by wide-spaced cameras for dynamical geodesy studies. These data were used to compute geodetic positions for observing sites over 1000 km apart. AFCRL scientists believed that the discrepancies between various satellite geoids and between satellite and terrestrial geoids could be resolved by investigating the following: the accuracy of gravitational harmonic coefficients from orbit analyses, reasons for disagreement of geoidal features, the effect of smoothing gravity anomalies at satellite altitudes, an error analysis produced by the distribution of observations, the ill-conditioning of solutions for harmonics, the inadequate coverage by gravity observations of large parts of the earth and the possibility of filling in gaps in terrestrial coverage by airborne gravity surveys.

4.16 Handbooks and Reports

4.16.1 Air Force Surveys in Geophysics March-1952

This report was intended to communicate the results of electronic and geophysical research to other agencies.

4.16.2 Handbook of Geophysics for Air Force Designers – November 1957

This handbook was developed from the extensive experience of the Air Force Cambridge Research Center's Geophysics Research Directorate and its capacity as a source of natural environmental data for the Air Force. It authoritatively provided the best geophysical information available for publication at this time.

4.16.3 Revised US Standard Atmosphere – December 1962

A 1962 revision of the United States standard atmosphere was published. The high-altitude part of the previous standard was based upon a small number of relatively inaccurate pressure and density data available in 1955. High-altitude atmospheric data obtained with IGY rockets and satellites demonstrated the inadequacies of the previous standard and provided the basis for a major revision above 20-km altitude. The definitions of this revised atmospheric model were adopted by the Committee on Extension to the United States standard atmosphere on March 15, 1962, and thereby this model became the basis for the 90- to 700-km region of the revised United States standard atmosphere.

4.16.4 Geophysics and Space Data Bulletin – July 1964

A large amount of geophysics and space data were collected, much of it on a routine basis, by AFCRL and associated contractors in the normal course of research work. Because of this potential usefulness, it was decided to consolidate these data within a publication that would be issued periodically. This bulletin, a first attempt to provide such information, was a compilation of both reduced and raw data that were voluntarily given by AFCRL contractors and in-house scientists. Topics included in this bulletin were: component magnetometer, cosmic ray neutron intensity monitor, oblique backscatter radar, riometer, and solar radio emission-spectral observations.

4.16.5 Handbook of Geophysics and Space Environments – November 1965

The space, atmospheric, and terrestrial environments influenced the functioning of all Air Force systems. As technology advanced, the role of the environment became more important to system performance. In many cases, the environment determined the limit in technical capability. This Handbook reflected the world of geophysics as honed and shaped by the special needs of the Air Force.

4.16.6 U.S. Standard Atmosphere Supplements – January 1966

The U.S. Standard Atmosphere is a series of models that defined values for atmospheric temperature, density, pressure and other properties over a wide range of altitudes. The first model, based on an existing international standard, was published in 1958 by the U.S. Committee on Extension to the Standard Atmosphere, and was updated in 1962 and later in 1966.

4.16.7 Earth Sciences Applied to Military Use of Terrain – December 1970

A survey of the state-of-the-art in the evaluation of natural terrain by earth-science techniques and measurement systems was presented in response to a need that existed for many years. This report considered the terrain as an envelope of the environment and all related parameters that were basic in an evaluation for relevant military applications such as unimproved landing areas, trafficability, site selection for operational facilities, terrain reconnaissance and surveillance, and target detection within a masked terrain complex. Methods of terrain-data acquisition, analysis, and evaluation and their limitations were reviewed. The report forecasted the requirement for an automated terrain-data acquisition, storage, and display system. Information pertaining to the classification of terrain data, field devices to measure bearing strength, and a visualized optimum remote sensing system were also given.

4.16.8 Microwave Acoustics Handbook – October 1973

Information essential for the design of acoustic surface wave filters, signal processors, and other miniature, low cost, reliable devices for use in communications and electronic sensing were given in this report. Computations of surface wave velocity and electromechanical power flow angle, and estimates of surface wave coupling to interdigital transducers were given for various orientations of the following surface wave substrate materials: $Ba_2NaNb_5O_{15}$, $Bi_{12}GeO_{20}$, CdS, Diamond, $Eu_3Fe_5O_{15}$, Gadolinium Gallium Garnet, $GaAs$, Germanium, $InSb$, $InAs$, PbS, $LiNbO_3$, MgO, Quartz, Rutile, Sapphire, Silicon, Spinel, TeO_2, YAG, YGaG, YIG, and ZnO. Particular cuts of interest provided more detailed numerical calculations of mechanical and electrical parameters governing acoustic wave propagation in crystalline media. Similar data were given for common metals. A list of material constants and a bibliography of 520 surface wave papers were also included.

4.17 AFCRL Sponsored Conferences

During this extremely productive period of AFCRL history, AFCRL scientists and engineers played a lead role in hosting many international conferences and symposia, some of which are listed below.

- First International Conference on Exploding Wire Phenomena – April 1959
- First Plasma Sheath Symposium – December 1959
- First International Conference on Silicon Carbide – December 1959
- First Satellite Geodesy Conference – January1960
- First International Conference on the Ultrapurification of Semiconductor Materials – April 1961
- Second International Conference on Exploding Wire Phenomena - November 1961
- Second Plasma Sheath Symposium – April 1962
- Third International Conference on Exploding Wire Phenomena – March 1964
- Working Group for World Standard and First Order World Gravity Network – April 1967
- Fourth International Conference on Exploding Wire Phenomena – October 1967
- First Tethered Balloon Workshop – October 1967
- International Antennas and Propagation Symposium – September 1968
- Second International Conference on Silicon Carbide – November 1968
- First International Conference on Fourier Spectroscopy – March 1970
- Second Conference on High Power Infrared Laser Window Materials – October 1972

Chapter 5: The Declining Years (1976-2004)

5.1 The Abolishment of AFCRL

Although AFCRL had weathered the repercussions of the Chapman Report which would have moved the Geophysics Research Directorate to Kirtland AFB, NM and would have established a new C3 Center at Hanscom AFB, of which the Electronics Research Directorate would have become a part, along with personnel from RADC, the next reorganization would prove to be devastating, namely the abolishment of AFCRL. Although Secretary of the Air Force McLucas had decided not to follow through with the Chapman Report recommendations, he quickly made plans to abolish AFCRL. The Chapman report had recommended that all basic research be conducted outside the research laboratories so this was his way of accomplishing this.

As background, there were three senior managers who, with some effort, might have been able to prevent the disestablishment of AFCRL: Alan Gerlach, Deputy for Technical Plans and Operations, Robert Barrett, Chief of the Solid State Sciences Laboratory, and Carl Sletten, Chief of the Microwave Physics Laboratory. Gerlach was the most powerful civilian manager and historically had been with the Geophysics Research Directorate for many years. Barrett and Sletten, on the other hand, had been with the Electronics Research Directorate, also for many years, and had felt that they were not being treated fairly by Gerlach since he tended to favor the geophysics laboratories. Thus, they believed that getting out from under Gerlach might be better for their labs. Since, GRD would become the Air Force Geophysics Laboratory, Gerlach made no effort to preserve AFCRL. Although the SAVE Committee attempted to prevent this from happening, they were not successful due in part from the lack of support from management. Thus, it was announced, that effective 1 January 1976, those laboratories and branches that were C3 oriented would become the Detachment 1 Deputy for Electronics Technology of Rome Air Development Center (RADC); namely, the Microwave Physics Laboratory, the Solid State Sciences Laboratory, the Laser Physics Branch of the Optical Physics Laboratory and the Electromagnetic Environment and Ionospheric Radio Physics Branches of the Ionospheric Physics Laboratory. The geophysics-oriented laboratories would become the Air Force Geophysics Laboratory (AFGL).

This closure was without doubt the most unfortunate event in AFCRL history and would eventually lead to its downfall. It was a classic example of "divide and conquer."

5.2 Further Reorganization and Downsizing

The group that was originally the Geophysics Research Division (GRD) was fortunate to retain their identity as the Air Force Geophysics Laboratory (AFGL) and they would keep that name until they were redesignated the Geophysics Laboratory of the Air Force Systems Command in February 1990. The group that was originally the Electronics Research Directorate (ERD) of AFCRL did not fare as well. ERD lost its identity immediately when AFCRL was closed; it became a Deputy of Electronic Technology of the Rome Air Development Center (RADC). As a development center, very little basic research was done at Rome and as a result basic and applied research funds became harder to come by.

In 1986 the Secretary of Defense released the Defense Management Report detailing how the Pentagon would implement the recommendations of the Packard Commission, a panel to improve the acquisition process. Although the research laboratories were not directly included in this report, they would be subjected to a freeze on civilian hiring. As part of this report, the DoD initiated a study on consolidating the AFSC Laboratories. In November 1989, the Air Force Systems Command announced that it would be taking a 10% cut in personnel over the next three years. This would lead to a further downsizing of Hanscom Research Site personnel. In February 1990, an Air Force Space Technology Center study proposed that the Geophysics Laboratory, once again, be relocated to Kirtland AFB as part of a new Space and Missiles Laboratory. In October 1991, the Secretary of the Air Force, Dr. Donald Rice, asked for briefings to assist on the physical consolidation of the former Geophysics Laboratory to Phillips Laboratory. However in January 1992, with the help of Senator Ted Kennedy, the Secretary of the Air Force, Dr. Donald Rice announced that this move would be deferred.

5.3 Four Superlabs

In December 1990, another major reorganization took place. The 16 research laboratories were consolidated into four "Super Labs," namely, the Wright, Phillips, Rome, and Armstrong Laboratories. The former ERD of AFCRL became the Electromagnetics and Reliability Division of Rome Laboratory. The Geophysics Laboratory was disestablished and became an Operating Location of the new Phillips Laboratory at Kirtland AFB. In July 1993, the Civilian Personnel Office at Hanscom AFB announced that it was authorized to offer retirement incentives to Phillips and Rome Lab employees. This option would help avoid layoffs.

5.3.1 <u>Attempted Closure of the Geophysics Directorate</u>

In June 1994, the Geophysics Directorate learned that the 1996 Program Objective Memorandum (POM) would zero fund the Geophysics Directorate Exploratory Development (6.2) and Advanced Development (6.3) funding. Since this action would essentially eliminate the Directorate, a new SAVE Committee was formed. Sen. Ted Kennedy visited Hanscom AFB in July and pledged his support to reverse the planned zero funding. In July 1994, he wrote the following letter to John Deutch, Deputy Secretary of Defense.

United States Senate
WASHINGTON, DC 20510-2101

July 11, 1994

The Honorable John M. Deutch
Deputy Secretary of Defense
1010 Defense Pentagon
Washington, DC 20301-1010

Dear John:

I am writing about the Air Force's plan, contained in its Program Objective Memorandum (POM) for fiscal year 1996, to delete all funding for the Phillips Laboratory Geophysics Directorate, located at Hanscom Air Force Base in Massachusetts. The Geophysics Directorate is a vital asset for the Air Force and for our national security. I urge you to rescind the Air Force decision and include funds for the Geophysics Directorate in the fiscal year 1996 budget request.

The Geophysics Directorate is the home of one of the world's leading geophysics laboratories. This institution, which will celebrate its fiftieth anniversary in 1995, is the sole Air Force laboratory conducting research into the effects of the atmospheric, space, and terrestrial environments on weapons systems and military equipment. Moreover, under the inter-service division of research responsibilities contained in Project Reliance, the Geophysics Directorate is the sole provider of these research services to all branches of the armed forces.

If the Air Force's programming decision is allowed to stand, our defense establishment will be left without this indispensable research capability. This decision will come at a time when the technological sophistication of our defense systems continues to grow, making detailed information about the impact of environmental factors increasingly important to their successful design and operation.

The Air Force decision to eliminate the Geophysics Directorate contradicts the guidance provided by your own office. In a May 25 memo to the service secretaries and directors of defense agencies on programming for fiscal year 1996, Dr. Anita Jones, the Director for Defense Research and Engineering, directed that the science and technology accounts should be funded at a level representing zero percent growth compared to fiscal year 1995. Despite this directive, the Air Force cut the science and technology accounts by 2.28 per cent in their POM submission.

70

This past Friday, I had the opportunity to visit Hanscom and the Geophysics Directorate. I was briefed on the laboratory's programs and met many of the impressive and dedicated men and women who make this institution an irreplaceable national asset. The people of Massachusetts are justifiably proud of the Lab's contribution to our national security. The commitment and talent reinforce my view that it would be a serious mistake to allow the Air Force decision to stand.

I understand that as the defense draw-down proceeds, the Department will have to reduce defense laboratory infrastructure by an appropriate amount. Nevertheless, I urge you to reinstate funding for the Geophysics Directorate in the POM for fiscal year 1996 and beyond. If reductions must be implemented in the Directorate's programs, this step will allow the intact laboratory to take part in a rational process to determine where those reductions should be applied.

I believe the Department should take the advice of the Air Force's own Scientific Advisory Board. This body, after reviewing the programs of the Geophysics Directorate, wrote last December that "The overall technical quality of the work in the Geophysics Directorate is outstanding and includes efforts that are world class and at the leading edge of technology. The outstanding capabilities of the in-house staff have been the key to the success of the Geophysics programs. It is important that the Air Force preserve this particular capability in order to accomplish present and future Air Force missions."

I urge you to reject the Air Force recommendation, and restore funding for the Geophysics Directorate.

Thank you very much for your attention to this important matter.

Sincerely,

Edward M. Kennedy

In September, Sen. Kennedy visited Hanscom AFB again and informed the Geophysics Directorate workforce that the majority of the funding would be restored. In September of 1994, the Civilian Personnel Office at Hanscom AFB announced another voluntary civilian retirement and separation incentive for Hanscom Research Site personnel. Once again, this action was a somewhat painless method of further reducing the workforce, since many spaces were lost due to attrition.

5.3.2 Plan to Establish a Hanscom Directorate

In April 1995. Gen Yates, Commander of the Air Force Material Command, in the following letter announced that effective 1 October 1985, the Geophysics Lab would be realigned from Philips Laboratory to Rome Laboratory. It would now join the Electromagnetics and Reliability Directorate in support of the ESC C3 Program.

10 APR 95

DEPARTMENT OF THE AIR FORCE
HEADQUARTERS AIR FORCE MATERIEL COMMAND
WRIGHT-PATTERSON AIR FORCE BASE, OHIO

MEMORANDUM FOR ESC/CC
                SMC/CC

FROM: AFMC/CC
      4375 Chidlaw Road Ste 1
      Wright-Patterson AFB OH 45433-5001

SUBJECT: Realignment of the Geophysics Directorate

1. I have decided to realign the Phillips Laboratory Geophysics Directorate (PL/GP) from Phillips Laboratory (PL) to Rome Laboratory (RL) effective 1 Oct 95. Rationale for this organizational realignment is as follows:

   a. Realignment under RL will help realize our long-term vision of having our laboratories colocated with their parent product centers without the expense or disruption of a physical move, since RL is attached organizationally to ESC and the Geophysics Directorate is already colocated with ESC at Hanscom AFB. I place an especially high value on maximizing personnel stability as we continue to experience significant manpower reductions over the rest of the decade. This realignment will help us maintain that stability by avoiding the disruption that would accompany relocation of the Geophysics Directorate to another product center location.

   b. Geophysics is a corporate technology that serves a broad spectrum of aeronautical, space, and C3I programs as well as a host of other customers who reimburse the Geophysics Directorate for technical work. Given the corporate nature of this technology, we have more flexibility in terms of its organizational alignment than we do for product-specific technology directorates associated with the aeronautical, space, or C3I disciplines. The corporate nature of the Geophysics technology area will continue to necessitate an interdisciplinary planning process including Wright Laboratory for aeronautical needs, Rome Laboratory for C3I needs, and Phillips Laboratory for space and missile related needs. In particular, I recognize that space-related work will continue to be a major portion of the Geophysics Directorate's activities and want to be sure that we maintain appropriate emphasis in that area. Accordingly, I expect AFMC/ST, in collaboration with SAF/AQ and the various laboratory commanders, to assure that we maintain a robust interdisciplinary planning process for the Geophysics science and technology budget.

2. Rome Laboratory should assume responsibility for leading the planning activities related to the FY97 Geophysics Technology Area Plan, and should begin an active dialogue now with Phillips Laboratory to assure a smooth transition as we complete planning for the FY97 APOM and posture ourselves for planning the FY98 POM. From a programmatic perspective, there will be

no changes in the 6.2 and 6.3 budget program elements associated with the Geophysics Technology area, other than financial management provided by RL/FM as opposed to PL/FM effective 1 Oct 95 (the start of FY 96).

3. Please develop a Program Plan (P Plan) to implement the above realignment and submit it through AFMC/ST to AFMC/XP by 1 Jul 95. AFMC/ST will orchestrate any needed headquarters staff support to assist you in formulating the P Plan.

RONALD W. YATES
General, USAF
Commander

There was no immediate response to this directive, so on 13 May 1997 all of the members of the Massachusetts Congressional Delegation signed the following letter to Secretary of the Air Force, Sheila Widnall, in which they referenced the previous letter from Gen Yates. It should be mentioned that AFRL in this latest consolidation had now planned to establish a number of Directorates for the new Laboratory. A valiant attempt was made to reunite the original ERD and GRD into a single Directorate at Hanscom AFB.

Congress of the United States
Washington, DC 20515

May 13, 1997

The Honorable Sheila Widnall
Secretary
Department of the Air Force
Room 4E871
The Pentagon
Washington, D.C. 20330

Dear Secretary Widnall:

We are writing regarding the current Air Force plan to consolidate research functions into a single laboratory system. We would like to express our strong support for a variation of an option that we have been informed has been recommended by at least two of the reorganization advisory committees. Specifically, as the existing directorates of the four laboratories are reorganized and consolidated into the Air Force Research Laboratory, we urge you to consider creating a new Battlespace Environment Directorate at Hanscom Air Force Base within this new structure. This new Directorate would be built around the present Geophysics Directorate, but would also include the current Electromagnetics Directorate as well.

The Geophysics research efforts performed at Hanscom Air Force Base are vital to one of Department of Defense's (DOD's) core technology areas, the Battlespace Environment. Understanding how natural and man-made environments affect military systems is critical to many operations including communications, navigation, flight safety, and the effective deployment of sensors and weapons. The current Geophysics Directorate at Hanscom is one of the primary providers of such technology for all DOD, and it is the only location where geospace efforts tied to Air Force needs are being pursued. When the advisory committees recommended that Geophysics become a separate Directorate within the new laboratory structure, they affirmed two key points: 1) the Geophysics effort is a unique and valuable resource that is of vital importance to the Air Force now and in the future; and, 2) the Geophysics effort supports not just a particular Air Force mission, but all of DOD.

As you know, the Geophysics efforts are presently under the management of the Phillips Laboratory at Kirtland Air Force Base in New Mexico. We believe that maintaining Geophysics' affiliation with Phillips in the new laboratory structure poses serious problems. Although the Geophysics team at Hanscom has been widely regarded as a world class organization, we do not believe the current Phillips Laboratory management has fully appreciated the importance of its work. Several Air Force and DOD independent review committees have raised concerns about the current organizational structure. For example, the Phillips Laboratory's own independent assessment group (ISAG) recently concluded that the management "has not grown comfortable with the importance of the Geophysics Directorate's role as manifest in the lack of internal budget relief that appears to be within [their] authority." In addition, the Air Force Science Advisory Board (SAB) has noted that Geophysics has absorbed more that its proportionate share of funding and personnel cuts over the last several years. A series of manpower and budget cuts has resulted in a thirty percent reduction in authorized Geophysics personnel over the past several years, while the Phillips Laboratory Directorates in New Mexico have experienced less than a two percent reduction. Finally, a DOD Technology Area Review and Assessment (TARA) Team analysis concluded that the Geophysics effort at Hanscom is a "world class staff and program, [a] national asset, [with] strong linkage to customers/operators," while the only weakness the TARA Team found was that the program sustained a thirty percent reduction in funding over the past two fiscal years. The Electromagnetics Directorate has had a similar experience under the Rome Laboratory.

There is little reason to expect that the funding and personnel situation would improve if Hanscom elements remain under the current management in the new laboratory structure. Fortunately, the reorganization effort now underway provides an opportunity to preserve and protect these unique research assets. It is our understanding that the Air Force has already asked three special advisory committees to review the laboratory reorganization: the Grass Roots Review Team, the Lab Alumni Review Team, and the Independent Assessment Review Team. We have been informed that at least two of these reviews have expressed support for the creation of a new Geophysics Directorate at Hanscom. We urge you to accept this recommendation, with one modification.

As the smaller directorates of the four existing laboratories undergo further consolidation, we believe the Air Force should align the electronics element at Hanscom -- the Electromagnetics and Reliability Directorate -- with the new Geophysics Directorate to form a Battlespace Environment Directorate. We make this recommendation because we believe the geophysics and electromagnetic technology areas are complementary to each other in that both address the needs of military systems in their operational environments. In addition to supporting critical Air Force missions, the Electromagnetics Directorate makes substantial contributions to Battlespace Environment technology. Aligning these two functions would strengthen Air Force support of one of DOD's core technology areas. We note that in 1995, former Air Force Materiel Command Commander, General W. Yates, and his successor, General Vicellio, as well as the former Electronic Systems Center Commander, Lt. General Franklin, supported a plan to combine these two organizations within the present Rome Laboratory. The current restructuring offers an opportunity to revisit this matter. We believe that aligning the electromagnetics function with the geophysics organization makes sense, inasmuch as these two organizations are already practically merged due to their co-location at Hanscom, and their sharing of support services and personnel (including operations support, travel, purchasing, contracting, human resources, library support, and other services). Consequently, we believe that formal merger of these two organizations could be readily accomplished.

We applaud your continuing efforts to streamline the Air Force's laboratory system, and we trust that you will assure that critical Air Force and DOD functions will continue to be preserved and protected during this restructuring. We respectfully request that you give every possible consideration to our suggestion that you use the present restructuring to create a Hanscom Battlespace Environment Directorate within the new single laboratory. We thank you for your consideration of our views, and request that you promptly inform us of any actions taken by the Air Force in this matter.

Sincerely,

Edward J. Markey
Member of Congress

John F. Tierney
Member of Congress

Martin T. Meehan
Member of Congress

Barney Frank
Member of Congress

William D. Delahunt
Member of Congress

Richard E. Neal
Member of Congress

Edward M. Kennedy
United States Senate

John F. Kerry
United States Senate

Joseph P. Kennedy, II
Member of Congress

John Joseph Moakley
Member of Congress

John W. Olver
Member of Congress

James P. McGovern
Member of Congress

Having not received a response from SAF Widnall, Sen John Kerry wrote the following letter to Secretary of Defense, William Cohen.

United States Senate
WASHINGTON, DC 20510

August 11, 1997

The Honorable William S. Cohen
Secretary of Defense
The Pentagon
Washington, D.C.   20301

Dear Secretary Cohen:

I write regarding the pending reorganization of the Air Force research laboratories. I believe that the Air Force's plan to consolidate the existing four laboratories into a single Air Force Research Laboratory (AFRL) structure is now, or will be shortly, under review in your office.

As you know so well, we in Massachusetts are extremely proud of the defense research complex that is located in and around Hanscom Air Force Base. These are the facilities which trace their roots to the "Rad Lab" at MIT and other famous research facilities in Cambridge that contributed so much to American forces in World War II. They have made an enormous contribution to U.S. military strength ever since. The Hanscom research complex encompasses, not only military personnel and civilian scientist-employees of the Air Force, but an extensive infrastructure of scientific and engineering expertise located in area universities, not-for-profit research laboratories, and among area contractors.

The Geophysics Directorate at Hanscom plays a critical role in the complex centered at Hanscom, as it does in U.S. defense research in general, since its fundamental mission is to characterize the air and space environment in which every element of the Air Force operates. I write because of my particular concern for the future of the Geophysics Directorate at Hanscom.

My understanding of the AFRL restructuring plan currently under review is that the existing Geophysics Directorate at Hanscom will be downgraded to a division within a new Space Vehicles Directorate headquartered at Kirtland AFB in New Mexico. Moreover, I understand that the current Electromagnetics Directorate at Hanscom, which has always been closely associated with the Geophysics Directorate, will now be downgraded and divided among three separate directorates. Finally, I understand that of the nine new directorates that will operate under the new AFRL structure, none will be located at Hanscom.

I am concerned, not only because of the possibility that a historically significant research institution in my state will be weakened further, but because I believe that the case has been made by Air Force advisory groups for both retaining the Geophysics Directorate at Hanscom and strengthening it.

77

I have been informed that at least two out of three independent special advisory committees that have reviewed the existing directorate have expressed support for modifying the current AFRL reorganization plan to include a Geophysics Directorate within the new AFRL. The advisory committees recommended the formation of a separate directorate because the work performed by the Geophysics Directorate relates to, and supports all of the new directorates, not just Space Vehicles. The existing Geophysics Directorate has customers in every proposed directorate of AFRL and throughout DoD.

Indeed, while the Air Force advisory committees have not addressed this subject, I believe that the work performed by the existing Geophysics Directorate at Hanscom is so fundamental to such a broad range of Air Force programs that there is compelling reason for Geophysics to constitute its own directorate under the new AFRL structure.
A stand-alone Geophysics Directorate at Hanscom would preserve the directorate from the disproportionate level of personnel and budget cuts which the Hanscom facility has suffered since it began reporting through Kirtland AFB several years ago. You may or may not be aware of the fact that, as recently as 1994, Kirtland management sought to zero-out the Hanscom Geophysics Directorate's entire 6.2 budget, a move that was reversed by the then-Deputy Secretary of Defense, John Deutch.

As I noted above, the Electromagnetics Directorate currently located at Hanscom has traditionally been allied with the Geophysics Directorate; both were originally part of the famous Air Force Cambridge Research Lab. As with the Geophysics Directorate, the Electromagnetics Directorate performs work which, by its very nature, supports a broad range of Air Force activities. Both the Electromagnetics and Geophysics elements could be easily recombined to form a new directorate for battlespace environment. Such a concept has won support in the recent past from successive commanders of the USAF Materiel Command, Generals Yates and Vicellio, and the former commander of the Electronic Systems Center, Lt. General Franklin.

I believe that a newly-combined directorate at Hanscom would optimize the productivity from the deep and historically rich scientific infrastructure that exists there, and would be well within guidelines that the Air Force set for itself in reorganizing all the Air Force laboratory facilities. I urge you to give this proposal every consideration, and I look forward to discussing this with you personally.

Best wishes.

Sincerely,

John F. Kerry
United States Senator

Bill: I would very much like to discuss this with you. Hope all is well.

78

THE SECRETARY OF DEFENSE
1000 DEFENSE PENTAGON
WASHINGTON, DC 20301-1000

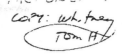

SEP 2 4 1997

Honorable John F. Kerry
United States Senate
Washington, DC 20510-2102

Dear John:

This is in response to your letter of August 11, 1997, regarding the proposed structure of the new Air Force Research Laboratory (AFRL) and planned operations at the Hanscom Air Force Base (AFB), Massachusetts, research complex.

We agree that the scientists and engineers at Hanscom AFB have made significant contributions to United States military strength for many years, and we look forward to their continued efforts as an integral part of AFRL. We have no desire to "downgrade" the organizations at Hanscom AFB, but rather to group similar technologies under a single manager so as to maximize technical synergy and promote the most efficient applications of resources. Although none of the AFRL technology directorates will be headquartered at Hanscom AFB, two of the directorates will have components there; these include the Space Vehicles Directorate (headquartered at Kirtland AFB, New Mexico) and the Sensors Directorate (headquartered at Wright-Patterson AFB, Ohio). In addition, the Associate Director for Space Vehicles and the Associate Director for Sensors, both members of the Senior Executive Service (SES)—general officer equivalent, will remain at Hanscom AFB.

We feel the proposed structure of AFRL will allow us to reduce management overhead while improving the focus on technical activities. Many options for technology directorate structure were considered, but we are confident the proposed structure will create a more efficient, effective laboratory enterprise postured to support the Air Force's Global Engagement vision. The research and development activities at Hanscom AFB remain an important part of the Air Force's vision for the future.

I appreciate your interest in the Hanscom AFB research complex and trust the information provided is useful.

Sincerely,

79

Unfortunately, it took about a month for Secretary Cohen to respond to Senator Kerry and he did not offer any hope to help establish a Directorate of AFRL at Hanscom AFB. Although this proposal had received the initial approval of Gen Yates, the Commander of the Air Force Material Command and his successor Gen Viccellio, politics once again reared its "ugly head" and rumors have it that this proposal was shot down by Sen. Domenici of New Mexico, who for many years had tried to move AFGL to Kirtland AFB. As a result, GRD and ERD each became a Division of each of two of the nine newly formed Directorates. If this Hanscom Directorate had been established, I believe that this would have given the Hanscom Research Site the long- term stability it desperately needed and this Directorate would have had a better chance of surviving the BRAC.

5.4 The Air Force Research Laboratory

In 1997 there was still another major reorganization in which the four "Super Labs" were further consolidated into a single Air Force Research Laboratory (AFRL) headquartered at Wright Patterson AFB in Dayton, Ohio. The former Geophysics Research Directorate became the Battlespace Environment Division of the Space Vehicles Directorate at Kirtland AFB. The Electromagnetics Technology Division became part of the Sensors Directorate, which was headquartered at Wright Patterson AFB. Thus, both Divisions were now at the mercy of their respective Directorates.

5.4.1 Congress Prevents AFRL from using S&T Funds for Air Force Systems

In August 1997, Maj Gen Paul, Commander of AFRL, announced that the Air Force Science and Technology (S&T) Program would take a substantial budget reduction. This would in turn result in a loss of 130 jobs at the AFRL Hanscom Research Site. The Electromagnetics Technology Division would be closed and the Tactical Environmental Support Branch of the Battlespace Environment Division would be downsized. A long drawn out battle between Congressional Delegations from many States and the DoD was waged in order to overturn this planned S&T budget reduction. In the following letters, you will see the concerted effort that was made by many of the Senators and Representatives to overturn the action of Maj Gen Paul. This announcement was initially made in the following letter from Maj Gen Paul.

Sweeney
X P
Gregory
Miller

FROM: AFRL/CC

SUBJECT: FY99 APOM Budget Reductions for S&T

TO: AL/CC
PL/CC
RL/CC
WL/CC
AFOSR/CC

1. As you are aware, the Air Force S&T program took a substantial budget reduction as part of the FY99 APOM deliberations. Attachment 1 shows the magnitude of that reduction for the FY99 APOM FYDP years as compared to the FY98 President's Budget (the FY99 Defense Planning Guidance baseline). The budget reduction deltas are shown for the 6.1 budget (top third of chart), the overall S&T budget to include 6.1, 6.2, and 6.3 (the middle third of the chart), and DDR&E's Defense Technology Objectives, or DTOs (the bottom third of the chart). Note that we are still assessing the impact of the budget reduction on the DTOs. The overall S&T reduction (middle third of Atch 1) has been approved through the Air Force Corporate Structure process and by the Chief and the Secretary. The next phase of the budget cycle will be OSD's response to the Air Force's APOM submission, and any directed OSD adjustments via Program Decision Memorandums and/or Program Budget Directives.

2. Attachment 2 shows the process we followed in determining how to absorb the overall directed budget reduction. Attachment 3 shows the top-level results of applying this strategy for FY99—the first year of the FY99 APOM FYDP—along with the change in percentage between the FY98 President's Budget and the FY99 APOM for our current eleven technology areas. As part of our AFRL Phase II standup, we will be translating the current eleven technology areas into ten technology areas that align directly with our nine Phase II technology directorates and AFOSR.

3. We know there is "broken glass" associated with Attachment 1, that is, within the context of the reduction strategy as contained in Atch 2, some things got deleted that should not have, and some did not get deleted that should have during the course of working program element and BPAC adjustments over a very short period of time. If possible, we will fix "broken glass" before the FY99 Adjusted BES submission in early Sep 97. Note this is not a reopening of the budget cut strategy, but merely making appropriate adjustments in how we are executing that strategy. As part of our assessment process, we also intend to ask the Air Force Scientific Advisory Board (SAB) for their assistance when we meet at Woods Hole MA for our annual S&T Quality Review offsite. The SAB's involvement will be in the context of a strategic reexamination of the entire S&T portfolio to help us shape our FY00 S&T POM submission.

4. AFRL/XP will soon release spread sheets which convert the top-level information in the attachments to specific PEs and BPACs. Let me remind you that the FY99 budget process is still in progress, and the specific results in Attachments 2 and 3 could change in the weeks and months ahead. AFRL/XP will be contacting you for assistance as we work the "broken glass" adjustments.

RICHARD R. PAUL
Major General, USAF
Director, Science and Technology

Attachments:
1. Budget Reduction Profile
2. Budget Reduction Strategy
3. Budget Reduction Results

cc:
SAF/AQ (Mr. Money, Lt Gen Muellner)
SAF/AQR (Dr. Hallwig)
AFRL/CD/XP
AFRL Phase II Directors (Dr. Janni, Mr. Neighbor, Ms. Anderson, Dr. Good, Mr. Korn, Dr. Russo, Mr. Urtz, Mr. McFawn, Mr. Brinkley, Dr. Curran)

Immediately after this announcement, our SAVE Committee sent the following letter to Steve Wolfe, Executive Assistant to Senator Kennedy along with similar letters to Tom Hubbard, Executive Assistant to Senator Kerry, and Bill McCann, Legislative Assistant to Congressman Meehan, asking for their assistance in rescinding this cut.

SAVE COMMITTEE

15 August 1997

Dear Steve

We have just seen the budget figures that General Paul has submitted for the Air Force Research Laboratory (i.e., the FY99 APOM numbers for S&T in the AF). This budget has been approved through the Air Force Corporate Structure and by both the AF Chief of Staff and the SAF. Final approval is needed by the Office of the Secretary of Defense. If this proposed budget is finalized, it will eliminate the former Atmospheric Sciences Division of the Geophysics Directorate by 1 Oct 98 and force the closure of the Electromagnetics Directorate by 1 Oct 99. These actions together will eliminate ~ 130 government researchers at Hanscom AFB plus a similar number of local contract personnel. This action alone will reduce the S&T workforce at Hanscom AFB by more than 30%. These new cuts are once again being applied disproportionately on the research activities at Hanscom AFB. We note that there are **no** cuts planned for the research elements at Kirtland AFB, NM.

We have enclosed a copy of the cover letter from Gen. Paul which accompanied the budget figures and one of the key charts which is referred to in the letter. In addition we have enclosed two other charts which show the impact of the proposed cuts on personnel at various sites. Of particular interest is Gen. Paul's attachment 3 (labeled Tech Area Summary). It shows which areas are being protected and which ones are scheduled for reduction or elimination. Under the Geophysics area, programs labeled Space environment will be protected whereas the Atmospheric Science (weather) programs will be eliminated (E). The $7.6M reduction indicated for FY99 is all of the 6.2 and 6.3 money associated with these programs. The 6.1 funding for these atmospheric programs (~$1M) has also been eliminated as part of the cuts included under Basic Research listed in Box 1. Generic across-the-board 6.1 cuts of 34% will account for another ~ $3+M in cuts to other geophysics programs as well.

Under the C4I area (item 6) $5.1M of the $29.9M savings is associated with the Electromagnetics Directorate (listed as Electronic reliability) at Hanscom which is scheduled for elimination (E) in FY00 according to the detailed numbers we have seen. Additional basic research money (6.1) for electromagnetics has also been eliminated in the Basic Research area in Box 1, under the label Electronics (sensors). The 6.1 numbers have not been broken out by line item (i.e., project element), so these cuts can only be estimated at this time.

It should be noted again that the Space and Directed Energy(DE) technology areas (items 2&3 in the table) which includes all of the research activities at Kirtland AFB are being fully protected in the budget (which indicates no 6.2 or 6.3 reductions). Whether they will be made to share in the 6.1 cuts is not known at this time.

Assuming that the 6.1 cuts are applied proportionately to all including Geophysics, the combined affect of these cuts on the Hanscom activities in FY00 will total ~ $36M. This corresponds to a 50% overall reduction at Hanscom whereas the overall S&T reductions are only 23%.

The other two charts showing the corresponding personnel reductions are self explanatory and reasonably consistent with the budget reduction numbers shown in Gen. Paul's attachment 3.

These recent planned reductions continue the pattern of disproportionate treatment of the Hanscom research functions and threaten the survival of all S&T at Hanscom AFB. Although this plan has been approved by the AF, there is a good chance that DoD may direct significant modifications before they finally approve it. We would appreciate your continued help in presenting our case to DoD during their upcoming review process.

Donald Smith
Ed Altshuler
SAVE Committee
NFFE, Local 1384
Geophysics Directorate
Hanscom AFB, MA

The Congressional Delegations from many States were strongly opposed to this cutback of S&T funds. As a result, a number of letters were written to Secretary of Defense, William Cohen and Acting Secretary of the Air Force, F. Whitten Peters regarding this proposed action. Below is a letter from the Massachusetts and New Hampshire Congressional Delegations to Secretary of Defense Cohen emphasizing the negative impact of the planned reductions of the S&T programs.

Congress of the United States
Washington, DC 20515

October 1, 1997

The Honorable William S. Cohen
Secretary of Defense
Department of Defense
The Pentagon
Washington, DC 20301

Dear Secretary Cohen:

We are writing to convey our serious concerns about the effect of planned reductions by the Air Force in its Science and Technology (S&T) programs beginning in fiscal year 1999. The recent FY 1999 preliminary budget request submitted to you by the Air Force would cut these Science and Technology programs by $1.5 billion over the next five years. These cuts would seriously damage U.S. capabilities in key defense technology areas and would harm the skilled, dedicated workforce at Hanscom Air Force Base.

These proposed cuts would affect two research elements at Hanscom: the Atmospheric Sciences Division of the Geophysics Directorate and the Electromagnetics Directorate of Rome Lab. The Geophysics Directorate at Hanscom AFB, a world-renowned research laboratory, is the only Air Force laboratory studying the effects of atmospheric and space environments on weapons systems and military equipment. As mandated by Project Reliance, the inter-service division of research responsibilities, the Geophysics Directorate is the sole provider of these research services to all branches of the armed forces. The recent Dorman study (DoD Laboratory Infrastructure Capability Study) stated that the Atmospheric Sciences Division is "unique in the nation in providing weather research for military operations. No other federal agency, industrial, or university source does or can provide this warfighter support."

Rome Lab's Electromagnetics Directorate at Hanscom is also a world-class research organization specializing in antennas, radar and electronic technology. The Electromagnetics Directorate's original research has supported the development of both military and civilian equipment. Their current research directly supports military satellite communications, including the MILSTAR system, the Airborne Warning and Control System (AWACS), and the Global Broadcast System (GBS), to name just a few. Other key research includes infrared imaging and low- observable tracking for unmanned aerial vehicles, space based radar antennas for cost effective global surveillance and small ultra-wideband antennas for vital DoD communications.

85

-2-

With the recent submission of its latest planning documents for fiscal year 1999, the Air Force has indicated it intends to cut its Science and Technology funding by approximately $250 million annually over the five-year plan, and to eliminate entirely the Electromagnetics Directorate and the Atmospheric Sciences Division of the Geophysics Directorate. We believe it would be a serious mistake to carry out these proposed reductions. To eliminate them would deny the entire Defense Department their unique research capabilities.

The Air Force's proposed reductions in its Science and Technology (S&T) budget contradict the specific guidance provided by your own office. In the Defense Planning Guidance (DPG) to service secretaries and defense agency directors on fiscal year 1999 programming, your office recommended that: (1) the science and technology accounts should generally be funded at the same funding level as fiscal year 1998, in real terms; (2) that special emphasis should be given to preserving funding for basic research; and (3) that the service should provide level funding for programs that support Defense Technology Objectives in designated technology areas of special interest to the Department.

The proposed Air Force cuts violate all three aspects of the DPG directive. The Air Force seeks to reduce its overall science and technology budget by 23% and to cut the basic research budget even deeper, by 33%. The elimination of the Electromagnetics Directorate and the Atmospheric Sciences Division will undermine direct support for the six Defense Technology Objectives that their work supports.

These proposed reductions are contrary to the guidance from your office, and they ignore the advice of several independent Air Force and DoD review committees. Most notable among these panels is the Air Force's Scientific Advisory Board, which has repeatedly highlighted the need to preserve these programs. These decisions come at a time when the technological sophistication of our defense systems continues to grow, making detailed information about the impact of environmental factors increasingly important to their successful design and operation.

Additional compelling testimony was provided by Air Force Director of Weather, Brig. Gen. Fred Lewis. Speaking of the proposed reductions in atmospheric research, General Lewis stated, "To us this cut represented an AF policy decision to discontinue research focused on the medium in which we 'fly and fight'. [W]e're convinced that the current trend in the reduction of organic research in the atmospheric sciences focused on Air Force-unique problems will have a significant long-term negative impact on understanding the environment in which we operate."

86

-3-

We recognize that as reductions in defense spending continue, the Department may have to reduce defense laboratory infrastructure. We urge you to reinstate funding for the Air Force environmental and electromagnetics programs in the Air Force budget for fiscal year 1999 and beyond. If reductions must be implemented in the overall research effort, this step will allow the directorates to participate in a fair process to determine where those reductions should most appropriately be applied.

If these Air Force decisions are allowed to stand, our defense establishment will be left without two critical aspects of an indispensable research capability. This loss would leave the Air Force and DoD without the expertise necessary to address current defense needs, and would terminate the long-range research necessary to modernize and reduce the cost of future military systems.

Thank you for your attention to this important matter.

Sincerely,

_____
Edward M. Kennedy

_____
Edward J. Markey

_____
Barney Frank

_____
John Joseph Moakley

_____
James P. McGovern

_____
William D. Delahunt

_____
Bob Smith

_____
John E. Sununu

_____
John F. Kerry

_____
John F. Tierney

_____
Martin T. Meehan

_____
Joseph P. Kennedy II

_____
Richard E. Neal

_____
John W. Olver

_____
Charles F. Bass

On 30 January 1998, I contacted Harry Hoglander of Rep. Tierney's office and explained that about 130 scientists and engineers along with over 100 on site contractors would lose their jobs if the planned budget cut remained. In addition, the Massachusetts economy would lose the financial support that our Divisions provided.

He asked for additional information so I sent him the following letter.

87

30 January 1998

Dear Harry,

Enclosed are:
AFRL Organization Chart
Sensors Directorate (SN) Organization Chart including the Electromagnetics
Technology Division (SNH) at Hanscom AFB
Space Vehicles Directorate (VS) Organization Chart including the Battlespace
Environment Division (VSB) at Hanscom AFB
Figure showing the locations of the AFRL Directorates
Summary of Electromagnetics Technology Division (SNH) Funding
Summary of Battlespace Environment Division (SNH) Funding
Graph of manpower history of predecessor organizations of SNH and VSB

Key Points:
The Tactical Environmental Support Branch of the Battlespace Environment
Division (VSBE), having over 30 people, has been targeted for elimination. This
Branch must give up about 10-12 spaces by the end of FY98. The current plan is
to offer a $25,000 incentive. If a sufficient number of people do not accept this
incentive, the remaining spaces will have to be obtained through a Reduction In
Force (RIF). The reason that all personnel in this Branch have not been eliminated
at this time is that they support a Defense Technology Objective (DTO) and the
DoD mandated that the Air Force restore all DTO funding. However this funding
will cease in the following year(FY00) and the remaining personnel will be
eliminated.
The Electromagnetics Technology Division (SNH) 6.2 Funding as of December
1997 is planned to decrease to $4.63M for FY00. This is 63% of the $7.34M in
PE62702F/4600 shown in Fig. 5; the remainder is for two SN Branches at Rome.
Only about $1.0 M of 6.1 funds are authorized for salaries; the rest must be used
for contracts. SNH does not receive 6.3 funding. Thus SNH would only have about
$5.6M. Since SNH needs as a bare minimum, at least $10 M to function, this cut, if
allowed to stand will essentially eliminate the Electromagnetics Technology
Division by the end of FY99.
Although the Battlespace Environment Division is not scheduled to receive cuts
beyond the elimination of their Tactical Support Branch, you can be sure that if the
Electromagnetics Technology Division is eliminated the departure of the
Battlespace Environment Division will follow shortly thereafter.

Note in Fig. 4 that there are 5 Directorates at Wright-Patterson, 2 Directorates at Kirtland and 1 each at Rome and Eglin. There is no Directorate at Hanscom. You may recall that we tried desperately to get a Directorate and failed. Gen Paul assured us that we would not be adversely affected, yet we are suffering the largest cut.

Note in Fig. 7 that the manpower at Hanscom has suffered a steady decline. We at one time had over 1200 personnel; we are now down to about 400. We have lost about 2/3 of our workforce. Unfortunately, each time we undergo a reorganization, the manpower decreases. This happened to Electromagnetics when they first became affiliated with Rome in 1976 and to Geophysics when they became affiliated with Phillips in 1990. Now it appears to be happening again.

Our major problem is that the Air Force Generals, who control the purse strings, have absolutely no understanding of the importance of research. Their attitude is that the Air Force does not need it and that the universities and industry will do it. For example, the S&T budget is slightly over 1% of the total budget. The Air Force had to find $1 B; to do this they initially cut our budget by 20% ($250 M). It was only after the DoD forced them to restore certain funds that the final cut came to about $60M. Gen Paul said that we should expect large cuts in FY00.

In summary, the Research Labs at Hanscom AFB are destined to be eliminated unless these cuts are rescinded. It is unfortunate that the Hanscom Labs which are the oldest and most productive Air Force Research Labs face extinction.

If you need any clarification regarding this material or need any additional information, please call me at (781) 377-4662, Fax me at (781)377-5040 or E-mail me at ed@crimson.rl.plh.af.mil. We appreciate your support!
Best regards,
Ed Altshuler

On 23 February 1998, I sent the following letter to the workforce informing them that Rep. Tierney would be visiting the Hanscom Research Site.

```
Date: Mon, 23 Feb 1998 12:10:16 -0800 (PST)
From: Ed Altshuler <ed@crimson.rl.plh.af.mil>
To: everybody@maxwell.rl.plh.af.mil, plh-subscribers@plh.af.mil
Subject: Congressman Tierney visit to AFRL at Hanscom AFB

We are pleased to announce that Representative John F.Tierney of the 6th
Congressional District, which includes Hanscom AFB, will be visiting the
Air Force Research Laboratory on Tuesday, 24 February at 9:30 am in the
auditorium.  Rep Tierney and his staff have been working very hard to
avert a RIF of some of our Laboratory personnel.  As you may know, about
10 to 12 positions from the Tactical Environment Support Branch are
slated to be abolished effective FY99 ( 1 October 1998).  It appears that
through Rep. Tierneys effort, this RIF can be avoided.

It is extremely important that the AFRL workforce show our appreciation
to Rep. Tierney by attending a" Town Meeting" with our Representative.
He will discuss the current status of his effort and also give us an
opportunity to discuss our concerns with him.

The loss of these positions is just a preview of what is in store for
AFRL-Hanscom.  In FY00 the Electromagnetics Technology Division is facing
a monumental cut and the remaining positions in the Tactical
Environmental Support Branch will continue to be reduced.  If we are to
survive, we will need all the Congressional support that we can get.  One
way to assure their continued effort is to show our appreciation.

IF YOU CARE ABOUT YOUR FUTURE YOU MUST ATTEND THIS MEETING AT 9:30 AM ON
TUESDAY. IT WILL LAST LESS THAN ONE HOUR.


ED ALTSHULER

Acting Chairman of the SAVE Committee and NFFE 1384 member
```

On 24 February 1998 Rep. Tierney and his Staffers Harry Hoglander and Toni Cooper visited AFRL Hanscom. Rep. Tierney stated that there would be no job losses during FY 98-99. I sent him the following thank you letter.

NATIONAL FEDERATION
OF
FEDERAL EMPLOYEES
PROFESSIONAL LOCAL 1384
L.G. HANSCOM AFB MA 01731

24 February 1998

Honorable John F. Tierney
2133 Rayburn House Office Building
Washington, DC 02155

Dear Congressman Tierney:

Just a note to thank you for visiting our Air Force Research Laboratory at Hanscom Air Force Base today. We are certain that our research is very important for the modernization of future Air Force systems. We have to somehow find a way of communicating this to the Air Force. As you know there is uncertainty as to our future at Hanscom. Your announcement that there will be no loss of jobs during FY 98 and FY 99 was very encouraging. We congratulate you on your presentation and the ease with which you fielded questions from the Workforce. We are cautiously optimistic that with your support along with that of the rest of the Congressional delegation, we will preserve one of the Air Force's oldest and most productive research laboratories.

Once again, we appreciate your effort and want to acknowledge the cooperation which we received from Harry Hoglander and Toni Cooper. We regret that our weather people were not able to provide better weather for your visit. We will work on that the next time around.

Best regards,

ED ALTSHULER
NFFE Local 1384 Union

There was no immediate response to the Congressional letter of 1 October 1997 to Secretary Cohen or an additional letter from Judd Gregg, US Senator from New Hampshire. The following letter was then written to President Clinton from John Young and Neal Lane, co-chairs of his Science and Technology Committee on 4 November 1998 in which they emphasized the importance of continued research support in the FY2000 S&T Budget.

November 4, 1998
President William J. Clinton
White House
Washington, D.C. 20500

Dear Mr. President:

Your vision for the future of America rests on a strong foundation of investments in science, technology, and education. The FY 2000 budget provides an important opportunity to expand your legacy of vigorous national commitment that will keep the United States at the leading edge of discovery across all frontiers of knowledge and innovation. We urge you to be bold in your FY 2000 budget requests and to support strongly a broad science and technology (S&T) portfolio.

At our September PCAST meeting, Reps. Ehlers and Brown and Senators Frist and Rockefeller briefed us about their efforts in the Congress to strengthen support for S&T. Their initiatives, as evidenced in the House of Representatives science policy study and S 2217, are generally supportive of your principles of substantial investment in S&T and echo the theme of maintaining balance in the research portfolio. Sustained investment in all fields allows us to exploit their interdependence and growing interdisciplinary cooperation. As budgets grow for the critically important and broadly admired biomedical research programs sponsored by the National Institutes of Health, for example, it will be important to make comparable investments in the other agencies' basic and applied research programs.

Federal investments in S&T are essential to the creation of new, well paying jobs; our competitiveness in the global economy; our national security; protection of the environment; and our health. The Council on Competitiveness report, Going Global: the New Shape of American Innovation, released last month emphasizes, in fact, that there is no room for complacency about the United States' current economic strength and technological leadership.

As you shape your FY 2000 budget request, we advise you to continue to focus Federal resources on strengthening the United States' research capacity through an approach such as the "Twenty-first Century Research Fund," which identifies important civilian research programs. Further, we recommend that this concept be broadened to encompass the basic research programs of the Department of Defense, since it is a major sponsor of research in the critical fields of mathematics, computing, complex systems, and engineering.

We are aware that the budget caps place tight constraints on the resources available for the FY 2000 budget. We urge you, nonetheless, to reaffirm the centrality and importance of S&T through strong and balanced investment increases in your budget. A firm commitment to FY 2000 R&D budget support will position the United States for even greater success in the 21st century.
Sincerely,

John A. Young, Co-Chair   Neal Lane, Co-Chair

This letter was followed by another from Neal Lane to Secretary Cohen, once again, stressing the importance of the need to maintain the support of Science and Technology.

THE WHITE HOUSE
WASHINGTON

December 17, 1998

The Honorable William S. Cohen
Secretary of Defense
1000 Defense Pentagon
Washington, D.C. 20301-1000

Dear Secretary Cohen:

I am writing to share with you my serious concerns about proposed FY2000-2005 budget reductions in the Air Force science and technology (S&T) program. This proposed 18 percent reduction of $219 million for FY2000 would seriously erode the Air Force's S&T base—people, facilities, technology products and programs. The Army and Navy are following this situation closely and will follow suit if DOD accepts the proposed cuts. Reductions of this magnitude would dramatically weaken our ability to develop and field advanced weapons and capabilities upon which our military will rely in the coming years.

Defense science and technology is essential not only to our military forces, but also to our nation as a whole. DOD for years has been entrusted with an essential stewardship role in science and technology, to a point where DOD now provides over half of America's technology base investment in the militarily and commercially crucial fields of electrical engineering, computer science, metallurgy and materials, and mechanical engineering. For all engineering fields, DOD funds over half of the federal technology base (6.1/6.2) support in our nation's universities and one third of our total federal R&D investment.

This technology support in years past has made possible the advanced weaponry on which our defense forces depend, as our current campaign in Iraq amply demonstrates. This support also has nurtured the growth of many of the fastest growing sectors of the American economy—microelectronics, telecommunications, the whole information revolution. As your acquisition reform initiatives have made clear, DOD will depend on the civilian sector more and more in the years to come for its products and services. And the dynamism of these sectors has provided the extra GDP growth that can allow us to envision the possibility of more resources made available for defense in the near future. It would be a mistake of historic proportions if DOD were to begin a policy of consuming its technological seed corn to meet near-term needs at a time when the fields of defense technology are so fertile with military and civilian potential.

Defense S&T cuts, particularly in basic research, would doubly hurt. Not only would we lose the research itself, but we would also devastate the university programs that train our next generation of military and civilian technical talent on which DOD and the nation vitally depend.

These cuts could be quickly inflicted, but the damage done would take years to restore, during which our global technological leadership could seriously decay. Students are already highly tempted to forego graduate training in favor of high paying jobs, as seen by the recent slowing in computer science enrollments. Major cuts in federal support would turn this technological trend into a flood, with serious national consequences.

President Clinton recognizes and has repeatedly emphasized the crucial role of defense S&T in our national and economic security. In his 1998 National Security Strategy, the President notes the importance of technological superiority and advanced military systems that exploit emerging technologies. In support of his policy, I understand that OMB has told DOD that 6.1/6.2 funding should be no less than the FY99 budget submission level. This is the minimum we should do. In light of the explicit congressional FY99 language calling for a 2 percent annual post-inflation increase in DOD S&T funding through 2003, we should go back with at least FY99 enacted levels, and preferably with the 2 percent real increase.

Technological superiority has been a longstanding pillar of our nation's military strategy, and history has shown the wisdom of DOD's role in supporting robust defense S&T investment. You have been a staunch supporter of this Administration's iron-clad commitment to the nation's overall national security and long-run economic well-being, which defense S&T has done so much to make possible. If the Department is now unwilling to continue its traditional, crucial role in supporting America's technology base, this will necessarily trigger a serious look at shifting this vital role—and the resources that have traditionally supported it—elsewhere in the government. My preference, which I hope is yours, would be for the Air Force, and DOD overall, to continue its past fruitful stewardship of much of the nation's S&T program. I strongly urge you to reverse the Air Force's unwise FY2000-2005 budget proposals.

Sincerely,

Neal Lane
Neal Lane
Assistant to the President
for Science and Technology

In spite of all of the letters to Secretary Cohen and the President, Maj Gen Richard Paul was still planning to use $94.6 M, which should have been used for S&T, to instead support the Space-Based Laser and Discoverer II Spaced Based Radar Programs as seen in the following letter.

DEPARTMENT OF THE AIR FORCE
AIR FORCE RESEARCH LABORATORY
WRIGHT-PATTERSON AIR FORCE BASE OHIO 45433

MEMORANDUM FOR SEE DISTRIBUTION   7 Jan 99

FROM: AFRL/CC
1864 Fourth Street, Suite 1
Wright-Patterson AFB OH 45433-7131

SUBJECT: Program Budget Decision (PBD) 753

1. As you know, we have been working the FY2000 science and technology (S&T) budget with the Air Staff for the past several months. The final budget iteration impacting S&T was PBD 753, signed on 4 Jan 99. AFRL/XP will provide the signed PBD 753 to you electronically. This PBD reflects a decision for the S&T budget to fund the AF portions of the Space Based Laser and the Discoverer II Space Based Radar programs (both of which are currently funded by non-S&T funds) from within the existing AF S&T topline. These two programs represent an investment of $94.6M in FY2000. Therefore, we must reduce our S&T POM submission by $94.6M in FY2000 with those reductions extending into the outyears at the levels reflected in PBD 753.

2. In determining how to take the $94.6M reduction, we considered our entire portfolio: Integrated Technology Thrust Programs (ITTPs), Enabling Technology, and Basic Research. I briefed the AF Council, CSAF, and SecAF on two separate occasions regarding options to absorb various levels of budget reductions, and we iterated (and modified) our proposals based on their collective feedback. As a result, for FY2000, the Air Force approved the following specific reductions to our budget:

  ITTPs (-$18.0M)
  - HyTech (eliminated)
  - Hyperspectral Imaging (reduced $1.4M)

  Enabling Technology (-$76.6M)
  - FY2000 impacts shown in Atch 1

  Basic Research ($0.0M)
  - No cut in FY2000, but outyear cuts begin in FY01

  Total = -$94.6M

PBD 753 translates these programmatic decisions into a table of 6.2 and 6.3 Program Elements (PEs), which also appears in Atch 2.

3. AFRL/XP will forward the final President's Budget (PB) detail to you, including any final adjustments, in the next few days. Based on the attached information and any final adjustments to the FY2000 PB, I would like each of you to prepare programmatic and manpower impacts for discussion at the 27-28 Jan 99 AFRL Corporate Board. Within the next week, AFRL/XP will provide additional details on expectations for your corporate board presentations and describe needed follow-on actions. So that you may begin work, we are providing the breakout of PBD 753 adjustments (Atch 2) to the FY2000 BES by PE and Budget Program Activity Code.

4. It is important to note this information is not releasable to the general public, contractors, nor congressional representatives until the budget is officially announced via OMB press release. I will expand on the FY2000 budget deliberations at our corporate board meeting.

RICHARD R. PAUL
Major General, USAF
Commander

Attachments:
1. Enabling Technology—FY2000 Impacts
2. PBD 753 Adjustments to FY2000 BES

cc:
SAF/AQR

DISTRIBUTION:
AFRL/DE
  HE
  IF
  ML
  MN
  PR
  SN
  VA
  VS
AFOSR/CC

As result of this letter, on 25 January 1999, the Congressional Delegations from a number of States wrote the following letter to Secretary Cohen clearly stating their concern regarding the Air Force plan to cut S&T funding.

Congress of the United States
House of Representatives
Washington, DC 20515

January 25, 1999

The Honorable William S. Cohen
Secretary of Defense
1000 Defense Pentagon
Washington, D.C. 20301-1000

Dear Secretary Cohen:

We write to express our serious concern with the Air Force's proposed reduction in Science and Technology (S&T) funding in its Fiscal Year (FY) 2000 budget. The proposed reduction would be in addition to the $160 million reduction incurred in FY 1999 and would have a long-term negative impact on future Air Force readiness and modernization.

The key to our Armed Forces' total dominance on the battlefield is superior technology and training. Investments in basic and applied defense research over several decades have made this superiority possible, and they are the most effective way to maintain our military's technological advantage. These investments not only play a paramount role in fostering a strong national defense, they also provide essential training for our nation's future scientists and engineers. However, today overall Defense Department S&T spending is at its lowest level since 1986, and the services' S&T funding is at a 22-year low.

It is our understanding that the Director of Defense Research and Engineering has reviewed the Air Force's proposed S&T budget and rejected the reduction. We strongly support the director's protection of basic and applied research. Although we fully realize the fiscal pressures the Air Force faces with pressing modernization and readiness needs, we urge you not to cut any funding for the service's future, its Science and Technology accounts.

In addition, Section 214 of the Strom Thurmond National Defense Authorization Act for Fiscal Year 1999 expresses the sense of Congress that, for each of the fiscal years 2000 through 2008, it should be an objective of the Secretary of Defense to increase the budget for the Defense Science and Technology Program for the fiscal year over the budget for that program for the proceeding fiscal year by a percent that is at least two percent above the rate of inflation as determined by the Office of Management and Budget. Reductions as proposed by the Air Force for FY 2000 are contrary to the direction of Section 214.

Thank you for your attention on an issue which is critical to maintaining our Armed Forces' dominance in the air, land and sea. Please feel free to contact us if you have any questions.

Sincerely,

Edward M. Kennedy, U.S.S.

Jeff Bingaman, U.S.S.

Pete V. Domenici, U.S.S.

John F. Kerry, U.S.S.

Mike DeWine, U.S.S.

Phil Gramm, U.S.S.

Kay Bailey Hutchison, U.S.S.

Ciro D. Rodriguez, M.C.

Sherwood L. Boehlert, M.C.

John F. Tierney, M.C.

Henry Bonilla, M.C.

Marty Meehan, M.C.

Tony P. Hall, M.C.

Allen Boyd, M.C.

As requested by Sen. Kennedy's office, on 5 February 1999, I sent the following letter to Menda Fife, Military Legislative Director, providing information that could be used to counter the Air Force plan to cut the S&T budget.

NATIONAL FEDERATION
OF
FEDERAL EMPLOYEES
PROFESSIONAL LOCAL 1384
L.G. HANSCOM AFB MA 01731

Dear Menda,

I am forwarding to you some documentation that I hope will be helpful in our quest to save the Hanscom S&T Labs from elimination. But at the same time let me emphasize that this is not only a Hanscom problem; it is an AFRL problem that will affect the future of Air Force research. I would like to share my thoughts with you regarding each of these documents which are presented chronologically.

1. 14 Dec 1998. – This congratulatory letter from Gen Paul, Commander of AFRL, to Rep. Tierney is intended to indirectly look to Tierney for support. Gen Paul knows that he has to abide by any cuts that are imposed on him by his superiors so we think that this is his way of hoping that Rep. Tierney will be able to help rescind these cuts, which on 14 Dec he knew would be coming.

2. 17 Dec 1998 -. This fantastic letter from the President's S&T advisor is an excellent summary of the problem with the Air Force S&T budget. Note that he is not only critical of the proposed cut but feels that the Air Force should increase the S&T budget by 2%, or at the very least keep it at the FY99 level. Also note that at that time the Air Force was originally planning a $219M cut. His point, "it would be a mistake of historic proportions if DOD were to begin a policy of consuming its technological seed corn to meet near term needs at a time when the fields of defense technology are so fertile with military and civilian potential," is an excellent philosophy that must be repeatedly emphasized.

3. 7 Jan 1999 – This letter from Gen Paul summarizes the planned S&T cut of $94.6M. I am also enclosing a list of the reductions; note that Hanscom was originally slated to take a total of over a $17M cut.

4. 13 Jan 1999 – This e-mail from Mr. McFawn, Director of the Sensors Directorate, to the workforce states that the Air Force is planning to cut its S&T budget by $94.6M

5. 14 Jan 1999 – After learning about the proposed reduction, we wrote this letter to Sen. Kennedy requesting his help. We also sent along an attachment that summarized two of the key space-related programs that are currently being worked on at Hanscom.

6. 2 Feb 1999 – This e-mail, from Mr. McFawn to the workforce, explains that the distribution of reductions listed in the 7 Jan letter have not yet been finalized. He also attached a Point Paper by Gen Paul on the FY00 S&T Budget. I prepared a clarification of this paper.

In summary we wish to congratulate your office for the preparation of the letter to Sec'y Cohen that was signed by Senators from MA, TX, NM and OH, and Representatives from MA, TX, NY OH and FL. We note that many of the signatories hold positions on both the Senate and House Armed Services and Appropriations Committees. It may be helpful if these members are made aware of the fact that the Air Force will probably imply that they are not decreasing their S&T Budget when they are indeed doing so. Also, we should mention that one of the key Hanscom programs, High Frequency Active Auroral Research Project(HAARP), is being conducted in Alaska. We believe that Sen. Stevens, Chairman of the Appropriations Committee is very supportive of this program and would not like to see it lost.

We hope that the DOD, and the Air Force in particular, will recognize the importance of S&T to the future of our country. We welcome your support! I apologize for the illegibility of some of the documents that are being faxed. If you have any questions on their content, please call me at (781)377-4662.

Best regards,

Ed Altshuler
NFFE Congressional Liason

As one of the signatories of the letter that was sent to Secretary Cohen on 1 October 1997, Rep. Tierney received the following letter from Acting Secretary of the Air Force, F. Whitten Peters, once again, not offering much hope in rescinding the S&T budget cut.

SECRETARY OF THE AIR FORCE
WASHINGTON

FEB 2 2 1999

Honorable John F. Tierney
U.S. House of Representatives
Washington, DC 20515-2106

Dear Congressman Tierney:

      This is in response to your letter to Secretary Cohen regarding the Air Force Science and Technology (S&T) budget for FY 2000. I agree, the key to dominance on the battlefield is superior technology and training. The Department's S&T Program seeks to develop the most critical technologies, and it provides ready opportunities for the education of future scientists and engineers.

      Last year's Air Force FY 1999 S&T reductions totaled approximately $90 million as compared to the projected amount for FY 1999 as reflected in the FY 1998 President's Budget. In FY 2000, the Air Force has maintained its basic research and overall S&T investment at the previous year's investment levels. The Air Force is currently in the process of restructuring its S&T Program to emphasize activities that support the development of an Expeditionary Aerospace Force (EAF). This restructure emphasizes the integration of air and space, as well as the critical role of space assets in EAF operations. The Air Force will double its S&T investment in space by FY 2005.

      While portions of the S&T Program will be redirected, the overall program remains focused on the most critical technologies needed for defense. Unfortunately, restructuring in a tight budget environment will lead to the discontinuation of certain programs with attendant reduction of personnel. I strongly support S&T and I assure you the Department will retain a healthy S&T Program.

      I appreciate your interest in this matter and trust the information provided is useful.

Sincerely,

F. Whitten Peters
Acting Secretary of the Air Force

Since not much progress had been made, a very strong letter was written to Secretary Cohen from Congressional Delegations from a number of states expressing their concern that the planned S&T reductions would have a long-term negative impact on future Air Force modernization.

Congress of the United States
Washington, DC 20515

March 3, 1999

The Honorable William S. Cohen
The Secretary of Defense
1000 Defense Pentagon
Washington, D.C. 20301-1000

Dear Mr. Secretary:

We are extremely concerned about the Air Force proposal to use Air Force S&T funding to fund the Space Based Laser and Discoverer II (space based radar) programs beginning in Fiscal Year 2000. These programs have not been funded out of the Air Force Science and Technology (S&T) Budget in the past. Our concern is that the Air Force appears to be proposing to insert these previously non-S&T programs into the FY 2000 Air Force S&T budget while providing no additional funding in the S&T budget to cover the costs of these programs. This equates to a significant cut to all other Air Force S&T programs in FY 2000 and the outyears. This decrease in real S&T spending will result in drastic cuts to critical Air Force research programs, force potentially severe reductions in force, and weaken the overall Air Force technology base.

Congress has taken a strong position on the need to maintain a stable Air Force Science and Technology investment. We recommended increased funding for the Department's S&T programs in Section 214 of last year's National Defense Authorization Act and we continue to believe in the importance of providing sufficient funding to ensure that the defense technology base remains strong and capable. We recognize that the Air Force will need to apply resources to a certain number of space-related technologies in order to address the need for an aerospace force. However, care must be taken to ensure that this effort does not cripple other critical components of the Air Force technology base. Because of the long lead time to develop new weapons and information systems, cutting S&T could make it impossible for our Nation to maintain technological supremacy in the future.

The Air Force recently reorganized its research functions and the Air Force Research Laboratory has made great strides in preparing to meet the national security challenges of the future. The proposed funding actions will seriously jeopardize the ability of the Air Force to meet those challenges.

102

Despite the enormous importance of S&T to ensuring both our current and future national defense, there has been a decline in funding for Air Force Science and Technology programs. Whether funding reductions are taken directly or as a result of inserting previously non-S&T programs into the S&T budget, the end result is the same. We are opposed to the proposed reductions to the Air Force S&T budget in Fiscal Year 2000. We urge you to take action to ensure that Air Force S&T programs are not further reduced in Fiscal Year 2000 and beyond. We must invest today to ensure our future security.

We are also concerned that the Air Force take no action to reduce manpower based on the proposed FY 2000 Air Force S&T budget until Congress has fully reviewed the budget proposal and indicated what level of funding Congress intends to provide for Air Force S&T programs in FY 2000. The sudden loss of large numbers of highly trained Air Force scientists and engineers could have a devastating long-term effect on the capability of the Air Force science and technology program.

Thank you for your time and attention to this matter. We look forward to hearing from you on this issue.

Sincerely,

The Honorable William S. Cohen
Page 3

[signatures]

George V. Voinovich   Charles E. Schumer

[signature]   _[signature]_

cc: The Honorable F. Whitten Peters
       Acting Secretary of the Air Force
       1670 Air Force Pentagon
       Washington, D.C. 20330-1670

       The Honorable Delores M. Etter
       Deputy Under Secretary of Defense
       (Science and Technology)
       Office of the Director of
       Defense Research and Engineering
       3040 Defense Pentagon
       Washington, DC 20301-3040

On 3 March 1999, there was also the following press release from the Senators Kennedy and Kerry and Representatives Meehan and Tierney.

Congress of the United States
Washington, DC 20515

FOR IMMEDIATE RELEASE
March 3, 1999

CONTACT: Will Keyser at 224-2633 (Kennedy)
Jim Jordan at 224-4159 (Kerry)
Dave Williams 225-8020 (Tierney)
Nicole Harburger 225-3411(Meehan)

Kennedy, Kerry, Meehan and Tierney Fight to Restore Air Force Science and Technology Budget Cuts

WASHINGTON, D.C. -- U.S. Senators Edward M. Kennedy and John F. Kerry and Representatives Marty Meehan and John Tierney today sent a letter to Secretary of Defense William Cohen to express their concerns about proposed reductions in the Air Force Science and Technology budget for Fiscal Year 2000. The cuts would have an adverse impact on the Rome research lab at Hanscom Air Force Base.

"I'm very hopeful that the Senate and House Armed Service Committee will restore the funds," said Kennedy, a member of the Senate Armed Services Committee. "The Air Force would be shooting itself in the foot to accept a reduction like this. Hanscom's cutting edge research is exactly what the Air Force needs for its high-tech missions of the future."

"Hanscom is a world-renowned research laboratory and I am extremely concerned that if this budget proposal comes to fruition, we will loose the critical research that is provided at this lab," said Kerry. "Senator Kennedy, Representative Tierney and I are fighting to preserve funding so that these researchers are able to continue their projects that are so vital to the strength of the United States Air Force."

"The Air Force's Science and Technology budget is critical to Hanscom. I am concerned with the scheme to fund the Space-Based Laser and Radar programs with Science and Technology money," said Meehan. "Senator Kennedy and Kerry, and Congressman Tierney and I have joined with a coalition of members to ensure that sufficient funding is provided to support our defense technology base.

Tierney said, "The successful track record of the Hanscom research lab makes a compelling case for the continued employment of current Air Force personnel. I intend to press that case, as I and my colleagues have in the past, in our conversations with Acting Air Force Secretary Whit Peters."

On 28 April 1999, Rep. Tierney sent the following letter to his House colleagues, asking them to sign the follow up letter to Rep. Curt Weldon, Chairman of the Subcommittee on Military Research and Development and Rep. Jerry Lewis, Chairman of the Subcommittee of Defense urging them to restore the $94.6M S&T budget cut.

Congress of the United States
House of Representatives
Washington, D.C. 20515

April 28, 1999

DID THE DEPARTMENT OF DEFENSE MAKE A MISTAKE?

Did you know that the current Department of Defense Science and Technology (S&T) budget could cut many programs important to the Air Force contained within their Air Force Research Labs (AFRL)? $94.6 MILLION to be exact from AFRLs across the nation. This reduction is contrary to the statements of senior Pentagon officials including Jacques Gansler, Under Secretary of Defense Acquisition and Technology, Dr. Delores Etter, Deputy UnderSecretary of Defense Science and Technology, and Lt. Gen. Gregory Martin, Principal Deputy Assistant Secretary of the Air Force for Acquisition who recently testified before the Senate Armed Services Committee, Subcommittee on Emerging Threats.

Specifically, Lt. Gen. Martin testified that the AFRLs would shift their research toward space-based programs including "increased research in Space-Based Laser, large deployable optics, space-based radar, reusable space vehicles, hyperspectral imaging, and microsatellites." Unfortunately, the Department of Defense appears to favor cutting the very programs it testified as important to S&T investments in space. For example, Hanscom Air Force Base, located in Bedford, Massachusetts, conducts research for space-based radar, hyperspectral imaging systems, and space based laser research.

In addition to the Department of Defense FY 2000 Budget proposal, which contains deep cuts in critical Science and Technology programs, the Defense Department is proposing to use Air Force S&T funding to fund space programs that have not been funded out of the Air Force Science and Technology (S&T) budget in the past. By inserting these previously non-S&T programs into the FY 2000 Air Force S&T budget while providing no additional funding in the S&T budget to cover the costs of these programs, the Air Force is essentially cutting all other Air Force S&T programs in FY 2000 and the out years. Thus, the reductions would result in termination of the very scientists that support new space technologies.

I invite you to join me in signing the attached letter to Chairmen Weldon and Lewis urging their support for restoring the $94.6 million in cuts. This funding is critical to maintaining our technological superiority in the military and is consistent with Air Force testimony before the Senate Armed Services Committee. Please have your staff contact Toni Cooper in my office at 5-8020, Sara Gray in Representative Boehlert's office at 5-3665 or Chris Schloesser in Representative Boyd's office at 5-5235 to sign on no later than May 5. Thank you.

Sincerely,

JOHN F. TIERNEY
Member of Congress

Hon. Curt Weldon, Chairman   Hon. Jerry Lewis, Chairman
Subcommittee on Military   Subcommittee on Defense
    Research and Development

Dear Mr. Chairman:

As you consider the National Defense Authorization Act/Department of Defense Appropriations Act for fiscal year 2000, we request that you restore $94.6 million in funding for research critical to the future readiness and modernization of the Air Force. This amount reflects a cut in funding for a number of important ongoing research programs within the Air Force Science and Technology (S&T) budget. This resulted from the Air Force's decision to include previously non-S&T funded programs in the S&T budget. The Air Force budget request includes cuts in research for air vehicles, directed energy, human effectiveness, hypersonics, sensors, command and control, computer technology, environment, weapons, and weather.

The cuts require the elimination of nearly 500 civilian personnel slots at Air Force Research Laboratory facilities in Florida, Massachusetts, California, New Mexico, New York, Ohio, and Texas. The sudden loss of large numbers of highly trained and irreplaceable Air Force scientists and engineers will have a devastating long-term effect on the capability of the Air Force science and technology program.

The failure of the Air Force to provide funding for these programs will cause the elimination of vital ongoing science and technology research. Unless money is restored, the Air Force's budget proposal will result in abrupt, disruptive, and wasteful cuts in Air Force science and technology. Eliminating these resources could increase costs to upgrade existing weapons systems in the future.

The Air Force's proposed cuts for these programs follow significant reductions already taken in the Air Force science and technology budget over the last decade. We are particularly concerned that the Air Force is the only service to cut its fiscal year 2000 science and technology budget below last year's request (in constant dollars).

The Air Force included the $94.6 million for science and technology on its unfunded requirements list submitted to Congress. Lt. Gen. Gregory Martin, Principal Deputy Assistant Secretary of the Air Force for Acquisition, testified before the House Armed Services Committee that the Air Force would welcome the additional funding.

Through Section 214 of last year's Strom Thurmond National Defense Authorization Act, Congress has taken a strong position on the need to maintain a stable defense science and technology investment. We continue to believe in the importance of providing sufficient funding to ensure that the defense technology base remains strong and capable.

Scientific research is the seed corn of tomorrow's information and weapons systems. Reducing scientific research will jeopardize our nation's future ability to maintain technological supremacy in an unstable world.

Sincerely,

107

Seventy-six House Members signed the letter to Weldon and Lewis and it was sent on 14 May 1999. The same letter was sent to President Clinton on 19 October 1999.

Altshuler, Edward E

From:	Cooper, Toni [Toni.Cooper@mail.house.gov]
Sent:	Friday, May 14, 1999 3:37 PM
To:	Altshuler, Edward E
Subject:	Correct List

Here is the list of members that signed the letter in support of restoring the funds to the AFRL's.

> George E. Brown, Jr. (D-Calif.)
> Dana Rohrabacher (R-Calif.)
> John B. Larson (D-Conn.)
> Allen Boyd (D-Fla.)
> Carrie P. Meek (D-Fla.)
> Joe Scarborough (R-Fla.)
> Karen L. Thurman (D-Fla.)
> Martin T. Meehan (D-Mass.)
> Michael E. Capuano (D-Mass.)
> William E. Delahunt (D-Mass.)
> Barney Frank (D-Mass.)
> Edward J. Markey (D-Mass.)
> James P. McGovern (D-Mass.)
> John Joseph Moakley (D-Mass.)
> Richard E. Neal (D-Mass.)
> John W. Olver (D-Mass.)
> John F. Tierney (D-Mass.)
> Ronnie Shows (D-Miss.)
> Charles F. Bass (R-N.H.)
> Gary L. Ackerman (D-N.Y.)
> Sherwood L. Boehlert (R-N.Y.)
> Joseph Crowley (D-N.Y.)
> Eliot L. Engel (D-N.Y.)
> Benjamin A. Gilman (R-N.Y.)
> Maurice D. Hinchey (D-N.Y.)
> Amo Houghton (R-N.Y.)
> Sue W. Kelly (R-N.Y.)
> Peter T. King (R-N.Y.)
> Rick Lazio (R-N.Y.)
> Nita M. Lowey (D-N.Y.)
> Carolyn B. Maloney (D-N.Y.)
> Carolyn McCarthy (D-N.Y.)
> John M. McHugh (R-N.Y.)
> Michael R. McNulty (D-N.Y.)
> Gregory W. Meeks (D-N.Y.)
> Charles B. Rangel (D-N.Y.)
> Louise McIntosh Slaughter (D-N.Y.)
> John E. Sweeney (R-N.Y)
> Edolphus Towns (D-N.Y.)
> James T. Walsh (R-N.Y.)
> Anthony D. Weiner (D-N.Y.)
> Tony Hall (D-Ohio)
> David L. Hobson (R-Ohio)
> Stephanie Tubbs Jones (D-Ohio)
> Marcy Kaptur (D-Ohio)
> Dennis J. Kucinich (D-Ohio)
> Steven C. LaTourette (R-Ohio)
> Robert W. Ney (R-Ohio)
> Michael G. Oxley (R-Ohio)
> Deborah Pryce (R-Ohio)

1

Thomas C. Sawyer (D-Ohio)
Ted Strickland (D-Ohio)
James A. Traficant, Jr. (D-Ohio)
Martin Frost (D-Tex.)
Charles A. Gonzalez (D-Tex.)
Ralph M. Hall (D-Tex.)
Ciro D. Rodriguez (D-Tex.)
Ron Kind (D-Wis.)

On 29 April 1999, I received a call from Sen. Kennedy's office stating that even if the $94.6M were restored, they were told that these funds may not revert back to the projects from which they were originally taken. Needless to say, our Congressional Delegation was furious and assured us that they would not allow Maj Gen Paul to take this action. On 14 May, I received another call from Sen. Kennedy's office to report that the Armed Services Committee had agreed to restore the funds and that they were confident that these restored funds would be approved by the Senate Appropriations Committee. Finally, on 27 May, after receiving a personal call from Sen. Kennedy, I was able to send the following announcement to our workforce.

Altshuler, Edward E

From:	Altshuler, Edward E
Sent:	Thursday, May 27, 1999 4:27 PM
To:	plh-subscribers
Cc:	'everyone@maxwell.rl.plh.af.mil'
Subject:	AFRL Budget-more good news

Dear Colleague

I just received a telephone call from Senator Kennedy. He stated that he now has succeeded in having the VSB and SNH funds that were previously restored by the Senate Armed Services Committee also restored by the Senate Appropiations Committee with the exception that Project 4600 has now been increased from $9.3M to $13.2M. This should provide SNH with the cushion it needs to continue. I have a call into Cong. Tierney's office to check on the status of the House Committees. I think that we are getting closer to opening that bottle of champagne! Great news for the Holiday weekend.

Ed Altshuler

Senate likely to reverse cuts to Hanscom lab research funds

The U.S. Senate yesterday overwhelmingly passed legislation that would restore funding cut from research labs at Hanscom Air Force Base.

Friday May 28, 1999

Senators voted 97-3 for the Department of Defense Authorization Bill of fiscal 2000.

The Senate is scheduled to consider and pass the appropriations bill after the Memorial Day recess, according to Massachusetts Sen. Edward M. Kennedy.

At Kennedy's insistence, the bills restore $13.2 million for Hanscom's research labs -- $9.3 million for the Electromagnetics Sensors Directorate and $3.9 million for the Battlespace Directorate. The restoration of these funds will protect the jobs threatened earlier this year when the Air Force cut almost $95 million from its science and technology research and development accounts, including $70 million form the Applied Research accounts.

"There is clear bipartisan support for the Electromagnetic Directorate and the critical science and technology programs at the Air Force Research Laboratories at Hanscom Air Force Base," according to Kennedy's press release.

-- JEFF SKRUCKSenate likely

to reverse cuts

to Hanscom lab

research funds

There were many letters written to Secretary Cohen from organizations within the scientific community. For example the following letter from IEEE-USA stating the importance of S&T funding was sent on 27 May 1999.

May 27, 1999

The Honorable William Cohen
Secretary of Defense
1000 Defense, The Pentagon
Washington, DC 20301-1000

Dear Secretary Cohen:

On behalf of the 240,000 members of the IEEE-USA, I am writing to urge your support to maintain the technological superiority the US currently possesses and assure our future strength by submitting a request for the DOD's Science and Technology Program sufficient to achieve these objectives.

The Defense Science Board Task Force on Defense Science and Technology Base for the 21st Century recommended a funding level of $8 billion for this program in FY 2000. We are concerned with the administration's request to fund these vital research activities at $7.4 billion, which continues a downward trend in this research area. Continuing cuts and reduction in R&D momentum cannot be imposed without jeopardizing the nation's future security.

DOD's S&T Program supports research in the nation's universities that is the bridge between fundamental science discoveries and future military applications. These activities make essential contributions to national defense by fueling innovation and training the scientists and engineers of tomorrow.

The S&T Program also funds research in the DOD laboratories and private sector industries that focus on technologies to support future DOD systems. This focus on the long-term revolutionary changes in military technology will keep US forces ahead of future adversaries and enable a quick response to emerging threats such as chemical and biological agents.

We fully understand the difficult position facing you and your colleagues of "doing more with less" that includes providing appropriate compensation to the men and women of our armed forces and adequate training to maintain our current superiority. However, we strongly

The Institute of Electrical and Electronics Engineers, Inc. - United States of America
1828 L Street, N.W., Suite 1202, Washington, DC 20036-5104
Office: (202)785-0017 ■ Fax: (202)785-0835 ■ E-mail: ieeeusa@ieee.org ■ Web: http://www.ieee.org/usab

encourage that an appropriate balance between current and future needs receive the highest priority. We therefore strongly endorse the Defense Science Board's recommendation raising the R&D funding level to $8 billion. We also urge that these funds be devoted exclusively to technology base activities and not to systems development.

If you have any questions, please contact Raymond Paul at IEEE-USA, (202) 785-0017.

Sincerely,

Paul J. Kostek
President
IEEE-USA

cc: The US Senate Committee on Armed Services
The US Senate Appropriations Subcommittee on Defense
The US House of Representatives Committee on National Security
The US House of Representatives Appropriations Subcommittee on National Security
The Secretary of the Army Louis Caldera
The Secretary of the Navy Richard Danzig
The Acting Secretary of the Air Force F. Whitten Peters

PJK/rp:bc

111

5.4.2 Senator Kennedy Saves Research Division at Hanscom AFB

However, when Maj Gen Paul briefed Menda Fife, Kennedy's Military Legislative Director on 25 June 1999, he told her that the restored funds would not be used to keep the Electromagnetic Technology Division open. This prompted Sen. Kennedy to write the following letter to Secretary of the Air Force F. Whitten Peters stating that he would like to meet with him.

EDWARD M. KENNEDY
MASSACHUSETTS

United States Senate
WASHINGTON, DC 20510-2101

June 28, 1999

The Honorable F. Whitten Peters
Acting Secretary of the Air Force
Pentagon
Washington, D.C. 20510

Dear Secretary Peters:

As you know, the Senate has restored nearly $70 million in science and technology funding in the Department of Defense Authorization and Appropriations Bills for Fiscal Year 2000, including $40.4 million for the Air Force Research Laboratories.

Funding was specifically restored by the Senate for the two Air Force Research Laboratories at Hanscom Air Force Base, which had been unexpectedly reduced by $14.2 million by the Air Force. The Senate restored $13.2 million of this reduction in the following manner:

62702F	Command Control Communications Technology	
	Electromagnetic Technology	+$9.3 million
62601F	Phillips Laboratory	
	Tropo-Weather	+$2.5 million
	Space Survivability	+$.6 million
	HSI Spectral Sensing	+$.8 million

The Senate Armed Services Committee report clearly details how the Air Force is to use these funds. These funds are intended to sustain the Air Force's science and technology infrastructure, which is critical to future Air Force technology developments. Without these funds, the Electromagnetic Technology Division would be closed and the BattleSpace Environment Division greatly reduced. Both of these divisions contribute to key Air Force research projects such as Space Based Laser, Hyperspectral Imaging, Discoverer II, Ballistic Missile Defense, TECHSAT 21, and Joint Strike Fighter.

Last Thursday, after your briefing from General Richard Paul, you sent him to brief my military legislative assistant, Menda Fife, on the Air Force's plans for the restored funding at the Hanscom labs. Unfortunately, my staff was told that the Air Force has no intention of using the $9.3 million to keep the Electromagnetic Technology Division open, but will use the funds only for these employees' payroll until the lab is closed in fiscal year 2000. Further, my staff was told that without this additional $9.3

The Honorable F. Whitten Peters
June 28, 1999
Page 2

million, the Air Force would have to take funding from other Air Force science and technology programs to complete this reduction in force. My effort to preserve the excellent research performed by the Hanscom Air Force Research Laboratory certainly was never intended to allow the Air Force to solve its budget problems at other locations, nor was it intended to allow the Air Force to proceed with the termination of Hanscom's outstanding scientists and engineers.

I'm deeply concerned that the Air Force apparently intends to disregard the Senate's instructions. I would welcome an early opportunity to meet with you personally to discuss this matter.

Respectfully,

Edward M. Kennedy
United States Senator

Both Secretary Peters and Maj Gen Paul met with Sen. Kennedy shortly after. I was told (off the record) that Senator Kennedy told them in no uncertain terms that they had better restore the funds to AFRL Hanscom, "or else."

On 2 August 1999, Maj Gen Paul wrote the following memorandum in which he stated that full funding would be continued for the AFRL Hanscom workforce. Evidently, they finally had to relent to Sen. Kennedy.

DEPARTMENT OF THE AIR FORCE
AIR FORCE RESEARCH LABORATORY
WRIGHT-PATTERSON AIR FORCE BASE OHIO 45433

0 2 AUG 1999

MEMORANDUM FOR THE AFRL/SN (HANSCOM) WORKFORCE

FROM: AFRL/CC
1864 4th Street, Suite 1
Wright-Patterson AFB OH 45433-7131

SUBJECT: FY2000 Budget and Manpower

1. There has been considerable activity in recent weeks regarding the FY2000 S&T budget and the AFRL workforce, including our workforce at Hanscom AFB. Because of the dynamic nature of activities surrounding the AFRL/SN (Hanscom) portion of our organization in particular, I want to use this means to communicate directly with you in the interest of providing the most factual and recent information possible.

2. Over the past few months, we have been in the process of evaluating planned manpower reduction actions at our various AFRL sites in the context of the FY2000 President's Budget. As you might expect, each site represents a different situation because of its current workforce size, specific reductions to the FY2000 S&T budget as a result of Presidential Budget Decision 753, timing of reduction-in-force (RIF) milestones, and status of Congressional marks (adds) in terms of restoring S&T dollars. Based on the current Congressional marks to the FY2000 S&T budget and the projected level of FY2000 reimbursable "in-house" funds for AFRL/SN (Hanscom), and in conjunction with dialogue between the Air Force and relevant Congressional principals/staffs, we have decided to retain 80 of the current 115 government civilian positions within AFRL/SN (Hanscom).

3. Our intent with respect to the 80-person civilian workforce is to continue full funding for activities in antenna technology, electromagnetic scattering, and infrared sensors technology, while reducing or eliminating funding in other research areas. Although work in each current area is both high quality and unique in nature, this decision reflects a philosophy of continuing full funding for those activities deemed to be of higher relative priority to the Air Force in order to preserve "critical mass," as opposed to taking a "peanut-butter" or pro-rata reduction across all areas, thereby risking "sub-critical mass" for all. AFRL/SN may give future consideration to some internal organization consolidation with the above-described workforce in FY2000 in order to maximize organizational efficiencies.

4. Because the current AFRL/SN (Hanscom) workforce numbers approximately 100 government civilians, we need to continue with the "voluntary" portion (VERA/VSIP) of the ongoing RIF process. Our hope is that sufficient volunteers come forth to preclude the need for involuntary RIF separations. The Hanscom AFB civilian personnel office will work with each of you to provide the information you need to make a thoughtful, well prepared decision regarding your own personal situation.

5. I plan to conduct a commander's call for our AFRL Hanscom site in early September 1999, and at that time will share my perspectives on both the current and future environments as they affect AFRL as a whole and Hanscom in particular. In the meantime, thank you for your patience and understanding as we work together through this difficult time of downsizing.

RICHARD R. PAUL
Major General, USAF
Commander

cc: AFRL/SN

114

On 29 September 1999, Senators from many States sent the following letter to Secretary of the Air Force Peters urging the Air Force to fund S&T Programs throughout the Future Years' Defense Plan at levels consistent with the FY2000 Defense Authorization Conference Report.

United States Senate
WASHINGTON, DC 20510

September 29, 1999

The Honorable F. Whitten Peters
Secretary of the Air Force
1670 Air Force Pentagon
Washington, D.C. 20330

Dear Secretary Peters:

As the Air Force continues its budget planning for Fiscal Year 2001, we urge you to fund Air Force Science and Technology programs throughout the Future Years' Defense Plan (FYDP) at levels that are consistent with Section 212 of the Fiscal Year 2000 Defense Authorization Conference Report which reiterates the Sense of the Congress expressed in Section 214 of the Fiscal Year 1999 Strom Thurmond National Defense Authorization Act. This section calls on the Department of Defense to increase funding for the Science and Technology programs of each military service annually by at least 2 percent above the rate of inflation.

The Air Force's Science and Technology programs are critical to our current and future Air Force and our overall national defense. Unfortunately, investment in Air Force S&T has dropped 53 percent in real terms over the last decade and at a rate much greater than overall defense spending, which has decreased 30 percent in real terms.

This past year was no exception with the Air Force again cutting its S&T budget. As you know, these budget cuts were met with strong, bipartisan action which restored most of these funds. Your leadership is needed to ensure that we do not face similar cuts in the FY2001 Air Force S&T budget.

Maintaining an effective science and technology program requires constant dedication. Once this dedication to ideas, scientific advances and key personnel is lost, it is virtually impossible to restore this critical scientific base. Cuts to the Air Force S&T program should not take place at a time when the sophistication of our defense systems continues to grow, and when science and technology are increasingly important for the successful design and operation of these cutting edge systems. If the Air Force continues with its current pace of S&T reductions, the Air Force and the Defense Department will be left without the expertise

115

The Honorable F. Whitten Peters
September 29, 1999
Page 2

needed to meet current defense needs, and without the long-range research needed to modernize future military systems. Our goal must be to preserve and strengthen the nation's science and technology infrastructure, not reduce or weaken it.

Congress has taken a strong and clear position in support of maintaining a growing investment in Air Force S&T. We hope our views on the necessity of a robust science and technology program have been heard, and that the Air Force will propose a Fiscal Year 2001 budget for S&T that is no less than $1.3 billion.

This amount will restore Fiscal Year 2001 Air Force S&T funding to the level that Congress intended. Additionally, while we expect future Air Force S&T budgets to include funding for Space Based Laser and Discoverer II, we do not expect funding for these programs to come at the expense of the Air Force's other S&T programs.

We hope that the Air Force shares our goal of a strong Science and Technology program as vital to our national security, and we look forward to receiving an Air Force S&T budget request that meets this important goal.

Sincerely,

Pat Roberts
United States Senator

Jeff Bingaman
United States Senator

Bob Smith
United States Senator

Edward M. Kennedy
United States Senator

Rick Santorum
United States Senator

Joseph I. Lieberman
United States Senator

Olympia J. Snowe
United States Senator

Jeff Sessions
United States Senator

116

The Honorable F. Whitten Peters
September 29, 1999
Page 3

Phil Gramm
United States Senator

Kay Bailey Hutchison
United States Senator

Bob Graham
United States Senator

Connie Mack
United States Senator

Dianne Feinstein
United States Senator

Barbara Boxer
United States Senator

Mike DeWine
United States Senator

George V. Voinovich
United States Senator

Daniel Patrick Moynihan
United States Senator

Charles E. Schumer
United States Senator

John F. Kerry
United States Senator

Pete V. Domenici
United States Senator

This letter was followed by another letter on 18 October 1999 to President Clinton from 76 Members of Congress stating that "Only a strong and invigorated defense technology base can ensure our Nation's security today and into the 21st century."

Congress of the United States
House of Representatives
Washington, DC 20515

October 18, 1999

The President
The White House
Washington, D.C. 20500

Dear Mr. President:

The continued long-term erosion of defense science and technology (S&T) funding will have a devastating effect on the future capabilities of the armed forces of the United States. Therefore, we strongly urge you to request in the fiscal year 2001 and Future Years Defense Budget funding levels consistent with Section 214 of Public Law 105-261, which calls for an annual spending increase for the Defense Science and Technology Program of at least 2 percent above the rate of inflation.

As recently as World War II, America's superior research power could overtake the enemy's technology through sudden spurts of scientific development. But today, defense technology development requires many years of research and development and the Nation no longer has the luxury of ramping up scientific research only during the times of crisis. Moreover, sudden spurts of activity followed by lulls contribute to overall costs with less effective results.

The technology base for our stealthy aircraft, precision guided munitions, and command, control and communications capabilities used this year in Kosovo was developed in the 1970s and 1980s. The effectiveness of our weapon systems twenty years from now will depend on the quality of the defense research we fund today.

Projected levels of spending are insufficient to ensure that the defense technology base remains strong and capable of providing the necessary foundation for the national defense. Total spending for the Department of Defense Science and Technology program has declined by almost 25 percent since 1993 (constant dollars). The decline is even more precipitous for the military services. For example, next year, spending for the Air Force Science and Technology program is projected to decline by 58 percent from its peak. This trend, if continued, will pose a serious threat to the national security of the next generation of Americans.

The President
October 18, 1999
Page Two

Only a strong and invigorated defense technology base can
ensure our Nation's security today and into the 21st century.

Sincerely,

Tony P. Hall, M.C.

Curt Weldon, M.C.

Ciro D. Rodriguez, M.C.

Christopher H. Smith, M.C.

Herbert H. Bateman, M.C.

Michael E. Capuano, M.C.

Neil Abercrombie, M.C.

James A. Traficant, Jr., M.C.

Ralph M. Hall, M.C.

Sherwood L. Boehlert, M.C.

Allen Boyd, M.C.

Mac Thornberry, M.C.

James P. McGovern, M.C.

Karen L. Thurman, M.C.

John E. Sweeney, M.C.

Dave Hobson, M.C.

Rodney P. Frelinghuysen, M.C.

Marcy Kaptur, M.C.

119

The President
October 18, 1999
Page Three

_____
Van Hilleary, M.C.

_____
Max A. Sandlin, M.C.

_____
John W. Olver, M.C.

_____
Wes W. Watkins, M.C.

_____
John M. McHugh, M.C.

_____
Bart Gordon, M.C.

_____
Carolyn McCarthy, M.C.

_____
Patrick J. Kennedy, M.C.

_____
Michael G. Oxley, M.C.

_____
Dana Rohrabacher, M.C.

_____
Joe Scarborough, M.C.

_____
Carrie P. Meek, M.C.

_____
James H. Maloney, M.C.

_____
John B. Larson, M.C.

_____
Robert T. Matsui, M.C.

_____
Maurice D. Hinchey, M.C.

_____
Robert E. Andrews, M.C.

_____
Amo Houghton, M.C.

_____
John F. Tierney, M.C.

_____
Benjamin A. Gilman, M.C.

The President
October 18, 1999
Page Four

Solomon P. Ortiz, M.C.

Lois Capps, M.C.

Edolphus Towns, M.C.

Ronnie Shows, M.C.

Steve Kuykendall, M.C.

Rick Lazio, M.C.

Martin T. Meehan, M.C.

Stephen C. LaTourette, M.C.

Tom Allen, M.C.

Bob Stump, M.C.

James P. Moran, M.C.

Ellen Tauscher, M.C.

Jerry Lewis, M.C.

John N. Hostettler, M.C.

Louise Slaughter, M.C.

Rush D. Holt, M.C.

Brian Bilbray, M.C.

Peter T. King, M.C.

Heather Wilson, M.C.

Charles A. Gonzalez, M.C.

121

The President
October 18, 1999
Page Five

Sue W. Kelly, M.C.

John Joseph Moakley, M.C.

Robert "Bud" E. Cramer, M.C.

Howard "Buck" McKeon, M.C.

Silvestre Reyes, M.C.

William M. Thomas, M.C.

James Talent, M.C.

Lynn Rivers, M.C.

Bob Franks, M.C.

Jim Turner, M.C.

Robert Ehrlich, Jr., M.C.

Deborah Pryce, M.C.

Carolyn B. Maloney, M.C.

Jim Saxton, M.C.

Thomas C. Sawyer, M.C.

Thomas M. Reynolds, M.C.

Frank Pallone, Jr., M.C.

Debbie Stabenow, M.C.

On 13 January 2000, Senator Kennedy and his staffers visited Hanscom AFB to accept congratulations from AFRL Hanscom for once again saving our jobs. I was given the privilege of extending the congratulations from our workforce in the following address.

"After a year-long battle, Senator Edward M. Kennedy has once again been able save the positions of over 100 scientists and engineers of the Air Force Research Laboratory (AFRL). As background, in January 1999, it was announced that AFRL would face a reduction of about $95 M in Fiscal Year 2000. This reduction would force AFRL to cut about 10% of the workforce or about 500 people. Unfortunately Hanscom was slated to take the brunt of this reduction; the Electromagnetics Technology Division with over 100 people would be eliminated and the Battlespace Environment Division would be downsized. If these reductions were allowed, they would eventually lead to the closure of AFRL–Hanscom. Our future was very bleak!

Recognizing the seriousness of this situation, the National Federation of Federal Employees Union (NFFE-1384) called upon Senator Kennedy to once again help, as he had done a number of times in the past, specifically in the years 1974, 1992, 1994 and 1997. It is also interesting to note that his brother John, as a Senator from Massachusetts in 1948 helped to prevent the predecessor organization Cambridge Field Station, from being moved to Rome, NY. When advised of this impending loss, the Senator launched a full-scale effort to save the Hanscom Research Site.

The Senator proceeded to meet with Secretary of the Air Force, F. Whitten Peters and the Commander of AFRL, Major General Richard R. Paul. He emphasized the importance of AFRL-Hanscom and how its loss could severely impact the future security of our nation. He and a coalition of Senators from other states, which would also have been affected by this reduction, wrote very strong letters to the Secretary of Defense, once again emphasizing the importance of retaining a stable Scientific and Technology budget and encouraging a restoration of the funds.

Massachusetts is truly fortunate to have a Senator who has the wisdom and the insight to recognize the importance of new technology to the future of the Air Force and to our country. He is aware of the rich history of AFRL-Hanscom. Immediately after the end of World War II, the Army Air Force began recruiting scientific personnel from the MIT Radiation Laboratory and the Harvard University Radio Research Laboratory for post-war employment at the newly established Cambridge Field Station, later to become Air Force Cambridge Research Laboratories (AFCRL) in 1949. Hanscom scientists and engineers, many who are recognized internationally, have been conducting innovative basic and applied research for over 50 years and have contributed significantly to the new technologies that are currently being deployed in military systems. Senator Kennedy also realized that AFRL-Hanscom is only the tip of the iceberg and that if this research site were lost it would severely impact many Massachusetts universities and businesses.

Senator Kennedy has once again been successful in saving the Hanscom Research Site. Since he does not want to fight this battle each year, he reached an agreement with Secretary Peters to keep funding and manpower levels for the Hanscom Research Site stable for the next 5 years. The Hanscom community deeply appreciates his support. This was certainly a hard fought battle. It showed that our Congressional Delegations do indeed have the clout that is sometimes necessary to reverse DoD plans. My congratulations to them for their outstanding effort."

Figure 12 Photo of Author with Senator Kennedy - 2000

5.5 Geophysics and Electromagnetics 50th Anniversary Celebration – 14 September 1995

Although the former AFCRL Laboratories were on the decline, there was good reason to celebrate the many productive years that led to our 50th anniversary. A gala banquet was held at the Crowne Plaza Hotel in Woburn, MA. There was a lot of nostalgia and fond memories of the past 50 years, particularly among those who had worked for the Cambridge Field Station in its early years and other long time employees. About 400 present and former employees and their guests enjoyed a delightful evening of wine, dinner, and dance. It was truly an evening to remember.

5.6 Research Accomplishments-1976 to 2005

In spite of the serious events that were taking place, the Hanscom Research Site continued to produce amazing research results.

5.6.1 New Surface Acoustic Wave (SAW) Cut for Reduced Spurious Signal Delay Line -1976

Since the 1950s, researchers had realized that sets of dispersive delay lines could be used to implement a high-speed analog Fourier transform by means of the chirp-transform algorithm. The advent of precision SAW dispersive delay lines reawakened this interest in the late 1970s. A surface-acoustic-wave (SAW) delay line is an ultrasonic delay line based on the effect of the propagation of an acoustic wave in the surface layer of the solid body. SAW delay lines were widely used in dispersive filters because of the simplicity in getting the required frequency responses. RADC scientists investigated surface acoustic wave orientations on anisotropic crystalline substrates having minimal diffraction spreading. The resultant conditions for the existence of these minimal diffraction cuts agreed with those derived from formal diffraction theory. These techniques were illustrated by the theoretical and experimental discovery of two new MDC orientations on lithium tantalite (LiTaO3), having diffraction retarded by a factor of 20 over isotropic materials. Spurious responses were reduced by 30 dB as compared to previous delay lines. Thus, the in-house discovery of a new orientation of lithium tantalite that had low coupling to spurious bulk waves solved the false target problem and was transitioned to industry and used with the AN/FPS-113 Combat Grande radar.

5.6.2 Rocketborne cryogenic (10 K) high-resolution interferometer spectrometer flight HIRIS: auroral and atmospheric IR emission spectra - 1976

A Michelson interferometer spectrometer cooled to 10° K by liquid helium was flown in an IBC Class III aurora on 1 April 1976 from Poker Flat, Alaska. The sensor, HIRIS, covered the spectral range 455–2500 wave numbers (4–22 μm) with a spectral resolution of 1.8 cm-1 and an NESR of 5 × 10-12 W/cm2 scrm-1 at 1000 cm-1. An atmospheric emission spectrum was obtained every 0.7 sec over an altitude range of 70–125 km. Atmospheric spectra were obtained of CO_2 (v3), NO (Δv = 1), O_3 (v3) and CO_2 (v2). Auroral produced excitations were observed for each band, this being the first known measurement of auroral enhancements of O_3 (v3), 9.6 μm, and CO_2 (v2), 15 μm, emissions.

5.6.3 SOLRAD 11A and 11 B Satellites – 1976

The two spacecraft were launched together on 15 March 1976, and positioned ~180 degrees apart at an altitude of ~20 Earth radii. The two satellites each carried an identical complement of 25 experiments to measure solar electromagnetic and charged particle emissions, earth auroral and stellar X-ray emission, terrestrial and interplanetary extreme ultraviolet emission, X-ray and charged particle emission from the anti-solar direction, and gamma-ray bursts. They carried AFGL instrumentation to monitor solar particle fluxes.

5.6.4 SPIRE – 1977

A Spectral Infrared Rocket Experiment (SPIRE) was conducted by the Air Force Geophysics Laboratory under the sponsorship of the Defense Nuclear Agency (DNA) to investigate infrared emissions from the earth limb. The payload was launched on a Talos Castor rocket on September 28, 1977, at local dawn from the University of Alaska's Poker Flat Research Range. It achieved an apogee of 285 km. The sensors on board the payload included a pair of infrared spectrometers covering the wavelength region from 1.40 to 16.5 nm. These spectrometers employed cryogenic cooling of the optics and detector telescopes for high off-axis rejection, and circular-variable filter wheels. Also, a dual channel photometer was included on the payload to measure visible scatter emissions in narrow, molecular-emission-free bands centered at 497.7 and 697.2 nm. The SPIRE sensors were coaligned with one another. The payload attitude during ballistic flight was controlled by an inertial control system programmed to accomplish limb scanning through the day and night portions of the earth limb region. The observation of infrared emission from the earth's upper atmosphere with a limb-viewing geometry was accomplished using a highly baffled spectrometer flown aboard a rocket. Cryogenic cooling was required to measure in the infrared at the sensitivities required. The recorded infrared spectra, as a function of tangent height, showed many atmospheric gas radiators in the 1 to 18 nm spectral range. This experiment demonstrated that it was possible to isolate weak IR emissions from much more intense emissions which originated near the surface of the earth.

5.6.5 AFGL's Magnetometer Network – 1977

The AFGL Magnetometer Network recorded raw data from the seven network stations. The output was several series of tapes containing the edited data from the fluxgate magnetometer only. Each series had either a one-second or a one-minute (averaged) sampling interval and was written in a tape format selected for compatibility with one or more specific computer types used at the Air Force Geophysics Laboratory, the World Data Center, and other scientific institutions. Each plot, on a single page, contained all 21 traces from the fluxgate magnetometers of the network (three components at seven stations). Detailed instructions were given for the execution of each of the computer programs employed in the procedure as well as for the basic operation of the network minicomputer on which the procedure was carried out. The procedure was highly automated and the description provided was sufficient to permit its being carried out by an untrained operator. For the days that were more active, the plots were repeated at reduced amplitude. These magnetograms served to assess the general character of magnetic activity, identify events for scientific study, and indicated the coverage and quality of the data available from the World Data Center.

5.6.6 Low-Cost, Compact Surface Acoustic Wave (SAW) Filter Bank Electric Warfare Receiver -1978

RADC performed pioneering research on surface acoustic wave (SAW) components and advanced SAW filter and resonator technology with significant decreases in the size, weight, and cost of oscillators, fast frequency-measuring filter banks and compact fast frequency-hopping synthesizers. Their compact SAW resonator chip at 780 MHz had a Q factor of almost 5,000, five times that of larger electromagnetic equivalents. Their technique of designing withdrawal-weighted SAW transversal filters increased out-of-band rejection from 30 dB to more than 60 dB. This technology led to SAW filters much smaller, cheaper and lighter than the widely used lumped constant filters and were eventually used in B1-B and F-22 aircraft.

5.6.7 An Artificial Auroral Experiment: Ground-Based Optical Measurements – 1978

On April 13, 1975, a rocket-borne electron accelerator was launched from the Poker Flat Research Range near Fairbanks, Alaska. The launch, the second effort in the Excede series of artificial auroral experiments, was designated Excede 2 test. The pulsed accelerator operated for approximately 100 sec in the altitude range 106-135 km, providing a 3-kV electron beam with maximum currents of 10 A. A rocket-borne retarding potential analyzer indicated that the charge buildup on the electron-emitting payload never exceeded a positive potential of 200 V. Ground-based television systems and a dual channel telephotometer recorded the optical emissions induced in the night atmosphere by the rocket-borne accelerator. The fluorescent or luminous efficiency for the production of the N2 + 1 N (0-0) band at 3914 Å by energetic electrons at altitudes of approximately 110 km was determined to be equivalent to or greater than 3.2×10^{-3}. A value of 1.1 was measured for the steady state photon emission ratio of the O (^{1}S) 5577-Å to N2 + 1 N (0-0) 3914-Å emissions induced in the atmosphere at 110 km by the rocket-borne electron source. The ground-based telephotometer measurements were corrected for the effects of atmospheric extinction by measuring the apparent stellar radiance of Vega. The 5850 pound payload was the heaviest ever placed in a sounding rocket.

5.6.8 High-Latitude Topside Ionosphere -1978

Two Air Force Geophysics Laboratory low-energy spherical electrostatic analyzers were used in conjunction with simultaneous Lepedea observations to study the energetic and ambient thermal plasmas in the evening sector topside ionosphere. Significant thermal electron flux enhancements were observed in the vicinity of the inverted V structures, which could be due to either auroral return currents or ionospheric scale height changes. Enhanced hyperthermal (E > 28 eV) fluxes of positive ions, as well as vehicle potential modulations, were observed as the satellite passed through inverted V events. At 2500 km, the polar cap electron density, temperature, and energy density were 89 ± 41 cm-3, 2234 ± 480°K, and 16.2 ± 5.8 eV/cm^3, respectively. Higher energy densities were found during times of magnetic disturbance. Persistent fluxes of hyperthermal electrons were identified with the polar rain observed with Isis 2 experiments. Finally, evidence was cited for the existence of small-scale (20 km) structures within the region of plasma sheet precipitation.

5.6.9 AFGL Plumex Program -1979

AFGL launched rocket-borne ion mass spectrometers from the Kwajelin Atoll in the Pacific Ocean. The probes were part of the Defense Nuclear Agency's PLUMEX Program to study the causes of equatorial scintillations. A two - rocket operation that successfully executed coincident rocket and radar measurements of backscatter plumes and plasma depletions, was launched into the mid - phase of well - developed equatorial spread - F. Results showed large scale F - region irregularities only on the bottom side gradient. In addition, ion mass spectrometer results were found to provide further support for an ion transport model, which "captures" bottom side ions in an upwelling bubble and transports them to high altitudes.

5.6.10 Effect of Multiple Receiving Antennas on the Response of an R.F. Intrusion Sensor - 1979

A phenomenological theory was developed to analyze the response of an RF intrusion detection system. The system consisted of a loop of leaky coax cable, which acted as a distributed transmitting antenna and one or more receiving monopoles located inside the loop. The variation in received signal power was computed for two system configurations. The first used a single arbitrarily located receiving antenna; the second used two receiving antennas. The results showed an increase in system response in the sector where the receiving antenna was nearest the leaky coax cable. It was also shown that the local phase constant, which controlled the period of the interference pattern varied as the position of the intruder changes. The same characteristics were present in the response of a two-antenna system. However, the amplitude of the variation varied over a wider range because of the interference between the two received intruder signals.

5.6.11 Hemispherical Coverage of Four-Faced Aircraft Arrays - 1979

It was shown that the radiating characteristics of a four-faced array with faces arranged in a streamlined configuration could produce hemispherical coverage. This investigation presented new experimental and theoretical results giving coverage for a side array in the plane perpendicular to the cylinder and showed that the structure radiated both polarizations efficiently for angles from the zenith to the horizon. In the absence of mutual coupling effects, the circularly polarized radiation remained within approximately 1 dB of the array projection factor. Finally the investigation presented coverage contours for a four-faced array with the front and back faces half the size of the side faces. In this case, the proper choice of front array tilt angle resulted in a hemispherical gain projection factor within 3.5 dB of peak gain over nearly the whole hemisphere.

5.6.12 The International Energy Budget Campaign - 1980

In November/December 1980, AFGL participated in an international campaign of ground-based, balloon-borne and rocket-borne experiments that was carried out in northern Scandinavia to study different energy production and loss processes in the mesosphere and lower thermosphere. Some 50 rockets and 14 balloons were launched and an extended network of 56 ground stations was operated in widely spread parts of Europe. Atmospheric behavior during geomagnetically disturbed, as well as quiet, conditions was studied. In addition, specific results were summarized concerning currents and particles, the radiation field, atmospheric density, temperature and composition, wind systems, wave dissipation and turbulence.

5.6.13 Stratospheric Cryogenic Interferometer Balloon Experiment (SCRIBE) - 1980

A 0.1/cm resolution LiN2 cooled cat's eye interferometer was flown on 8 October 1980 from Holloman AFB. A description of the instrument was given as well as its performance with sample interferograms and spectra shown. It was demonstrated that the interferometer was capable of yielding resolutions of approximately 0.1/cm while in flight and cooled to 77 K. A spectrum showing the resolution capability of the instrument was presented, along with an analysis of the data.

5.6.14 Satellite Vacuum Ultraviolet Airglow and Auroral Observations - 1980

Global observations of the airglow, aurora, and solar scatter radiance of the earth's atmosphere were made in the 1100- to 2900-Å wavelength region. The spectrometer and photometer utilized were pointed toward the earth center at all times on the polar-orbiting Department of Defense satellite S3-4. The experiment was described, and initial measurements were discussed. These measurements included detection of the nitrogen Lyman-Birge-Hopfield bands in the nightglow as well as in the dayglow. In addition, nitric oxide delta and gamma bands and oxygen Herzberg bands were found in the nightglow. Vacuum Ultraviolet auroral enhancement and the tropical ultraviolet airglow due to atomic oxygen emission were also obtained.

5.6.15 Post Burnout Thrust Measurements - 1981

Research was conducted regarding the problems of avoiding collision between separated payloads and spent rocket motors due to post burnout thrust and also the problem of contamination of scientific instrumentation due to outgassing or the smoldering insulation. In order to measure this post burnout thrust, a payload instrument module was separated from an instrumented Black Brant VC Rocket in the exoatmosphere. In addition to measuring accelerations and velocities, the spent motor was observed by a TV camera on board the command attitude controlled payload module. Analysis showed that the payload separated cleanly from the vehicle.

5.6.16 The Moving Base Gravity Gradiometer Program – 1981

AFGL was designated as the lead laboratory of the Moving Base Gravity Gradiometer Program, which was funded by the Defense Mapping Agency (DMA). A description of the two modes of the system: the land based and the airborne modes, including mockup models and viewgraph sketches were described along with the accuracy requirements of the system, diagrams and pictures of the actual three-axis gravity gradiometer that was developed. AFGL and DMA were able to determine which aircraft would best suit the needs of the GGSS program.

5.6.17 Rocket-borne Infrared Sky-Survey Experiments – 1981

Attention was given to the rocket-borne infrared sky-survey experiments developed by the Air Force Geophysics Laboratory. The two survey instruments designed for the experiments were the Survey Program of Infrared Celestial Experiments (SPICE) sensor, and the Far Infrared Sky Survey Experiment (FIRSSE) telescope. The SPICE sensor was cooled by super-critical helium and covered the 8-30 micron spectral range in three bands. The FIRSSE instrument had a super-fluid helium reservoir and incorporated the three bands while also extending the measurements to 120 microns with two additional focal plane arrays. The instruments permitted extending previous measurements four to five times deeper into the galaxy. The experiments were designed to be flown on ARIES sounding rockets at 380 km.

5.6.18 SCATHA – 1981

The Air Force satellite P78-2 was designed to study Spacecraft Charging at High Altitude (SCATHA). The spacecraft contained a number of payloads for the investigation of spacecraft charging phenomena. The Air Force Geophysics Laboratory designed and developed three of the payloads. Due to the volume of data and the complexity of the analysis requirements, a Data Analysis System (DAS) was designed by the Analysis and Simulation section of AFGL. The Space Test Program satellite designated P78-2 was launched from the Eastern Test Range on 30 January 1979. The space vehicle (SV) was successfully placed in near synchronous orbit for the purpose of investigating spacecraft charging at high altitude. The mission provided data for the study of charging, discharging and plasma interaction phenomena. Prelaunch objectives included studies of the interaction of charging and discharging phenomena with SV operations and techniques designed to control SV charge; effects on spacecraft materials due to charging and discharging; studies of various particles over a wide range of energies; and determination of magnetic field intensities due both to the environment and the spacecraft.

5.6.19 Orbiting Geophysics Laboratory Experiment -1982

This was an investigation on the potential utility and technical feasibility of a new self-contained support system to be utilized repeatedly for different AFGL experiments in space, using the Space Transportation System (Shuttle) for launch and retrieval. This support system was designed to operate independently of both the STS and ground stations, therefore, data were stored rather than transmitted by telemetry. Angular pointing was the only maneuver planned; no propulsion was designed into this system.

5.6.20 CRRES/SPACERAD Program 1982-1990

The Space Radiation Effects (SPACERAD) Program emerged in 1982 with a group of sponsors in DoD, NASA, industry, and a large consortium of experimenters. SPACERAD instruments successfully functioned when they were turned on. For military planners, the survivability of microelectronics systems in space was a serious issue. The need for radiation hardening of microelectronics had become even more crucial with the strategic goal of creating autonomous spacecraft, which would rely on information processing on-board the vehicle. There were different requirements for hardening against natural and nuclear conditions. In the case of natural conditions, there were high-energy particles in near-Earth space that could affect space systems. Particles trapped in the inner (primarily proton) and outer (primarily electron) radiation belts could damage advanced electronic devices and other systems on board spacecraft. Their susceptibility to damage increased as the size of microelectronic cells decreased. By the end of 1990 the CRRES/SPACERAD Program had been in progress for nearly ten years and had both evolved and undergone many trials. The original scientific goal of the program, a very ambitious one, was to achieve comprehensive, simultaneous measurements of the Earth's radiation belts in order to create the first dynamic models of space radiation. Thus, in the end, against considerable odds, the obstacles to realizing CRRES as a functioning satellite in orbit were overcome. The Space Physics Division's extended investment of manpower and in-house exploratory development funds had paid off. After a decade of endeavor AFGL was on the way to realizing its goal of characterizing the Earth's radiation belts.

5.6.21 Comparison of Data from the Low Energy Electrostatic Analyzers on Satellite P78-1 - 1982

Air Force satellite P78-1 had aboard, on the wheel section, two detectors each consisting of a low energy and a high energy electron electrostatic analyzer. The low energy analyzer collected electrons in the energy range of 50 eV to 1 keV and the high energy analyzer collected electrons in the energy range of 1 keV to 20 keV. The two detectors were placed 90 degrees apart on the wheel section of the satellite.

5.6.22 Earth Limb Infrared Atmospheric Structure (ELIAS) – 1983

The ELIAS experiment was flown from the Poker Flat Research Range, Alaska in 1983 and successfully monitored visible and infrared emissions from an IBC III+ aurora. Measurements were performed in both staring and scanning modes over several hundred seconds. The data for short- and mid-wave infrared regions were analyzed in terms of auroral excitation of the NO and NO+ vibrational bands. Auroral excitation efficiencies and kinetic implications were determined.

5.6.23 Next Generation Weather Radar (NEXRAD) - 1984

The Boston Area NEXRAD Demonstration (BAND) was formulated to assess the operational utility of Next Generation Weather Radar (NEXRAD) algorithms and display products in three seasons of New England weather. BAND was a cooperative effort, which utilized the AFGL 10-m Doppler weather radar and data processing systems and the staff of the NEXRAD Interim Operational Test Facility to remote NEXRAD-like weather radar products to future joint agency users of this data. Operational users of BAND information included both central forecast facilities such as the USAF Global Weather Central at Offut AFB, NE and the National Severe Storm Forecast Center at Kansas City, MO, as well as local forecast facilities including the Base Weather Station at Pease AFB, NH, the National Weather Service Forecast Office at Boston, MA, and the Federal Aviation Administration Air Traffic Control Center at Nashua, NH. The BAND demonstration began on 16 November 1983 and ended on 1 July 1984. During this period more than 450 hours of NEXRAD-like data on all types of New England weather were provided in real-time to the operational users for their evaluation.

5.6.24 Polar Ionospheric Irregularities Experiment (PIIE) – 1985

Results were obtained from the Polar Ionospheric Irregularities Experiment (PIIE), conducted from Sondrestrom, Greenland, on March 15, 1985. An investigation of processes which led to the generation of small-scale (less than 1 km) ionospheric irregularities within polar-cap F-layer auroras was conducted. An instrumented rocket was launched into a polar cap F layer aurora to measure energetic electron flux, plasma, and electric circuit parameters of a sun-aligned arc, coordinated with simultaneous measurements from the Sondrestrom incoherent scatter radar and the AFGL Airborne Ionospheric Observatory. Results indicated the existence of two different generation mechanisms on the dawnside and duskside of the arc. On the duskside, parameters were suggestive of an interchange process, while on the dawnside, fluctuation parameters were consistent with a velocity shear instability.

5.6.25 Vibro-Acoustic Measurement System (VAMS) – 1985

AFGL shipped its Vibro-Acoustic Measurement System to the V23 launch site at the STS facility at Vandenberg AFB to measure vibro-acoustic behavior that occurred for several Ground Support System structures. The forecasts of this behavior were based on particular vibration and pressure responses determined by an explosive sounding program conducted at V23. Motion levels were found to be substantially below all levels of concern. However, companion studies showed that high accelerations could be anticipated in the OFS Room and the PCR. In addition, pounding could occur between PCR and PPR. Strong reverberations on acoustic records from V23 indicated that launch overpressures at V23 were significantly altered from those recorded at the Kennedy Space Center for the shuttle at altitude and clear of the ground.

5.6.26 Infrared Measurements of Zodiacal Light -1985

The shape and intensity of scattered sunlight and thermal emission from the interplanetary dust cloud were determined by the structure, size and chemical composition of the individual particles and their distribution through the solar system. The infrared zodiacal emission at wavelengths between 2 and 30 microns was measured with a cryogenically cooled absolute radiometer from a rocket platform. The in-plane measurements were well matched by a dust density distribution, which decreased as the inverse of the distance from the sun. The out of plane measurements were well matched by a dust density exponential distribution.

5.6.27 AFGL Sensors for the Defense Meteorological Satellite Program (DMSP) - 1987

The Defense Meteorological Satellite Program (DMSP) carried two AFGL designed sensors for space weather forecasting, the SSJ/4 particle detector and the SSIES plasma monitor. The SSJ/4 measured the flux of precipitating electrons and ions with energies between 30 eV and 30 keV. The data from these analyzers were processed at AFGL and were available to the scientific community. Both by itself, and in combination with other sensors on the satellite, the SSJ/4 detectors provided important data for the study of auroral processes.

The SSIES experiment monitored the ionospheric thermal plasma, which affected communications and operations. The total ionospheric electron content (TEC) determined the phase delay of radio signals. The plasma density and scale height measured by the SSIES instrument, together with other data sources, which described the lower ionosphere, were used to determine TEC on an operational basis. Finally, the SSIES and SSJ/4 measurements were combined to calculate the rate of joule heating of the lower ionosphere by currents driven by forces from the magnetosphere.

5.6.28 Cryogenic instrumentation and detector limits in FTS - 1987

The desire to measure atmospheric emission spectra of the upper atmosphere led to the development of cryogenically cooled infrared Fourier transform spectrometers (FTS). These spectrometers combine the sensitivity advantage of a Fourier transform spectrometer with the sensitivity gains obtainable with modern infrared detectors operated at low photon backgrounds. The temperature required to obtain maximum sensitivity was primarily determined by the wavelength region of interest, longer wavelengths requiring lower temperatures. In order to take full advantage of reduced background operation, the preamplifier was cooled in order to reduce the noise. Low noise preamplifiers capable of operation down to liquid helium temperatures were developed. Three cryogenically cooled spectrometers of significantly different design were considered. The first instrument was a standard Michelson interferometer cooled to 10 K with supercritical helium and capable of 1 wave number resolution. This interferometer was successfully flown on a rocket and obtained measurements of atmospheric limb emission at tangent altitudes from 70 km to 150 km. The second was a field widened prism interferometer, which operated at liquid nitrogen temperature and was flown on a rocket and obtained measurements of atmospheric emission in the 2 to 8 micrometer region during an aurora. The third was a balloon borne liquid nitrogen cooled interferometer, which incorporated cat's eye retroreflectors for end mirrors and was capable of 0.1 wave number resolution. This spectrometer was successfully flown on a balloon several times and obtained measurements of atmospheric limb emission at tangent altitudes from 0 km to 30 km.

5.6.29 Gamma Ray Advanced Detector Experiment – 1988

AFGL launched the first large helium-filled balloon in the Antarctica in support of the Gamma Ray Advanced Detector (GRAD) experiment. After a series of catastrophic balloon problems, only two balloon failures occurred in more than 100 flights. The success of the Gamma Ray Advanced Detector experiment by the Air Force Geophysics Laboratory resulted in numerous requests for long duration flights in Antarctica.

5.6.30 Operational Tactical Decision Aid - 1988

AFGL delivered to the Air Weather Service an Operational Tactical Decision Aid for infrared weapons systems. The Tactical Decision Aid (TDA) was an integrated target/atmosphere/sensor model that was used to estimate target acquisition ranges for infrared sensors. It employed an extensive 8000-plus line computer code, LOWTRAN-6, to evaluate the atmospheric extinction of infrared signals for various climatologically conditions. Compact atmospheric extinction models were developed for various types of atmospheric extinction, which were significant for the TDA application. The models were developed based on the LOWTRAN-6 computation and were verified through extensive accuracy analysis. For automated generation of a database for accuracy analysis, an interactive driver for LOWTRAN-6, called DGU, was developed.

5.6.31 Space-Qualified Fracture-Resistant Quartz - 1988

Until this work, stable GPS oscillators were not available. Scale-up and Tech transfer won the Federal Lab Consortium Award for Technology Transfer.

5.6.32 Auroral Photography Experiment - 1988

In the framework of this program, the Lockheed Palo Alto Research Laboratories performed a joint experiment with AFGL to make observations of the aurora, airglow, shuttle induced emission effects such as surface discharge, shuttle glow, and thruster induced effects. In this program the Air Force flew Lockheed instrumentation as a secondary payload on the shuttle and made observations through the orbiter windows with the specialized equipment. The hardware was essentially a re-flight of the Auroral Photography Experiment (APE), which was flown on mission 41-G.

5.6.33 High Frequency Active Auroral Research Program (HAARP) – 1990

The High Frequency Active Auroral Research Program (HAARP) was an ionospheric research program jointly funded by the U.S. Air Force, the U.S. Navy, the University of Alaska, and the Defense Advanced Research Projects Agency (DARPA). Built by BAE Advanced Technologies (BAEAT), its purpose was to probe the ionosphere and investigate the potential for developing ionospheric enhancement technology for radio communications and surveillance. The HAARP program operated out of a major sub-arctic facility, named the HAARP Research Station, on an Air Force–owned site near Gakona, Alaska. The most prominent instrument at the HAARP Station was the Ionospheric Research Instrument (IRI), a high-power radio frequency transmitter facility operating in the high frequency (HF) band. The IRI was used to temporarily excite a limited area of the ionosphere. Other instruments, such as a VHF and a UHF radar, a fluxgate magnetometer, a digisonde, and an induction magnetometer, were used to study the physical processes that occur in the excited region.

The HAARP project directed a 3.6 MW signal, in the 2.8–10 MHz region of the HF band, into the ionosphere. The signal could be pulsed or continuous. Then, effects of the transmission and any recovery period could be examined using associated instrumentation, including VHF and UHF radars, HF receivers, and optical cameras. According to the HAARP team, this advanced the study of basic natural processes that occur in the ionosphere under the natural but much stronger influence of solar interaction, and how the natural ionosphere affected radio signals. This enabled scientists to develop methods to mitigate these effects to improve the reliability or performance of communication and navigation systems, which would have a wide range of uses, civilian and military, such as an increased accuracy of GPS navigation, and advances in underwater and underground research and applications.

This led to improved methods for submarine communication, or an ability to remotely sense and map the mineral content of the terrestrial subsurface, and perhaps underground complexes, of regions or countries, among other things.

5.6.34 Platinum Silicide IR Pushbroom Camera -1990

Silicide focal plane array (FPA) technology continued to advance with better photodiodes, larger monolithic arrays and IR background limited cameras that had near television image quality. Those parameters which limited the performance of sensors along with work, which could give a ten-fold improvement in camera sensitivity were investigated. This camera was later used in a U-2 to map Iraqi mine fields. An article on this new technology was published in Aviation and Space Technology.

5.6.35 Showerhead MOCVD Technology – 1993

The Electromagnetic Technology Division conducted basic research on the Showerhead MOCVD Technology, which provided inherent advantages over other vertical reactor concepts such as a high level of deposition uniformity and material quality. The exceptional uniformity of thickness, doping, and composition of the deposited device structures combined to produce advanced GaN-based structures at the lowest overall cost per wafer in the industry. This technology was transferred to Spire Corporation and marketed by Thomas Swan for companies such as Northrop Grumman.

5.6.36 Platinum Silicide Staring Infrared Camera -1995

Methods were investigated to characterize infrared focal plane array (IR FPA) non-uniformity and infrared camera spatial noise. Techniques were examined which ranged from simple visual inspection of the video imagery to array characterization criteria. While the effect of spatially correlated noise patterns on sensor performance was impossible to quantify in a simple way, rather simple expressions could be derived to obtain a representative assessment of sensor performance. It was concluded that the temporal stability of the spatial noise pattern was most relevant to camera performance and that there was no simple parameter, which could predict sensor performance when spatial noise was present in the imagery. This technology produced a camera with three-fold increase in night vision warning and detection range. It was used by the entire B-52 fleet and the FBI.

5.6.37 Two-element dielectric antenna serially excited by optical wavelength multiplexing – 1999

A single pulsed laser beam containing multiple wavelengths (wavelength multiplexing) was employed to activate two semiconductor antennas in series. The dielectric nature of the semiconductors permitted serial cascading of the antenna elements. Recently observed nonlinear characteristics of the radiated field as a function of the free carrier accelerating (bias) voltage were used to minimize the small interactions between elements. It was demonstrated that the temporal electromagnetic radiation distribution of two serial antennas was sensitive to the three-dimensional pattern of the optical excitation source. One could, in turn, vary this distribution continuously by optical means to reconfigure the array.

5.6.38 A study of hydrogen evolution at irradiated p-InP electrodes in nitric acid solutions – 1999

Recent investigations of the photoelectrochemical (PEC) etching of p-InP in nitric acid showed an unusual property where hydrogen was not evolved with the formation of metallic indium. In order to find the cause of this lack of hydrogen evolution at the irradiated p-InP electrode, the inhibition of the reduction of nitric acid was studied. Sulfamic acid was shown to completely inhibit the reduction of nitric acid. With Sulfamic acid, hydrogen was evolved at the irradiated p-InP electrode in nitric acid. The lack of hydrogen evolution in the PEC etching was attributed to the reaction of the nascent hydrogen atoms, formed on the p-InP electrode, with an active species involved in the reduction of nitric acid. In the presence of Sulfamic acid, the hydrogen atoms combined to evolve hydrogen. Experiments showed that the reduction of nitric acid had no effect on the PEC etching of the p-InP in nitric acid.

5.6.39 Electric and Magnetic Current Sources in Infinite and Semi-Infinite Spaces-Expressions for the Radiated Fields in Cylindrical Coordinates - 1999

Expressions were derived for the electromagnetic fields due to a circular cylindrical axially-directed electric current source, a radial electric ring source, and magnetic frill in free space and above an infinite ground plane. The expressions were valid everywhere in space including the source region. The fields were given in cylindrical coordinates, and the results were applicable, among others, to the analysis of coaxially-fed cylindrical antennas.

5.6.40 Investigation of microstrip radial stub CAD models from 2 to 60 GHz - 2000

The accuracy of microstrip radial stub computer-aided design (CAD) models was investigated both experimentally and against electromagnetic simulations. A dual-resonator technique was used to eliminate confounding variables and to obtain accurate experimental data. This technique was extended beyond the earlier perturbation analysis applied to discontinuities to enable checking models that have significant electrical length. Model phase errors in excess of 16° were found for the microstrip radial stub.

5.6.41 The Midcourse Space Experimental Survey of the Galactic Plane - 2001

The Midcourse Space Experiment (MSX) surveyed the entire Galactic plane within |b| ≤ 5° in four mid-infrared spectral bands between 6 and 25 µm. These survey data were combined to create 1680 1.5 × 1.5 degree images that covered the region with 6" pixel spacing in each of the spectral bands. The images preserved the inherent resolution of the data but had up to twice the sensitivity of a single scan. The individual survey observations had to be extensively conditioned to achieve the co-add advantage. Additionally, 36 lower resolution 10° × 10° images were generated in each band that spanned the full latitude and longitude range of the survey. These panoramic images had a resolution of ~1.2 with 36" pixel spacing and a six-fold improvement in noise equivalent radiance, making them an ideal product for comparison with radio surveys of the Galactic plane. An ancillary set of images was created from other MSX astronomy experiments that lied within 10° of the Galactic plane. These images either extended the latitude coverage of the survey or provided deeper probes of Galactic structure either by themselves or when added to the survey images.

5.6.42 Improving the accuracy of antenna and scattering computations with Incremental Length Diffraction Coefficients - 2001

Incremental length diffraction coefficients (ILDC's) provide a convenient, efficient method for determining high frequency scattered fields for arbitrary angles of incidence and scattering. Under the assumption that high-frequency scattering is a local phenomenon, the fields radiated by each differential element of the induced sources on a general three-dimensional scatterer will be the same as the fields radiated by the differential length of the two-dimensional canonical scatterer that conforms locally to the geometry of the three-dimensional scatterer. The far fields radiated by a differential length of the canonical scatterer are called ILDC's. Thus, the high-frequency fields radiated by a general scatterer or antenna can be determined by integrating the appropriate ILDC's (multiplied by the incident field) over boundary curves on the scatterer or antenna. A straightfoward, convenient substitution method was developed for the determination of ILDC's that form the basis to improve upon the accuracy of high-frequency electromagnetic fields computed with some of the more widely used radar cross section and antenna computer codes such as XPATCH and GRASP. The line integration of these ILDC's along discontinuities and shadow boundaries eliminates singularities in caustic and transition regions and yields corrections to physical optics fields that are valid for all angles of observation. Neither cumbersome ray tracing nor searching for critical points are involved in the application of ILDC's.

5.6.43 Population-Inversion and Gain Estimates for a Semiconductor TASER - 2001

A solid-state design advanced to achieve a terahertz-amplification-by-the-stimulated-emission-of-radiation (TASER) was investigated. The original design was based on light to heavy-hole inter-subband transitions in SiGe/Si heterostructures. This work adapted the design to electron inter-subband transitions in the more readily available GaAs/Ga1 Al As material system. It was found that the electric-field induced anti-crossings of the states, derived from the first excited state with the ground states of a superlattice in the Stark-ladder regime, offered the possibility of a population inversion and gain at room temperature.

5.6.44 A Multi-Josephson Junction Qubit-2002

A persistent super current multi-Josephson junction (JJ) qubit whose circuit was based on a flattened JJ triangular prism was designed. The Schrödinger equation for the 1D constrained system was equivalent to the Whittaker Hill equation, for which the exact solutions were found. Symmetric or antisymmetric coupling of the qubit to an external magnetic field, excited only the corresponding symmetric or antisymmetric terms in the Hamiltonian. This specificity allowed coupling to a system bus comprised of an LC resonant loop. It was indicated how separate buses might be coupled into a larger branching network.

5.6.45 Geodesic Sphere Phased Array Antenna For Satellite Control And Communication - 2002

It was realized that within the next decade there will be a dramatic increase in the number of commercial and military satellite constellations providing world-wide telecommunication, environmental, navigation, and surveillance services. The satellites will need a network of ground stations to serve as the gateways for satellite tracking, telemetry, and command operations and/or payload message/data routing. A typical ground station requires one or more large, high performance antennas at L and S-band with hemispherical coverage for communicating with the satellites. Two types of antennas can be used for the ground station: mechanically steered reflectors or electronically steered arrays (ESA). Due to their relatively low initial cost, satellite operations have almost exclusively used reflector antennas, however, their effectiveness and operability were limited due to their high operation and maintenance cost, susceptibility to single point of failure, low antenna utilization, inflexibility to adapt to new mission and operational requirements, long down times, and inability to be maintained under operational conditions.

Thus, there was a great need to improve the operating efficiency and mission capabilities of the present satellite control network with a better antenna. It was shown that the Electronically Steered Array can provide superior performance and greatly enhance present system capability and capacity and that a spherical array was the optimal choice for ground-based satellite control antennas in terms of performance and minimum number of radiating elements, However, since the fabrication and assembly of curved surface arrays was difficult and expensive, the Electromagnetic Technology Division of the Air Force Research Laboratory proposed a low-cost, multi-function, multi-beam GDPAA for horizon-to-horizon satellite operations and that the spherical array surface be approximated by a number of flat panel subarrays. In this manner, the design preserved all the advantages of spherical phased arrays while maintaining the ease of fabrication afforded by well-developed planar array technology. The Electromagnetic Technology Division designed and fabricated one of the 675 flat panel subarrays. The initial results showed that the construction of the full array was feasible.

5.6.46 Large Variations in Balloon Ascent Rate over Hawaii -2002

A sequence of nine weather balloons were launched over the island of Hawaii during the nights of 12, 13, and 17 December, 2002, providing measurements of ascent rate, horizontal wind speed and direction, temperature, and other quantities. The measurements showed short intervals of altitude with a large increase in ascent rate, occurring only near the tropopause, indicating regions of strong upward air velocity at this location. The large ascent rates correlated well with the strength of a jet stream, and with the presence of a local critical level, indicating mountain waves as the primary cause. No corresponding decreases in ascent rate were measured, suggesting strong three-dimensional effects.

5.6.47 Antenna Design using a Genetic Algorithm - 2004

The design of antennas using a genetic algorithm (GA) was invented by scientists of the Electromagnetics Technology Division of the Air Force Research Laboratory. The GA starts with a large population (trillions, for typical problems) of potential wire configurations. These configurations are determined by the constraints of the problem and the method of encoding all configuration information (e.g., start and end points and wire sizes) into a string of 1s and Os, called a binary chromosome, or a set of numbers, called a real chromosome. The GA randomly selects a sample population, of wire configurations from a very large population. It then evaluates the performance of each member of this population, with a cost function that compares individual performance with the desired or ideal performance. The cost function returns a single number to the GA that is a measure of its fitness. In antenna design with a GA, evaluating the cost function involves simulating each member with an electromagnetics code, and comparing the results with those desired. As in the evolutionary process of "survival of the fittest," high-quality strings (chromosomes) mate and produce offspring, while poor quality strings perish. Offspring are created by combining randomly selected parts of two chosen parent strings. With succeeding "generations," the quality of the strings continually improves, and an apparent optimal solution is ultimately obtained. It should be mentioned that the GA does not necessarily produce the "best possible" design, however it does produce a design that generally performs better than others that have been derived, and with a configuration that has not been predicted.

Antennas designed using a genetic algorithm have been used for many applications, in particular for two NASA missions, the ST5 and the TDRS-C. NASA's Space Technology 5 (ST5) launched three small spacecraft to test innovative concepts and technologies. Genetic algorithms were used to design antennas having wide beamwidth for a circularly polarized wave and wide impedance bandwidth. These constraints made this a challenging antenna design problem. The evolved antenna had a number of advantages in regard to power consumption, fabrication time and complexity, and performance. Lower power requirements resulted from achieving high gain across a wider range of elevation angles, thus allowing a broader range of angles over which maximum data throughput could be achieved.

In addition to the ST5 antenna, an S-band phased array antenna element design that met the requirements for NASA's TDRS-C communications satellite was also designed. A combination of fairly broad bandwidth, high efficiency and circular polarization with high gain made for another challenging design problem. The specification called for two types of elements, one for receive only and one for transmit/receive. The genetic algorithm produced a single element design that met both specifications thereby simplifying the antenna and reducing testing and integration costs. Aerospace component design is an expensive and important step in space development. Evolutionary design can make a significant contribution wherever sufficiently fast, accurate and capable simulators are available to implement the appropriate fitness function.

One of the applications for which genetic algorithms was applied was the design of an electrically small antenna for satellites and unmanned aerial vehicles. Below is a design that produced an antenna configuration that could not have been obtained using any other design approach.

Figure 13 Electrically Small Genetic Antenna

Chapter 6: The Base Realignment and Closure (BRAC) – 2005

On 15 November 2002, the Secretary of Defense, Donald Rumsfeld, initiated the Base Realignment and Closure (BRAC), the purpose of which was to eliminate excess capacity within the DoD. He established the Infrastructure Executive Council (IEC) to oversee and operate the Department's BRAC 2005 process. The IEC, with inputs from the Military Departments, would then generate a list of installations that would be either realigned or closed. The IEC recommendations would then be submitted to the Secretary for his review and approval. The services would base their recommendations on the military value of an installation and its capacity to support other core missions as well as current missions. The BRAC time line was as follows:

- NLT 16 May 05 SECDEF Recommendations are given to the BRAC Commission and released to the Public
- NLT 1 July 05 Comptroller General (GAO) Analysis of Recommendations is released
- NLT 8 September 05 Commission's Recommendations are forwarded to the President
- NLT 23 September 05 President must Approve or Disapprove of the list in its entirety
- NLT 20 October 05 If the President disapproved the list, the Commission Submits Revised Recommendations to the President
- NLT 7 November 05 President approves or disapproves of resubmitted list +45 Legislative Days or adjournment
- Congressional Approval or Disapproval following President's submission to Congress

At the time, Hanscom AFB, which had escaped the previous BRAC, was being considered for BRAC 2005. Hanscom personnel were relieved to learn that the Base was not on the BRAC list. However, on 13 May 2005, the Base Realignment and Closure (BRAC) Commission announced that the Air Force Research Laboratory (AFRL) would relocate the two Divisions that made up the Hanscom Research Site; the Electromagnetics Technology Division would move to Wright Patterson Air Force Base (WPAFB), Dayton, OH and continue to be part of the Sensors Directorate; the Battlespace Environment Division would move to Kirtland Air Force Base (KAFB), Albuquerque, NM and continue to be part of the Space Vehicles Directorate. After the BRAC announcement, we were cautiously optimistic that our Congressional Delegation would once again prevent the closure of the AFRL Hanscom Field Site. Members of the BRAC commission had visited our Laboratory and spoken with our management. They had been told that we were a relatively small research laboratory and that most of the senior scientists and engineers (S&E's) would probably not relocate to KAFB and WPAFB. Thus the Air Force would lose their expertise in the areas of Geophysics and Electromagnetics. The BRAC personnel said that they understood our situation and that we would probably be removed from the list. Unfortunately when the list was released on that fateful day of 13 May 2005, our AFRL Hanscom Research Site was on it. We were blindsided! In retrospect, we believe that we may have been the "sacrificial lambs" that were included on the BRAC list so that the larger organizations at Hanscom AFB could survive. The following is a letter that was written by Senator Kennedy after this announcement.

"From the Office of Sen. Edward M. Kennedy

May 13, 2005

KENNEDY ANNOUNCES VICTORY FOR MASSACHUSETTS BASES
Massachusetts sees net gain of 491 Jobs, Hanscom gains 1,104 Jobs

"I'm very pleased to see that the Pentagon proposed moving the Air Force's Air and Space Information Systems R&D center to Hanscom. This is an acknowledgement of the excellent work that is done at Hanscom. It will bring over 1100 new jobs to Massachusetts, and new high-tech mission. It will make Hanscom, in their words, "a multi-functional center of excellence in the rapidly changing technology area" of command and control technologies. It will provide our Air Force with a more efficient structure for developing the needed information network to keep our military's technological advantage.

I am concerned to see that the list proposes closing Otis Air Guard Base and proposes moving those planes to Atlantic City, New Jersey. We need to look carefully at that proposal and determine its effect on national security.
This list is not the final step in the process. It's the Pentagon's proposal. The BRAC Commission will now consider it over the summer, with a final vote in Congress in the Fall. We'll continue to fight for our bases as we've done all along. We have a team of experts scrutinizing the results now to find out whether the Pentagon's analysis properly evaluated our bases. We'll use that information to make the strongest arguments we can that our bases are needed for national security, and we will continue to make that case before the commission.
This BRAC round has been a long journey. Since the initial legislation was passed in September 2001, we've been hard at work to ensure that Massachusetts' bases are not closed. As soon as it was enacted, Governor Jane Swift and I began discussing our BRAC strategy. Governor Romney joined the effort when he was elected in 2002 and has been strongly committed preserving our bases ever since.

We've looked carefully at past BRAC rounds to determine which bases were most vulnerable. For high-tech research and development facilities like Natick and Hanscom, we found that past BRACs couldn't properly analyze the complex factors that make them so successful. We worked hard to see that the Pentagon understands what is needed to maintain high-tech military advantage—a skilled workforce, and access to the best research institutions and industry. We've got that here in Massachusetts for our bases. Other bases in other states don't have that advantage.

We enlisted the support of Senator Sununu and Senator Gregg because of the impact that base closings would have on southern New Hampshire. We brought senior BRAC officials up to Hanscom and Natick to see firsthand the impressive work being done there.

We offered the government the opportunity to do even more in the state, and worked hard on an expansion plan. We visited senior military officials in the Pentagon and Ohio. We worked hard in the state to back up the expansion plan with a bond bill to pay for it.

Our communities have rallied around our bases in an unprecedented show of support. We've made sure that the BRAC officials know how strongly Massachusetts supports them. And we'll continue to do that as the process continues. The results today show that our efforts have paid off."

Note that Sen. Kennedy's principal concern was Otis Air Guard Base. Although research at Hanscom and Natick was mentioned, it will be seen that a genuine effort was not made to save the AFRL Hanscom Research Site.

In the original BRAC announcement, the following statements were issued:

Realign Air Force Research Laboratory, Wright Patterson AFB, OH, by relocating the Information Systems Directorate to Hanscom AFB, MA. Unfortunately, the Information Directorate was relocated to Rome NY, rather than Hanscom AFB as was originally stated for the following reason.

"Through this consolidation, the Department would increase efficiency of RDT&E operations resulting, in a multi-functional center of excellence in the rapidly changing technology area of C4ISR. Environmentally, this recommendation would have the potential to impact air quality at Hanscom. Additional operations at Hanscom might impact archeological sites, which might constrain operations. This recommendation might require building on constrained acreage at Hanscom. The hazardous waste program at Hanscom would need modification. Additional operations might impact wetlands at Hanscom, which might restrict operations."

Thus,

"Relocating all Information Directorate activities from WPAFB, OH to Rome Research Site, NY – Consolidating Information and Cyber research to enhance collaboration, teamwork and innovation to carry out the stated mission to lead the discovery, development and integration of affordable warfighting information technologies for our air, space and cyberspace force."

Another BRAC recommendation:

Realign Wright-Patterson AFB, OH (MSG) Maxwell AFB, AL (SSG), and Lackland AFB, TX (CPSG Crypto Mod/Depot), by relocating Air & Space Information Systems Research and Development & Acquisition to Hanscom AFB, MA.

This never happened. These are two examples of how the New York and Ohio Congressional Delegations successfully changed the BRAC recommendations, whereas the Massachusetts Congressional Delegation failed.

6.1 Letters Objecting to the BRAC

Realizing that we had to persuade the BRAC Commission to remove our Hanscom Research Site from their list before it went to the President, we immediately formed a new SAVE Committee, which I chaired, to attempt to save our Hanscom Research Site. On many previous occasions, when our Divisions had been threatened, our Congressional Delegation had always emphasized the importance of basic and applied research at Hanscom AFB and they had been very supportive of our research laboratory. As a result, our SAVE Committee wrote letters to our Massachusetts Congressional Delegation, to the BRAC Commission and to the Chief Scientist of the Air Force. Letters were also written by our Congressional Delegation to the BRAC Commission and by the Lexington and Concord Boards of Selectman to the BRAC Commission.

NATIONAL FEDERATION
OF
FEDERAL EMPLOYEES
PROFESSIONAL LOCAL 1384
HANSCOM AFB MA 01731

19 May 2005

Honorable Edward M. Kennedy
United States Senate
315 Russell Building
Washington DC 20510

Dear Senator Kennedy,

First let me congratulate you on your outstanding effort in saving Hanscom Air Force Base from the 2005 BRAC closure list. Unfortunately, we at the Hanscom Research Site of AFRL received the BRAC announcement with mixed emotions. On the one hand we were pleased that Hanscom Air Force Base will remain open; however, we were very disappointed to learn that the Electromagnetics Technology Division and the Battlespace Environment Division of the Air Force Research Laboratory (AFRL) are slated to be relocated to Wright-Patterson AFB (WPAFB) and Kirtland AFB (KAFB) respectively.

As you know, this is not the first time that the Air Force has planned to close down the Hanscom Research Site. With your support we have succeeded in preventing this from happening in the past. We call upon you once again to prevent the Hanscom Research Site from being relocated.

As background, you know that the Hanscom Research Site has a long and rich history. In 1945, the then Army Air Forces had the wisdom to recruit scientists from the MIT Radiation Laboratory and the Harvard Radio Research Laboratory for post-war employment at Air Force Cambridge Research Laboratories (AFCRL). This organization grew and flourished for many years, producing numerous significant scientific achievements. Yet, in spite of this success, during the past 20 odd years the workforce has been repeatedly reorganized and downsized. You and Governor Romney have mentioned the importance of building a strong R & D capability at Hanscom AFB. If the Hanscom Research Site is relocated, as planned, all research that has been conducted at Hanscom AFB will be lost. At one time we had a workforce of about 1200 people; that workforce has now dwindled down to about 225 scientists and engineers. We should be increasing the R&D workforce, not eliminating it.

On paper, the proposed realignment may seem reasonable. However when one examines the details of the realignment, we note that it is unlikely that it will accomplish what is intended and the end result could severely impact the research capabilities of the Air Force. Let us review some of these details:

- In principle, about 225 civilian S & E's are scheduled to be relocated to WPAFB and KAFB. In reality, it is expected that only about 10 % of these people would be willing to relocate. Thus the Air Force would lose many highly skilled scientists and engineers who have been conducting cutting edge research in the areas of sensors and geophysics.
- In addition, there are close to 200 people who are working as on-site contractors; these people would lose their jobs. Finally, the Hanscom Research Site provides support to many local universities and companies. This move would result in the loss of close to ($30 M) to the Massachusetts economy as well as another 100 jobs.
- It has been pointed out that there are mistakes in the BRAC report. For example, the proposal to move the AFRL Information Systems Directorate from WPAFB to Hanscom AFB was in error and will not happen. Thus, we would ask that you verify the number of positions that would for certain be transferred to Hanscom AFB. It could be that the actual gain of civilian positions coming to Hanscom AFB is a lot less than the 800 positions estimated in the BRAC report.

About 6 years ago, the Air Force reorganized their research laboratories into a single Air Force Research Laboratory. At that time there was concern as to whether a Directorate with Divisions in several locations could function effectively. Our experience has shown that the Divisions at the Hanscom Research Site have not only been very successful in coordinating their research efforts with their respective Directorates but they have actually produced major products that are essential to key Air Force programs, including products currently in use by the troops in Iraq. The availability of E-mail and video teleconferencing have contributed to this success.

In summary, we have presented some of the reasons why it would not be in the best interest of the Air Force to relocate the Divisions that make up the AFRL Hanscom Research Site to WPAFB and KAFB. Thus, the bottom line is that although new non-research positions may be moving to Hanscom AFB, there may be a potential loss of almost as many research positions. In addition, the cost to relocate the employees will run into millions of dollars. Is this plan in the best interest of the Air Force?

We deeply appreciate all of the support that you have provided in the past; we hope that with your continued support, we will able to overcome the current plan to abolish our Hanscom Research Site.

Sincerely,
Ed
Dr. Edward E. Altshuler
NFFE Local 1384 Liaison to Congress
Air Force Research Laboratory
Electromagnetics Technology Division
80 Scott Drive
Hanscom AFB, MA 01731-2909
(781)377-4662

Similar letters were sent to Sen. Kerry and Gov. Romney

6.1.2 Presentation to Congressional Staffers

Since we did not receive a response to the Kennedy, Kerry and Romney letter, I contacted the local offices of our Congressional Delegation and on 8 June 2005 we gave a power point presentation to the staffers of Representatives Meehan, Tierney, Markey, Senators Kennedy and Kerry and Gov. Romney. We provided an overview of our laboratory along with a summary of our key research areas and the importance of our research to the Air Force and the Department of Defense. We explained that although there were currently only 223 government scientists and engineers in the Hanscom Research Site, there were also over 200 on site contractors who would lose their jobs; in addition, local companies and universities would lose an estimated $200M dollars in business.

Unfortunately, we did not receive a response to our appeal. This was another indication that we were not going to receive the same kind of support that we had received in the past.

6.1.3 BRAC Commission Visit to Boston – 6 July 2005

We learned that the BRAC Commission would be visiting Boston on 6 July and that Senator Kerry would have a chance to address the Commission. I sent the following message to his staffer, Mark Sternman, to ask if he needed any additional information beyond that which was in our briefing.

-----Original Message-----
From: Altshuler Edward E Civ AFRL/SNHA
[mailto:Edward.Altshuler@hanscom.af.mil]
Sent: Tuesday, June 21, 2005 10:16 AM
To: Sternman, Mark (Kerry)
Subject:
Dear Mark,
Just a note to ask if you have had an opportunity to discuss with Senator Kerry the relocation of the Hanscom Research Site to Wright-Patterson AFB and Kirtland AFB. In view of the fact that the 6 July meeting with the BRAC Commission is rapidly approaching, we want to make sure that the Senator has all of the information that he will need to avert this move. Also, if the Senator believes that it would be helpful for one or more of our committee to attend the meeting with BRAC and even give a briefing, we would be happy to do so.
Please let us know the Senator's plan and will he need any additional info.
Best regards,
Ed
Dr. Edward E. Altshuler
NFFE Local 1384 Liaison to Congress
Air Force Research Laboratory
Electromagnetics Technology Division
80 Scott Drive
Hanscom AFB, MA 01731-2909
(781)377-4662
(781)377-1074 Fax

His reply:

Thank you for your message.
We plan to use your information in Sen. Kerry's remarks for July 6. Since he has only a six-minute speaking slot, I'm not sure that he's going to be able to touch on any other bases besides Otis, but he will certainly discuss Hanscom in his statement that he plans to submit for the record.
Attending the July 6 meeting is entirely up to you and your colleagues. Given that the hearing covers all of New England, I expect more than 1000 people to attend. If we need more information from you before July 6, I hope that you will not mind our contacting you.
Thanks again, mss

Several of us did attend that meeting and since I had met Senator Kennedy on previous occasions I did say hello to him. Unfortunately, he was too occupied for me to have much of a conversation with him. However, Reps. Tierney, Markey and Meehan did send the following letter to Chairman Principi of the BRAC Commission.

Congress of the United States
Washington, DC 20515

**Testimony Submitted for the Record by U.S. Representatives
Edward J. Markey (MA-7), Martin T. Meehan (MA-5), and John F. Tierney (MA-6)
to the
Defense Base Closure and Realignment Commission
Regional Field Hearing
Boston Convention and Exhibition Center
Boston, Massachusetts
July 6, 2005**

We would like to thank you, Chairman Principi, and members of the Commission for holding this regional hearing in Boston. We welcome the opportunity to submit testimony as you continue your deliberations about the future structure of the United States Armed Forces. We represent the towns surrounding Hanscom Air Force Base (AFB) – Rep. Markey (Lexington and Lincoln); Rep. Meehan (Concord); and Rep. Tierney (Bedford). In addition, Rep. Markey represents the Natick Army Soldier Systems Center (SSC).

Given the vital importance to our national defense of Hanscom AFB and Natick SSC, we are pleased that the Pentagon's recommendations rightfully recognized the military value of Hanscom and Natick. The proposal to realign five organizations to Hanscom and preserve nearly all of the functions at Natick SSC reflects an understanding of the fact that the experienced workforce and the complex work that occurs at these installations cannot be easily or effectively replicated elsewhere.

Enduring partnerships with nearby academic centers and a cluster of cross-service, cutting edge, defense technology entities have helped Hanscom AFB and Natick SSC become such critical technical research assets. The presence of an unparalleled workforce serves as the engine behind the thriving industries and institutions that support Hanscom and Natick. The strength of the technology cluster in our region helped Natick SSC earn the number one ranking in military value for both Human Systems Research and Human Systems Development and Acquisition by the Technical Joint Cross Service Group. Both Hanscom and Natick earned several top ten rankings in other Technical Joint Cross Service Group categories.

We are concerned, therefore, that the decision to realign the Air Force Research Laboratory (AFRL) at Hanscom by relocating the Sensors Directorate to Wright Patterson Air Force Base, Ohio, and the Space Vehicles Directorate and Geophysics Lab to Kirtland Air Force Base, New Mexico may be inconsistent with aspects of the Pentagon's analysis of Hanscom, and could disrupt key programs. For instance, Hanscom scored highly across key Development and Acquisition (D&A) areas, including sensors, electronics, and electronic warfare. Additionally, as the AFRL components at Hanscom Air Force Base draw heavily upon regional human capital capabilities in science and technology, the proposed relocation of the Sensors and Space Vehicles Directorates appear to carry significant costs with few gains. It may prove virtually impossible to reconstitute the seismic work of the Geophysics Lab at another location, and a previously attempted transfer of the Lab's mission in 1997 was overturned in 2003 at the urging of the Massachusetts Congressional Delegation and the Nuclear Threat Monitoring Group within the Air Force Technical Applications Center with the full support of the Air Force.

We understand that internal polls of employees at these Directorates and past BRAC rounds suggest that less than 20% of professionals currently employed in the Directorates would be likely to relocate, should Hanscom AFRL's Sensors and Space Vehicles Directorates be moved in accordance with the Department of Defense's proposals. Without access to a similar strong employee base, the AFRL mission may be negatively and unnecessarily impacted.

We respectfully request that you re-examine the Pentagon's analysis as it relates to the Sensors and Space Vehicles Directorates and appropriately weigh the difficulty of reconstituting the formidable intellectual and business cluster that exists in Massachusetts, as well as the value of the highly skilled workforce currently serving at these Directorates' facilities at Hanscom.

Finally, we want to add our voices in support of Massachusetts workers and our colleagues U.S. Senators Edward M. Kennedy and John Kerry, and U.S. Representatives William Delahunt (MA-10) and Stephen Lynch (MA-9), as well as Governor Mitt Romney, in their efforts to have the Commission reexamine the recommendations of the Department of Defense with respect to the Otis Air National Guard Base, and the Naval Shipyard Puget Sound – Boston Detachment.

We appreciate the challenging task confronting you as you work toward a final recommendation. We thank you for your service and for your time and attention to our concerns.

This was certainly a very strong letter, but to no avail. Unfortunately it fell on "deaf ears."

6.1.4 Letter to Air Force Chief Scientist – 18 August 2005

From: Altshuler Edward E Civ AFRL/SNHA
Sent: Thursday, August 18, 2005 2:05 PM
To: 'lewis@eng.umd.edu'
Subject: BRAC recommendation to relocate the AFRL Hanscom Research Site

Dear Dr. Lewis,

We, at the Hanscom Research Site, were very disappointed to learn that the Pentagon BRAC recommendation proposed that the Air Force Research Laboratory (AFRL) Electromagnetics Technology Division of the Sensors Directorate and the Battlespace Environment Division of the Space Vehicles Directorate be relocated to Wright-Patterson AFB (WPAFB) and Kirtland AFB (KAFB) respectively. We welcome this opportunity to bring to your attention the negative impact that this relocation would have on the AFRL.

As you know that the Hanscom Research Site has a long and rich history. In 1945, the then Army Air Force had the wisdom to recruit scientists from the MIT Radiation Laboratory and the Harvard Radio Research Laboratory for post-war employment at Air Force Cambridge Research Laboratories (AFCRL). This organization has flourished for many years and has produced numerous significant scientific achievements relevant to the Air Force operations.

On paper, the proposed realignment may seem reasonable. However, a close examination of the realignment shows that instead of accomplishing its stated intent, its end result would severely impact AFRL research capabilities. Let us briefly review some of these details:

In principle, about 225 civilian S & E's are scheduled to be relocated to WPAFB and KAFB. Based on past moves within our organization and elsewhere, it is expected that only about 10-20 % of these people would be willing or able to relocate. Thus, AFRL would lose many of its highest skilled scientists and engineers (about half of whom hold doctorates) who for decades have been conducting cutting- edge sensors and geophysics research. The inevitable result is essentially the irreplaceable loss of the Electromagnetics Technology Division of the Sensors Directorate and the Battlespace Environment Division of the Space Vehicles Directorate. The synergism currently available with greater Boston universities and research establishments does not exist in either Dayton or Albuquerque. We do not believe it prudent for the Air Force to write off these two critical research areas.

There are close to 200 university and research establishment S&E's who work as on-site contractors. Their expertise would also be lost since they will not be given any financial incentive to move. Finally, the lost financial support that the Hanscom Research Site provides to these universities and companies would result in the additional loss of another 200 jobs.

About 6 years ago, the Air Force reorganized their research laboratories into a single Air Force Research Laboratory. At this time there was concern as to whether a Directorate with Divisions in several locations could function effectively. Our experience has shown that the Divisions at the Hanscom Research Site have not only been very successful in coordinating their research efforts with their respective Directorates but they have actually produced major products that are essential to key Air Force programs, some of which are currently used by our troops in Iraq. The availability of e-mail and video teleconferencing has also contributed to this success. If you feel that a list of our most valuable research products would be helpful, we will provide it to you immediately on request.

In summary, we have presented several key reasons why it is not in the best interest of the Air Force to relocate the Divisions that make up the AFRL Hanscom Research Site to WPAFB and KAFB. We deeply appreciate any support that you can provide to help reverse the BRAC plan and will supply you with any desired information, if needed.

Best regards,

Ed
Dr. Edward E. Altshuler
NFFE Local 1384 Liaison to Congress
Air Force Research Laboratory
Electromagnetics Technology Division
80 Scott Drive
Hanscom AFB, MA 01731-2909
(781)377-4662
(781)377-1074 Fax

His reply:

"Ed,
I am indeed very much aware of the history and capabilities of the Hanscom Research Site, so you are preaching to the proverbial choir. I am frankly concerned about what the realization of these BRAC recommendations would mean for several capabilities currently housed at Hanscom, and have been asking questions about this, including a direct tasker to AFRL. I suspect that your estimate of 10-20% might even be too high, and even worse, I fear that the most talented people would be least likely to relocate.
Unfortunately, I was not at all involved in the BRAC decisions, and my role in influencing the final recommendations would be limited at best. Not quite sure what I can do frankly, and especially not sure if I could reverse the BRAC decisions from my position on the Air Staff, but I am exploring options. I know that time is of the essence.
MJL"
Dr. Mark J. Lewis
Chief Scientist of the United States Air Force
AF/ST

This was certainly a very sincere letter, however nothing came of it.

6.1.5 Letter to the BRAC Commission – 30 August 2005

30 August 2005

To the BRAC Commission:

We at the Hanscom Research Site were devastated by the news that your Commission plans to relocate the Electromagnetics Technology Division of the Sensors Directorate to Wright- Patterson Air Force Base (WPAFB) and the Battlespace Environment Division of the Space Vehicles Directorate to Kirtland Air Force Base (KAFB). The fact that the Hanscom Research Site was not even mentioned in your presentation makes us wonder whether your Commission is truly aware of the consequences that will result from this realignment. For your information, the Hanscom Research Site has a long and rich history. In 1945, the Army Air Force had the wisdom to recruit scientists from the MIT Radiation Laboratory and the Harvard Radio Research Laboratory for post-war employment at Air Force Cambridge Research Laboratories (AFCRL). This organization has flourished ever since and has produced numerous significant scientific achievements relevant to the Air Force operations.

While on paper the proposed realignment may seem reasonable, a close examination of this realignment shows that instead of accomplishing its stated intent, its end result will severely impact Air Force Research Laboratory (AFRL) research capabilities. In principle, about 225 civilian scientists and engineers (S & E's) are scheduled to be relocated to WPAFB and KAFB. Based on past moves within our organization and elsewhere, it is expected that only about 10-20 % of these people would be willing or able to relocate. In addition, several hundred on-site and off-site contractors, would also lose their jobs. Thus, AFRL would lose many of its highly skilled S&E's (about half of whom hold doctorates) who for decades have been conducting cutting- edge sensors and geophysics research. The inevitable result is essentially the irreplaceable loss of the Electromagnetics Technology Division of the Sensors Directorate and the Battlespace Environment Division of the Space Vehicles Directorate. The synergism currently available in the greater Boston area, with universities and research establishments, does not exist in either Dayton or Albuquerque. Aligning research conducted in DoD laboratories with the economic imperatives of consolidation can lead to unperceived incompatibilities. We do not believe it prudent for the Air Force to write off these two critical research areas.

In the previous BRAC, the Army Research Laboratories were consolidated and most of the researchers did not relocate. As a result, research relevant to Improvised Explosive Devices (IED's) was discontinued. Because our soldiers in Iraq encounter IED attacks daily, this is considered one of our most serious problems. I am sure that the personnel who made that fateful decision to realign the Army laboratories had good intentions; but look at how many lives would have been saved, if that research had been allowed to continue.

We would also like to bring to your attention two extremely relevant research programs that could also improve the safety of our troops. The first is called the Crossed Dispersion Prism (CDP) sensor; it holds great promise for the warfighter in detecting, identifying and locating enemy threats such as IEDs, mortars, MANPADS (Man-Portable Air Defense Systems), Anti Aircraft Artillery, and small arms. The second relevant program relates to the effect that energetic electrons and ions trapped in the Earth's magnetic field have on microelectronic components that control computers on DoD satellites. In the late fifties and early sixties the US and USSR detonated nuclear devices in the upper atmosphere, creating new radiation belts. Today, such explosions would wreak havoc on our fleets of C3I satellites. What could we do if an enemy with nuclear capability detonated a bomb in space? AFRL scientists at Hanscom Research Site are designing innovative ways of using low-frequency radio waves to sweep killer particles out of the radiation belts before they can seriously harm our satellites.

These are just two examples which justify the importance of the Hanscom Research Site to the Air Force Research Laboratory; there are many more. In conclusion, we hope that it is not too late for your Commission to reverse the Pentagon recommendation. Do you really want to be responsible for making another fateful decision that would leave our fighting men and women more vulnerable to enemy fire?

Dr. Edward E. Altshuler
NFFE Local 1384 Liaison to Congress
Air Force Research Laboratory
Electromagnetics Technology Division
80 Scott Drive
Hanscom AFB, MA 01731-2909
(781)377-4662
(781)377-1074 Fax

No reply.

NATIONAL FEDERATION
OF
FEDERAL EMPLOYEES
PROFESSIONAL LOCAL 1384
HANSCOM AFB MA 01731

Dear Senator Kennedy,

Just a note to let you know that we truly appreciate the effort that you and your staff made in trying to reverse the BRAC decision to relocate the Hanscom Research Site to Wright-Patterson AFB, Ohio and Kirtland AFB, New Mexico. We truly feel that the BRAC Commission has made an irrevocable decision, which will prove to be a major setback in the research areas of sensors and geophysics for many years. Unfortunately, this loss is bound to have a serious impact on our military capability.

As a last ditch effort, which will probably fall on "deaf ears," we have sent the attached letter to the BRAC Commission using their "public input" website. If there is a way to send this letter more directly to the Commission, I would appreciate hearing from you.

Sincerely,

Dr. Edward E. Altshuler
NFFE Local 1384 Liaison to Congress
Air Force Research Laboratory
Electromagnetics Technology Division
80 Scott Drive
Hanscom AFB, MA 01731-2909
(781)377-4662
(781)377-1074 Fax

Similar letters were also sent to Senator Kerry, our Representatives and Governor Romney. Regretfully, no response.

6.1.7 Letter to Maj Gen Paul Nielsen (ret.), Former Commander of AFRL 7 September 2005

Altshuler Edward E Civ AFRL/SNHA wrote:
Dear Paul,

I hope that your new position is working out well. As you know these are dire times for us at the Hanscom Research Site. We have been seeking support from Senators Kennedy and Kerry, Congressmen Markey, Meehan and Tierney and Governor Romney. The Congressmen did write a strong letter to the BRAC Commission but so far it seems to have fallen on deaf ears. Part of the problem is that they have been focusing their effort on saving Otis Air Guard Base and we do not feel that they have given us as much support as they would have done otherwise. In any case we are still in touch with them and we haven't given up.

I have been in contact with Dr. Mark Lewis, Chief Scientist of the Air Force. He is extremely sympathetic of our situation, however he did not feel that he could help our cause.

My main reason for contacting you is the following: We have been told that Dr. Ron Sega, Director of DDR&E, was involved in the decision to relocate the Hanscom Research Site. I do not know whether you know him, but if you do, we would like to know whether he may be able to help reverse the BRAC decision. It is hard to believe that in knowing that most of the key S&E's would probably not relocate, that AFRL would still essentially eliminate our Divisions. We are very proud of our history and it just doesn't seem right for it to end this way.

We would truly appreciate any support or advice that you may have.

Best regards,

/Ed/
Dr. Edward E. Altshuler
Air Force Research Laboratory
Electromagnetics Technology Division
80 Scott Drive
Hanscom AFB, MA 01731-2909
(781)377-4662
(781)377-1074 Fax

Ed,
Just got home from a trip and I have a meeting that will tie me up most
of tomorrow. I will try to call you later in the day.
Paul

(Gen Nielsen did call me the following day and explained that he thought that Dr. Sega was one of the people who suggested that the Hanscom Research Site be placed on the BRAC list, so he would be of no help. Gen Nielsen was without doubt the best of all the Commanders of AFRL history. He had a deep appreciation of the role of research for the Air Force.)

6.2 The Relocation Process – 13 September 2007

The next step in the relocation process was the procedure that would be followed. There were two options for transferring an employee to the new location, a Transfer of Function (TOF) or a Transfer of Work (TOW). The TOW was also referred to as a Non-Transfer of Function.

6.2.1 <u>Transfer of Function</u>

What is a Transfer of Function?

TOF

- ✓ Function ceases in one location and moves to another location not performing the function at the time of transfer
- ✓ No rights to a transfer unless the alternative is separation or demotion
- ✓ All eligible employees receive an offer at the new location
- ✓ If more employees than positions, RIF at gaining activity (prior to transfer)

Not TOF

- ✓ Function already exists in the new location
- ✓ Transfer of work that does not meet the official definition of a TOF
- ✓ May or may not be offered employment at the new location
- ✓ Function is contracted out or jobs are abolished

7

 Notification Process

- Employees will receive Management Directed Reassignment (MDR) letter from management
    - Letter will be issued 6-8 months in advance of reporting date
    - MDR will have <u>specific date </u>when they are required to report to duty location
- Employees will have 10 calendar days to accept or decline the reassignment

For Official Use Only 3

162

6.2.2 Letter to the Workforce by the Director of the Sensors Directorate - 4 September 2007

Directorate to the Electromagnetics Technology Division of the Sensors Directorate at Hanscom Air Force Base. The process for transferring positions of employees from HAFB to WPAFB could be either a Transfer of Function (TOF) or a Transfer of Work (TOW).

Team RY and interested parties in WRS RI,

Hope you're all enjoying the transition to fall – certainly came fast here in Dayton – one day if was 92 degrees and the next it dropped to the 50's, with breezy winds and rain!

Monday and Tuesday of this week we met up at Boston with the Hanscom civilian personnel team, the AFMC A1 team and Hq AFRL DP folks who will be working with us over the next several months as we work through the process of making a recommendation and determination of whether our BRAC moves will be a TOF (Transfer of Function) or a Non-TOF move. The primary purpose of this meeting was to introduce the players in this process to each other, to familiarize the personnel folks with what we do mission wise, to define at what level in the organization we would define the "function" to be at for the determination and to state management's desired outcome.

From RY we had myself, the affected BRAC division chiefs, most all of the Branch Chiefs, Emil Martinsek and Ron Kaehr. I made a presentation (that I'll get Dave to post to Livelink for you to look at since it's a 28Mb file) which provided some insight to the team about who we are, what we do and how we do it/have done it over the past 10 years as an integrated function/team. Bottom line is that our information was received well by the personnel team. I asked that our "function" be defined at the Division level and though I haven't received final concurrence of that recommendation from the personnel crowd – I believe this will be accepted. I also told them that I would like to see the final determination be made for our BRAC to be a Non-TOF, specifically because this is in the best interest of my employee's (you) and that it allows us to operate at each site up into 2011 until we're ready to pack up and move to Wright Patterson and provides us the most flexibility in terms of accommodating individual situations across the next three to four years. I know that many of you had concerns with a Non-TOF decision because you weren't guaranteed a job at the gaining site – I raised this with the personnel folks and said I'd like to give you a letter of intent if this is the case – they said I couldn't do that – but that this isn't an issue in their eyes – because anyone who wants to move in either situation will get moved. I've told you repeatedly for the last two and a half years that I'd like all of you to move to Dayton and continue on with our team – so the bottom line on this is that if we get a Non-TOF determination I will management reassign all those that want to make the move from Rome or Hanscom to WP by 15 September 2011.

So I feel that we successfully made our case, got the information across that the personnel folks needed and stated our position.

We have taken another step in this journey – keep the faith we'll get through this.

Cheers,

Joe
Joe Sciabica, SES
Director, Sensors
Air Force Research Laboratory
937.255.2620 Work DSN:785
937.371.8604 Cell
937.656.4325 Fax DSN:986

6.3 Letters of Support

Many of the companies that we supported in the local area wrote letters to the BRAC Commission but to no avail. A letter to the BRAC Commission was sent by the Boards of Selectman of Lexington and Concord and was published in the local newspaper.

6.3.1 Lexington, Concord send letter to BRAC

By Maureen O'Connell
Posted September 07, 2005 @ 08:00 PM
Following the lead of the Lexington Board of Selectmen, the Concord board met Tuesday afternoon to draft a letter to the chairman of the Base Realignment and Closure Commission asking it to spare the 230 jobs it plans to take from Hanscom Air Force Base.
On August 25, the BRAC Commission dashed the hopes of Bedford, Concord, Lexington, Lincoln and other friends of the Air Force Base when it recommended Hanscom not expand, as it has been announced in May, but continue to operate minus two operations. With the Sensors Directorate and Space Vehicles Directorate moving to Ohio and New Mexico, respectively, under BRAC's August recommendation, approximately 200 jobs are expected to move from Hanscom.
The letter, signed by Selectman Chairman Anne Shapiro, expresses gratitude to BRAC for recognizing Hanscom's importance to both the Defense Department and the region, but asks it to reconsider its recommendation to remove the two units from Massachusetts.
"The deadline for decision-making is fast approaching, but we believe strongly that the analysis of this proposal should be reviewed immediately, before the final recommendations are made," the letter states. "This decision should be reversed."

It continues, "The proposed move would result in an enormous loss of valuable technological know-how for the Air Force. (Department of Defense) operations at Hanscom benefit from the constant, daily collaboration between personnel at the base and the Boston scientific and academic community.

"Many of the civilian researchers working on (Department of Defense) projects are unlikely to relocate to these other bases, and it is quite likely that their experience and expertise will be lost," Shapiro wrote.

Lincoln selectmen did not consider a letter at its meeting Tuesday night, but Bedford's board said such a letter was not something it would be undertaking. Calling the letter a "bad move," Bedford Selectman Sheldon Moll said the letter was discussed at the last selectmen's meeting, but was not signed.

"This is not something that I think is appropriate at this time. We are basically blessed in having the base remain," he said.

Moll said he felt sympathy for the 200 people that would be asked to move or retire, but noted he was happier the bulk of jobs at the base would remain unaffected by any BRAC decisions.

We should be thankful for what we have," he said. Concord board members disagreed."

"The loss of these operations from Hanscom (Air Force Base) will not only be a significant economic loss for our region, but it will also represent a very real loss to our nation's defense capability," wrote Shapiro.

Staff Writer Paul Furfari contributed to this report.

6.4 BRAC Letters

Many letters were written by our SAVE Committee and by our Congressional Delegation to the Secretary of the Air Force to rescind the BRAC and to change the date of the Transfer of Function.

6.4.1 Letter to Massachusetts Congressional Delegation

With rumors that BRAC might run into financial problems, I sent the following letter to Sen. Kennedy and similar letters to the rest of the Massachusetts Congressional Delegation.

NATIONAL FEDERATION
OF
FEDERAL EMPLOYEES
PROFESSIONAL LOCAL 1384
HANSCOM AFB MA 01731

24 October 2007

Dear Senator Kennedy,

As of now, the BRAC resolution to close the Air Force Research Laboratory Hanscom Research Site (AFRL/HRS) is in the process of being implemented. The need for Congressional intervention has become more urgent, due to efforts by AFRL to complete the transfer of a large portion of HRS positions to Ohio and New Mexico by early 2009 rather than the BRAC completion date of September 2011. This acceleration toward closure is causing a severe disruption to our important on-going research in support of our warfighters. We cannot overemphasize the negative impact that this BRAC decision will have on Massachusetts. The Hanscom Research Site, which evolved from the MIT Radiation Laboratory and the Harvard Radio Research Laboratory after World War II, has had a long and rich history. The current Air Force Research Lab at Hanscom AFB is considered one of the premier research laboratories in the world. We have many unique facilities and equipment that enable us to do cutting edge research. We have a dedicated workforce of over 200 scientists and engineers, about half of whom hold doctorates. We receive close support from 300 on-base contractors who work side by side with us. If the BRAC is not overturned, all of these assets will be lost! This runs counter to the American Competiveness Initiative (ACI), a high priority of the Administration and Congress. Our Senators, Congressmen and Governor have emphasized the importance of expanding research at Hanscom AFB. Doesn't it make sense to figure out a way to preserve the Hanscom Research Site so as to avoid the loss of about 500 hi-tech jobs and the financial support that we provide to our local universities and industry?

There are reports that the costs of the BRAC commission's recommendations were grossly underestimated. The 2005 cost was $22.3 Billion; now the Defense Department is asking for $30.7 Billion, a 38% increase. For example, we have learned that the cost to relocate the Hanscom Research Site to Ohio and New Mexico is approximately double the initial estimate. Fort Monmouth officials warned in a memo, before the BRAC costs were finalized, that incorrect data used to calculate the cost of operating the post were mistakenly supplied to the DoD; the correct data were later provided but unfortunately this information was ignored. As a result, the

166

cost rose from $780 Million to $1.5 Billion. Inflation has also struck other BRAC recommendations. The realignment of Fort Knox, KY to Fort McCoy, WI has increased 94%; mothballing Fort Monroe, VA, 288%; closing portions of the Naval Weapons Station, CA, 221%. Maryland is slated to to have an influx of about 45,000 new jobs; Maryland officials estimate that $16 Billion will be needed to accommodate this additional workforce; and the list goes on and on. The BRAC costs are skyrocketing to a point where what was originally supposed to be a savings to the DoD, may likely turn into a loss. We understand that a bill has been introduced in the Senate that would require the Secretary of Defense to report to Congress twice a year on the cost of implementing the BRAC plan, so as to introduce transparency and place a fiscal leash in the base closure process. We hope that our Congressional Delegation along with the Congressional Delegations of other states that are also being negatively impacted, will follow the BRAC costs very closely. Our country is fighting wars in Afghanistan and Iraq, which are costing hundreds of billions of dollars; the Air Force is looking for an additional $100 Billion above current budget plans over the next 5 years if it is to buy enough aircraft and satellites to handle future requirements handed down by DoD leaders. As a result, the DoD is strapped for funds. Should the DoD now be spending billions of dollars of up front money to implement the BRAC, when there is a strong possibility that we will never, even in the long term, realize a savings? Under the circumstances, we hope that you and your fellow Senators will vote to either rescind the BRAC or at the very least delay its implementation.

Over the years, the Air Force, on a number of occasions, has attempted to close our Laboratory. You have always found a way to prevent our closure. Once again, we desperately need your support.

Best regards,

Ed
Dr. Edward E. Altshuler
NFFE Local 1384 Liaison to Congress
Air Force Research Laboratory
Electromagnetics Technology Division
80 Scott Drive
Hanscom AFB, MA 01731-2909
(781)377-4662
(781)377-1074 Fax

Once again, there was no response to this letter so I sent a "follow-up" letter to our Congressional Delegation on 2 November 2007.

This letter is a follow up to the letter that I sent several weeks ago. I hope that you will find some time in your busy schedule to review the negative impact that the BRAC decision to close the Hanscom Research Site will have on our workforce and the State of Massachusetts. I would appreciate receiving a response to our letter.

Best regards,

Ed

Dr. Edward E. Altshuler
NFFE Local 1384 Liaison to Congress
Air Force Research Laboratory
Electromagnetics Technology Division
80 Scott Drive
Hanscom AFB, MA 01731-2909
(781)377-4662
(781)377-1074 Fax

This time I did receive a response from most of the Congressional Delegation. They said that they would follow any Congressional activity regarding this issue. Unfortunately, I do not believe that it surfaced in either the House or the Senate.

6.5 BRAC Acceleration of TOF Date – December 2007

The BRAC was scheduled to be completed by 15 September 2011. In December 2007, a letter was circulated stating that the Air Force may accelerate the relocation process by requiring employees at the HRS to sign letters of intent in early 2009 to indicate whether they planned to relocate. Refusing the transfer would result in termination within two months. The remaining employees would become an operating location (OL) for WPAFB or KAFB. At this point we finally received support from our Congressional Delegation. On 3 January 2008, the following letter was sent to Secretary of the Air Force, Michael W. Wynne and signed by Senators Kennedy and Kerry and Representatives Frank, Markey, McGovern, Tierney and Tsongas.

6.5.1 Letter from the Massachusetts Congressional Delegation to Michael W. Wynne, Secretary of the Air Force – 3 January 2008

Congress of the United States
Washington, DC 20515

January 3, 2008

The Honorable Michael W. Wynne
Secretary
U.S. Department of the Air Force
1690 Air Force Pentagon
Washington, DC 20330-1670

Dear Secretary Wynne:

We are writing to request information about the transfer of responsibilities of the Air Force Research Laboratory (AFRL) from Hanscom Air Force Base to Kirtland Air Force Base and Wright-Patterson Air Force Base as part of the implementation of the Base Realignment and Closure (BRAC) Commission process.

On December 21, 2007, our staff received a briefing from Air Force personnel on the BRAC-directed transition of the AFRL. We appreciated the information we received on this important matter and are writing to request additional follow-up information.

It is our understanding that the BRAC implementation is to take place in 2011. However, we have been informed that the Air Force may be accelerating the relocation process by requiring that AFRL personnel sign letters in early 2009 to indicate whether they intend to continue working in their current position when it is moved, which presumably will require employees to move from the New England region to an area in closer proximity to Kirtland AFB or Wright-Patterson AFB. We have been advised that employees who refuse the transfer may be terminated within two months of the date they indicate their intention not to transfer, while the remainder will become an operating location of Kirtland AFB or Wright-Patterson AFB at Hanscom AFB. Our constituents are also concerned that employees who intend to move but later change their minds could be penalized. Please confirm whether our understanding of these requirements is accurate and provide related clarification as necessary.

A move to Kirtland AFB or Wright-Patterson AFB would have a profound effect on hundreds of AFRL scientists and engineers, support staff, contractors and their families, since it is expected that many AFRL employees will elect not to move to New Mexico or Ohio. This would lead to significant attrition rates and have an adverse effect on the continuity of the Air Force mission.

Please provide us, by January 31, 2008, with information about the schedule and details of the relocation process for AFRL personnel, including copies of all forms that AFRL personnel are being asked to sign to indicate their employment plans. Please also describe how the Air Force intends to ensure that the vital activities of the AFRL continue uninterrupted during the transition, especially in the event that significant numbers of personnel decide not to follow the mission to Kirtland AFB and Wright-Patterson AFB.

Thank you for your attention to this very important matter.

Sincerely,

Edward J. Markey
U.S House of Representatives

Edward M. Kennedy
U.S. Senate

John F. Kerry
U.S. Senate

Barney Frank
U.S. House of Representatives

John F. Tierney
U.S. House of Representatives

James P. McGovern
U.S. House of Repres

Niki Tsongas
U.S. House of Representatives

cc:

Major General Daniel J. Darnell
Director of Legislative Liaison
U.S. Department of the Air Force
1160 Air Force Pentagon
Washington, DC 20330-1160

6.5.2 Reply to the Wynne letter from Gen Bruce Carlson, Commander of the Air Force Material Command 11- February 2008

DEPARTMENT OF THE AIR FORCE
HEADQUARTERS AIR FORCE MATERIEL COMMAND
WRIGHT-PATTERSON AIR FORCE BASE, OHIO 45433-5001

OFFICE OF THE COMMANDER

1 1 FEB 2008

AFMC/CC
4375 Chidlaw Road
Wright-Patterson AFB OH 45433-5001

The Honorable Edward M. Kennedy
United States Senate
Washington DC 20510-2101

Dear Senator Kennedy

Thank your for your inquiry on January 3, 2008 regarding our implementation of the Congressionally mandated Base Realignment and Closure (BRAC) Commission transfer of Air Force Research Laboratory (AFRL) responsibilities from Hanscom Air Force Base to Kirtland and Wright-Patterson Air Force Bases (AFBs). I recognize the Air Force's implementation of this BRAC decision is of great concern to you and your constituents. Be assured the Air Force is doing everything possible to take care of our valued team members at Hanscom during this difficult transition period.

As you are aware, the AFRL functions were directed to be realigned to Kirtland and Wright-Patterson AFBs no later than September 2011. In order to balance mission accomplishment with our personnel goals, the AFRL team has determined the process should begin April 2008 with the Transfer of Function/Transfer of Work (TOF/TOW) determinations. Although this may be perceived as accelerating the process, the timeline is based on historical data from previous BRAC transfers, personnel regulations, and employee rights/entitlements.

For example, when BRAC directed the closure of Kelly and McClellan AFBs less than 20 percent of those offered job relocation packages accepted. This left the Air Force with a critical gap in depot capability as new workers had to be hired and trained. For the Hanscom BRAC-directed transfer, the capability gap concern is amplified by the fact 66 percent of the Hanscom AFRL team is retirement eligible. I am certain you will agree replacing an estimated 180 scientist and engineers will take both time and energy. In fact, we estimate a full 2 years is required to complete the process (advertising, search, interviews, job offers, acceptances, relocations, and training).

By regulation, the BRAC transition process must begin no later than 18 months prior to the BRAC mandate of September 2011. This means the Air Force must begin to offer applicable entitlements and benefits to affected employees no later than February 2010. During our continued consultations at Hanscom, however, many of the affected employees indicated a desire to begin the process in the summer when schools are out and relocations are easier on families. In order to balance our employee concerns, regulatory guidance, and our mission needs the AFRL leadership made the decision to establish temporary operating locations at Hanscom in

War-winning capabilities ... on time, on cost

June 2009 for employees affected by TOF determinations in order to aid a seamless transfer of workload by September 2011.

A key milestone in establishing employee rights, benefits, and entitlements is the April 2008 TOF/TOW decision. Under a TOF decision, AFRL employees have the right to voluntarily transfer with the work and will be asked to declare their intentions (forms attached). Personnel who elect to relocate are entitled to all Permanent Change of Station entitlements allowed by regulation including household goods shipment, travel, a house hunting trip, temporary quarters, and miscellaneous expenses. The Air Force will attempt to place employees who decline transfer on local job vacancies (for which they are qualified) for approximately 14 months until the June 2009 effective date. If the employee cannot be placed on a job vacancy by this time they may retire, if eligible, or will be separated with all applicable reemployment rights offered by the DoD Priority Placement Program. Employees who elect to geographically relocate, but later decline may choose to retire or will be separated.

If the April 2008 decision is TOW, the Air Force is under no obligation to offer employees the opportunity to move with the work, but we still plan to offer relocation opportunities none-the-less. Employees not volunteering to relocate, however, are classified 'surplus' and would be entitled to pre-Reduction in Force (RIF) placement efforts where mandatory matching rules apply--the Air Force must fill local area job vacancies using the surplus list if an employee is qualified to perform the job. Unfortunately, under TOW rules if employees cannot be placed in a vacancy they will undergo RIF procedures that could result in their being reassigned at grade, changed to lower grade, or separated.

I hope you now share in my confidence that this plan meets the BRAC-directed relocation of the Hanscom workload by balancing the needs of our employees with the AFRL mission. On behalf of the entire Air Force Materiel Command team, thank you for your continued support to the Air Force, our personnel, and their families. A copy of this letter will be sent to all signatories of the January 3, 2008 letter.

Very respectfully

BRUCE CARLSON
General, USAF
Commander

Attachments:
1. BRAC Planning Schedule for AFRL Hanscom
2. Relocation/Mobility Agreement
3. Sample Transfer of Function Canvass Letter
4. AFRL Communications Plan
5. TOF/TOW Talking Paper

Similar letters were sent to all of the other signatories This was a rather bold response and was not well received by our Congressional Delegation as indicated in the letter that I received from Cindy Buhl of Rep. McGovern's office.

6.5.3 Internal Letters from Massachusetts Congressional Delegation – 11 February 2008

---Original Message-----
From: Buhl, Cindy [mailto:Cindy.Buhl@mail.house.gov]
Sent: Monday, February 11, 2008 6:57 PM
To: Altshuler Edward E Civ AFRL/RYHA
Cc: Bisceglia, Joe; O'Brien, Joseph (MA03); Pacheco, Matthew
Subject: FW: Reply to 3 January08 Letter- AFRL Personnel Transition Due to BRAC

Dear Mr. Altshuler,

As you can see, we aren't particularly pleased with this information.

And as Will Huntington with Rep. Markey's office says below, we will be pushing back on this --

Cindy Buhl
Legislative Director
Rep. McGovern (MA-3)

-----Original Message-----

From: Huntington, Will
Sent: Monday, February 11, 2008 6:04 PM
To: Trivedi, Atman (Kerry); Bassett, Bethany; Maroney, Jay (Kennedy); Rose, Markus; Buhl, Cindy; McDermott, Kevin; Hardwick, Dak

Subject: FW: Reply to 3 January08 Letter- AFRL Personnel Transition Due to BRAC

Folks-

Attached is the AFRL response to our joint letter of Jan. 3 concerning the Hanscom BRAC process. The physical copies should be sent today to everyone, but Lt. Col. Liu asked me to pass along the digital version.

I haven't had a chance to digest it fully quite yet, but from a quick reading I think that AFRL could use some nudging to improve how this process flows for the folks at Hanscom. In particular, the 10-day response required in the draft Transfer Function Canvass Letter (Attachment 3) seems very short.

Best,

Will

>Will Huntington
>Legislative Assistant
>U.S. Rep. Edward J. Markey (D-MA)
>will.huntington@mail.house.gov
>tel: (202) 225-2836
>fax: (202) 226-0092

-----Original Message-----

From: Liu Alan Lt Col SAF/LLP [mailto:alan.liu@pentagon.af.mil]
Sent: Monday, February 11, 2008 5:01 PM
To: Huntington, Will
Cc: RSS - SAF/LLS; RSS - SAF/LLH; SAF/LLP Workflow
Subject: Reply to 3 January08 Letter- AFRL Personnel Transition Due to BRAC

Will,

Please see the attached. Per our discussion, request you provide the letters and attachments to each of the respective members. I will deliver the hardcopies to their offices once I receive them from AFMC.

Again, thank you for your patience on this issue. Let me know if you have further questions.

Cheers,

Alan
ALAN S. LIU, Lt Col, USAF
Senior Legislative Counsel
Secretary of the Air Force Legislative Liaison 1160 Air Force Pentagon Washington, DC 20330
DSN: 227-7114; Comm: (703) 697-7114
Fax: (703) 697-3520

6.5.4 SAVE Committee Review of Gen Carlson Letter

Paragraph by paragraph rebuttal of General Carlson's letter dated 11 February 2008. Before we discuss by paragraph the potentially misleading and erroneous content of General Carlson's, we summarize our main points as follows:

- The Air Force has established a TOF effective date 2+ years before the actual move
  - That will prematurely decimate the workforce, undermining the AFRL mission

- This has the effect of transferring MA jobs to New Mexico and Ohio in June 2009
    - This contradicts the AF stated schedule of moving in September 2011
- The Air Force plan suspends employee BRAC rights 2 years before the move
- The Air Force plan does not provide for mentoring or effective transfer of knowledge

Paragraph one of Gen. Carlson's letter states that you should "Be assured the Air Force is doing everything possible to take care of our valued team members". The current plan has us sign a letter in April 2009 asking if we will move. Refusing this transfer of function (ToF) will result in termination within 2 months. Forcing employees to leave government service more than two years before the BRAC requirement is not consistent with Gen. Carlson's quoted objective, or with the guidance in the attached letter from Deputy Secretary of Defense Gordon England. We note that OPM regulations allow retirement incentives until the day of the move. Instead, the Air Force is effectively suspending those rights two years before the move. Examples of the rights no longer available after June 2009 are discontinued service retirement and severance pay. Both management and the union expect that the early ToF date will result in a large number of scientists leaving. New hires will be made in OH or NM, effectively transferring jobs in June 2009 instead of September 2011.

In paragraph two, there are basically two statements. One concerns the balancing of mission accomplishment and their personnel goals. We believe that the present plan has mission accomplishment as a very low priority and that their personnel goals are never clearly described. There is no doubt that the AFRL mission will be severely impacted by the departure of a significant fraction of the staff in 2009 under the current ToF schedule, and this is not consistent with any reasonable personnel goals. This early ToF effective date is not required, or even consistent with BRAC provisions.

Paragraph three addresses the concerns of Air Force management on replacing the portion of the workforce that chooses not to move. The argument for an early decision letter uses the example of a depot closure during a previous BRAC cycle, which has little relationship to replacing scientific personnel. This comparison is very misleading. Scientists take years of training and are continually learning and therefore the current workforce has an enormous corporate knowledge base. Precisely because it will be difficult to replace the vast scientific experience presently at AFRL Hanscom, everything should be done to keep the current scientists employed as long as possible. This allows the non-moving scientists to act as mentors for younger scientists who will be hired in the time the laboratories will remain at Hanscom. If the current senior scientists leave in April 2009, as a result of an early decision process, the few new employees will not have the opportunity to overlap with the current scientists and their mission critical corporate knowledge will not be transferred. It seems obvious that the mission would be best served by such mentoring. In contrast with replacing personnel at a depot, the proper transfer of scientific knowledge takes years of intensive work.

Paragraph four discusses three topics. The letter states (1) that it is necessary to start the process 18 months prior to September 2011, (2) the employees have a preference for a summer move, and (3) the early decision process in April 2009 is necessary to "aid in a seamless transfer of workload". We believe a clarification is needed to understand exactly what process needs to be started 18 months prior to September 2011. We noted previously that OPM allows for "adverse action conditions" as late as the moving date. Moving during the summer season is obviously preferable to employees with families. However, the June 2009 date is not the moving date but the date present employees are terminated if they refuse the ToF. We have been told that construction schedules set the moving dates as summer or fall of 2011. Therefore requiring us to sign a ToF letter in April 2009 has no relevance to the season of the move. In addition, once employees have accepted the move, management retains the right to move them at management's discretion whether the new buildings are finished or not. This could include non-summer moves at management discretion. Thus, the argument about desiring summer moves is completely disingenuous. Finally, as discussed above, the seamless transfer of knowledge will take place only if there is a significant period of employment overlap between the experienced scientists and the junior scientists who will be hired to replace them. We also want to remind you that the research being performed at Hanscom AFB has been determined to be "world class" by the Air Force Scientific Advisory Board. There is an extremely small pool of similarly experienced scientists outside AFRL who could continue our work "seamlessly".

Paragraph five is particularly confusing as it states that the Air Force will begin helping those employees who choose not to be part of the transfer of function in April of 2008. This is in contrast to the April 2009 date in the timetable that the Air Force enclosed and what our management has been telling us. This discrepancy needs to be clarified.

Paragraph six discusses the implications of a Transfer of Work (ToW) determination. This has become moot since the decision has been made that all but two employees are ToF.

Paragraph seven addresses the balancing of employees' needs against Air Force mission. The proposed early change in operating location in April 2009 will neither address the needs of the employees nor that of the AFRL mission. The first is true because the vast majority of employees (estimates are 20% will move) will benefit from a later ToF effective date and the second because an early decision date will remove the majority of the corporate knowledge of this prestigious laboratory.

We look forward to your help in protecting our rights and will gladly provide more information if needed.

6.5.5 Letter from Our Congressional Delegation to Acting Secretary of the Air Force Michael Donley – 20 June 2008

Congress of the United States

Washington, DC 20515

June 20, 2008

The Honorable Michael Donley
Acting Secretary
U.S. Department of the Air Force
1690 Air Force Pentagon
Washington, DC 20330-1670

Dear Acting Secretary Donley:

Thank you for your response dated February 11, 2008 to our letter of January 3, 2008 regarding the implementation of the Base Realignment and Closure (BRAC) Commission transfer of Air Force Research Laboratory (AFRL) responsibilities from Hanscom Air Force Base to Kirtland and Wright-Paterson Air Force Bases. We write to request further clarification on the AFRL BRAC process as it relates to this transfer. We appreciate your ongoing cooperation on this important issue as well as your responses to the questions that follow.

Desirability of Increased Overlap between Retiring and New AFRL Personnel

We are concerned that the decision to implement a Transfer Of Function (TOF) effective date of June 2009 instead of 2011 may have a deleterious effect on the AFRL mission. Specifically, we are concerned that the current Air Force plan will not allow for the adequate transfer of knowledge from retiring AFRL staff to the large number of new personnel.

The February 11th response notes that: "For the Hanscom BRAC-directed transfer, the capability gap concern is amplified by the fact [that] 66 percent of the Hanscom AFRL team is retirement eligible. I am certain you will agree [that] replacing an estimated 180 scientist [sic] and engineers will take both time and energy." We agree wholeheartedly that the Air Force will face a significant challenge in replacing the world-class AFRL personnel likely to decline to transfer. In addition, given the current plan for a TOF effective date of 2009, the Air Force will have lost many of its best AFRL personnel prior to the hiring of new staff. This lack of overlap between veteran and newly-hired personnel will prevent crucial and much-needed knowledge transfers, resulting in a significant loss of institutional memory to the detriment of AFRL's vital mission.

We urge you to consider establishing a TOF effective date of 2011, instead of June 2009. Pushing back the TOF effective date would allow you to hire new personnel before BRAC-related departures, improving knowledge transfers and maximizing AFRL's ability to successfully fulfill its mission.

Penalties for Changing an Initial Acceptance of Transfer

The "Relocation/Mobility Agreement" included in the February 11th response (Document 2) requires signatories to agree to a number of conditions. Sections 6.E and 6.F require signatories to agree that, should they "refuse to relocate to (gaining location) when directed," they will become "ineligible for discontinued service retirement, severance pay, unemployment

177

6.5.6 <u>Reply of Letter to SAF Donley from Gen Carlson – 27 June 2008</u>

AFMC/CC
4375 Chidlaw Road
Wright-Patterson AFB OH 45433-500
The Honorable Edward M. Kennedy
United States Senate
Washington DC 20510-2101

Dear Senator Kennedy

Thank you for your request for further clarification on June 20, 2008 regarding our implementation of the congressionally mandated Base Realignment and Closure (BRAC) Commission transfer of Air Force Research Laboratory (AFRL) responsibilities from Hanscom Air Force Base to Kirtland and Wright-Patterson Air Force Bases (AFBs). I recognize the Air Force's implementation of this BRAC decision is of great concern to you and your constituents. Be assured the Air Force has carefully considered our BRAC-directed plans and schedule for the relocation of the Hanscom workload by balancing the needs of our employees with the AFRL mission.

We share in your concern regarding the need to enable crucial and much-needed knowledge transfers between veteran and newly-hired personnel and have developed a three-pronged strategy for ensuring that critical intellectual capital is preserved through the BRAC transfer. The Transfer of Function (TOF) effective date of 1 June 2009 is a crucial component of that strategy as outlined below.

First - New Hires: Knowing that we will have losses in critical personnel as a result of the BRAC move, we are actively and aggressively hiring new personnel in advance of the TOF. Because of the BRAC rules, we are unable to hire into the organization at the gaining location prior to the TOF, so we are limited to new hires who are willing to move to the losing location (Hanscom AFB) and then later to the gaining location (Kirtland AFB and Wright-Patterson AFB). While we have been able to entice a number of excellent candidates under these conditions, this constraint is quite limiting. Once the TOF occurs, we will have the option to hire at the gaining location. It is a fact that this will open up opportunities to hire key, critical personnel who are unwilling or unable to make the temporary relocation to Hanscom AFB.

Regardless of whether a person is hired in Massachusetts or in New Mexico or Ohio, these individuals will spend a period of intense interaction with existing (nonmoving) personnel at Hanscom to learn their jobs, responsibilities, and unique knowledge about their particular area of research or development.

Second - Incentivizing current personnel: We are incentivizing existing personnel at Hanscom AFB to continue to work for AFRL for as long as possible (and preferably after the physical move to Kirtland or Wright-Patterson AFB) through retention and relocation bonuses. The more individuals that we can convince to stay with the laboratory, the better able we will be to execute our mission in the short term as we reestablish capability at the new locations.

Third - Retaining key experts: We are utilizing available authorities and resources, such as Reemployed Annuitants, Term Hires, and contract positions to retain specific key personnel who will not be moving, but are critically needed to support the mission as we transfer knowledge from our current employees to those who will support the mission at the new location.

In addition to these three strategies, we are also ensuring that impacts to our capability to perform our mission are minimized by carefully planning our activities in concert with the TOF and physical move schedules. The primary advantage of a TOF in FY09 is that we can more gradually shift resources from Hanscom AFB to Kirtland AFB or Wright-Patterson AFB and avoid prolonged downtime at the time of the physical move in FY11. Without an early TOF, we would need to cease operations while we shut down the Hanscom facility, move, and bring up our laboratory facilities at the new locations while simultaneously facing the challenge of replenishing 80% or more of our workforce. With the TOF in FY09, we are able to gradually build up a staff and capability at the gaining location between FY09 and FY11, thus allowing for more flexibility in the actual transition and--most importantly--a decreased down-time. In our estimation, the risks associated with transitioning intellectual capital are significantly lower with a TOF in FY09 versus FY11.

In the AFRL Transfer of Function, employees are reassigned from their losing organization into the gaining installation's Operating Location (OL). Before the employee reassigns into the OL, he/she is required to sign a relocation-mobility agreement. This is a necessary precondition of movement into the OL since the OL is designed to identify those employees who have agreed to move to the gaining location. Signing of this agreement requires the employee to accept a follow on assignment to the gaining organization outside of his/her commuting area as dictated by mission requirements. Your reference to the 5 CFR 351.302(g) no longer applies when an employee signs a relocation-mobility agreement and later declines to move. In such instances, the follow on reference, 5 CFR 351.303, does not apply either. There are separate regulations governing each benefit and entitlement, which have distinct stipulations concerning employees who decline to move after signing a mobility agreement. The following regulatory information addresses the denial of entitlements to employees who agree and then later decline to move to the gaining activity:

Employees who decline to move under a mobility agreement are considered voluntary separations and are not eligible to receive severance pay under the 5 CFR, Subpart G, 550.703.

Discontinued Service Retirement is governed by the CSRS and FERS Handbook, Chapter 44, Section 44A2-1.3 which states "An employee who accepts a position that has a mobility requirement is not eligible for Discontinued Service Retirement if he or she subsequently declines a position outside the commuting area.

An employee is only eligible to register in the Priority Placement Program if he/she is not on a mobility agreement, does not occupy a position where the position description requires mobility, and has not signed an agreement to move as a condition of employment, per Department of Defense Manual 1400.25, Chapter 3, Section B, 1a (d).

Separation Incentives are used when a workforce shaping or a Reduction in Force (RIF) occurs. Employees who accept a TOF, move to the Operating Location and then later decline to move do not meet the conditions of workforce shaping nor do they meet the requirements under the 5 CFR Part 351 Reduction in Force.

While we are more than willing to do whatever is feasible to ease the problems of our employees at Hanscom AFB who choose not to move with the workload to our gaining installations, we must abide by governing regulations as we execute this transfer.

I hope you now share in my confidence that this schedule balances the needs of our employees with the AFRL mission and our requirements for the existing Relocation/Mobility Agreement are necessary. On behalf of the entire Air Force Materiel Command team, thank you for your continued support to the Air Force, our personnel, and their families. A copy of this letter will be sent to all signatories of the June 20, 2008 letter.

> Very respectfully
> BRUCE CARLSON
> General, USAF
> Commander

On 27 June Sen. Kennedy and all of the signatories of the 20 June letter received the above response from Gen Carlson. Once again, he would not change the planned June 2009 ToF date.

6.5.7 Letter to the Commander of AFRL – 7 August 2008

Since it appeared that we had run into a dead end regarding our attempt to delay the ToF date, I decided to appeal to Maj Gen Bedke, the Commander of AFRL. I knew that it would be unlikely that a 2-star General would question a 4-star General, but nothing ventured, nothing lost so I sent the following letter.

7 August 2008

Dear Gen Bedke,

I am writing to you because I believe that we share a common interest in that we both want the very best for the future of the Air Force Research Laboratory. I read with interest your WIT #41 and appreciated the sincerity of your response to the anonymous letter that was sent to you regarding recent Air Force decisions that have not been looked upon favorably by the DoD and Congress. It appears that AFRL is now on the brink of further aversely affecting the Air Force's relationship with Congress. On 3 January of this year, Senators Kennedy and Kerry along with five members of the Massachusetts House of Representatives sent a letter to SAF Wynne asking that the TOF date of June 2009 be moved to the final date of the BRAC, September 2011. Our Congressional Delegation questioned the need to accelerate the relocation process. Gen Carlson replied to this letter and made the following comments regarding the TOF.

"Be assured the Air Force is doing everything possible to take care of our valued team members at Hanscom during this difficult transition period." Yet, the current plan is for employees to receive a Transfer of Function Offer Letter in March of 2009 with a suspense to sign and return the letter to the local Civilian Personnel Flight (CPF) in April of 2009. An employee who declines to relocate will be separated from government service effective 1 June of 2009. This action does not seem consistent with the above statement, considering the fact that the employees are being forced to make a very important career decision, well in advance of the final BRAC relocation date of September 2011.

Our Congressional Delegation was not pleased with Gen Carlson's response so they sent another letter on 20 June 2008, this time to Acting SAF Donley, in which they stated, "We are concerned that the decision to implement a Transfer of Function (TOF) effective date of June 2009 instead of 2011 may have a deleterious effect on the AFRL mission. Specifically, we are concerned that the current Air Force plan will not allow for the adequate transfer of knowledge from retiring Air Force staff to the large number of new personnel. In addition, given the current plan for a TOF effective date of 2009, the Air Force will have lost many of its best AFRL personnel prior to the hiring of new staff. This lack of overlap between veteran and newly-hired personnel will prevent crucial and much needed knowledge transfers, resulting in a significant loss of institutional memory to the detriment of AFRL's vital mission.

We urge you to consider establishing a TOF effective date of 2011, instead of June 2009. Pushing back the TOF effective date would allow you to hire new personnel before BRAC-related departures, improving knowledge transfers and maximizing AFRL's ability to successfully fulfill its mission."

At the time BRAC was initially announced, the Hanscom workforce was advised that they would be able to work until September 2011. The change to 1 June of 2009 has created considerable turbulence and concern in our workforce. They feel very strongly that they have been betrayed and the consensus is that these decisions have been made to facilitate the relocation without any regard for the workforce.

Since more than 80% of our personnel are not planning to relocate to either Dayton or Albuquerque, our lab will become a skeleton workforce of mostly junior scientists and engineers with very few support personnel. We have already lost many scientists, engineers and support people and they have not yet been replaced. AFRL management must realize that it will be next to impossible to replace our experienced workforce with qualified new hires within the next 10 months. We fear that we will become a non-functional research laboratory and that our effectiveness will be severely compromised. If on the other hand, the TOF date were delayed until 2011, then there would be a much higher likelihood that the transition could be accomplished in a more orderly way, since there would then be more than an additional two years available to recruit new scientists, engineers and support people and to have them mentored by the senior personnel who would still be at the lab. In closing, all I ask is that the personnel responsible for making this decision be completely aware of the unnecessary havoc that they will be creating if they keep the TOF date of June 2009. AFRL has the authority to change the TOF date and as stated in your WIT#41, "You should arm yourself with the facts."

If the TOF date is not changed to 2011,

Fact #1 The USAF will risk further antagonizing Congress.

Fact #2 AFRL will prevent the Electromagnetics Technology Division and the Battlespace Environment Division from fulfilling their respective national missions in a time of war, when the technologies that they are developing are essential.

Fact #3 AFRL will also be doing a disservice to a dedicated Hanscom workforce, in that they will be forced to make a decision some two years in advance of the move.

For the productivity of the laboratories and the care and well being of our current workforce, please take into account the above facts and consider changing the TOF date to September 2011. Doing so would allow the Hanscom personnel, who are not planning to relocate, additional time to mentor the new hires who will eventually fill their positions.

    ⸍cerely,

Ed
Dr. Edward E. Altshuler
Air Force Research Laboratory
Electromagnetics Technology Division
80 Scott Drive
Hanscom AFB, MA 01731-2909
(781)377-4662

As expected, no response.

6.5.8 Letter to Governor Patrick – 13 November 2008

In November, after Barack Obama had been elected president, we decided to write to Gov Patrick and seek his help, since he was a friend of Obama. I sent him the following letter.

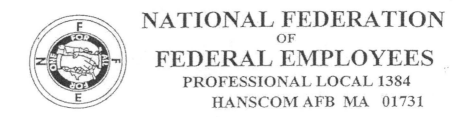

NATIONAL FEDERATION
OF
FEDERAL EMPLOYEES
PROFESSIONAL LOCAL 1384
HANSCOM AFB MA 01731

13 November 2008

Dear Governor Patrick,

We are very pleased that our new President-elect is Barack Obama, since we believe that he will provide much-needed support to the Nation's scientific community. At present, the Base Realignment and Closure (BRAC) resolution to close the Air Force Research Laboratory / Hanscom Research Site (AFRL/HRS) in September 2011, is in the process of being implemented. I am writing on behalf of the HRS Workforce to appeal to you to engage with the Massachusetts Congressional Delegation to preserve the HRS and avoid the loss of over 400 high-tech jobs along with the financial support that the HRS infuses into our local universities and businesses.

The Air Force Research Lab at Hanscom AFB, which evolved from the MIT Radiation Laboratory and the Harvard Radio Research Laboratory after World War II, is one of the premier research laboratories in the world. We have many unique facilities and equipment that enable us to do cutting-edge research. We have a dedicated workforce of over 200 scientists and engineers, about half of who hold Doctorates.

183

We receive additional support from close to 200 on-base contractors who work side by side with us. We cannot overemphasize the negative impact that this BRAC decision will have on Massachusetts. To make matters worse, the Air Force is planning to accelerate the BRAC process by some two years by having a Transfer of Function (TOF) date of 1 June 2009, instead of the originally planned date of September 2011. In April 2009, the employees will be asked to sign a mobility agreement to relocate. If they do not sign the agreement, they will be terminated on 1 June 2009. If they sign the agreement and later change their mind, they will be penalized. Our Senators and Representatives, along with you, have emphasized the importance of the research at Hanscom AFB, hence this appeal.

There are reports that the costs of the BRAC commission's recommendations were grossly underestimated. The 2005 cost was $22.3 Billion; now the Defense Department is asking for over $33 Billion, about a 50% increase. The BRAC costs are skyrocketing to a point where what was originally supposed to be a savings to the DoD may likely turn into a loss. For example, we have learned that the cost to relocate our Hanscom Research Site to Wright-Patterson AFB, Ohio and Kirtland AFB, New Mexico is now estimated to run over $100 Million. What will the Air Force get in return for this BRAC investment? Very little! Since fewer than 15% of the employees are expected to relocate, the Air Force will lose the expertise that is needed to conduct research in support of our warfighters. Of course, the Air Force's position is that this transition can be accomplished seamlessly. However, the reality is that it will be next to impossible to replace the HRS's experienced workforce with similarly qualified scientists and engineers, thus losing most of the technical expertise that Congress was promised by the BRAC Commission. The bottom line is that the Air Force will spend over $100 Million to move a handful of largely inexperienced employees to the new locations. These gaining locations will in turn receive all of our positions; unfortunately, these will probably go unfilled for many months, if not years.

Our country is fighting wars in Afghanistan and Iraq, which are costing hundreds of billions of dollars and our economy is in shambles; yet the Air Force is looking for an additional $100 Billion above current budget plans over the next five years if it is to buy the military systems that are needed to meet future DoD requirements. As a result, the DoD is strapped for funds. I respectfully submit that the DoD should not now be spending billions of dollars of up-front money to implement the BRAC when there is a strong possibility that we will never, even in the long term, realize a savings! In view of the fact that Massachusetts is slated to lose over 400 jobs and the millions of dollars that the Hanscom Research Site provides to Massachusetts businesses and universities, we ask your support in appealing to the Massachusetts Congressional Delegation to do everything in their power to either rescind the BRAC or, at the very least, to delay its implementation.

I would appreciate an acknowledgement that you have received this letter and would be pleased to provide any additional information.

        ʼt regards,

Ed

Dr. Edward E. Altshuler
NFFE Local 1384 Liaison to Congress
Air Force Research Laboratory
Electromagnetics Technology Division
80 Scott Drive
Hanscom AFB, MA 01731-2909
(781)377-4662
(781)377-1074 Fax

Once again, no response.

6.5.9 Letter to Head of Obama Pentagon Review Team – 14 November 2008

I saw an article in the Boston Globe that President-elect Obama had appointed John P. White, Chairman of the Middle East Initiative of the John F. Kennedy School of Government at Harvard University to head the Pentagon Review Team. White had previously served as Deputy Secretary of Defense in the Clinton Administration. I decided to write him the following letter.

NATIONAL FEDERATION
OF
FEDERAL EMPLOYEES
PROFESSIONAL LOCAL 1384
HANSCOM AFB MA 01731

14 November 2008

Dear Prof. White,

As the head of President-elect Obama's Pentagon Review Team, I am writing to ask that your Committee review a very important and costly DoD plan, the Base Realignment and Closure (BRAC) Resolution of 2005. The planning for BRAC-2005 took place in the early 2000's, a time when our Nation was at peace and financially stable. The conditions today are vastly different in that we are now fighting two wars and the global economy is in shambles. The original reason for the BRAC was cost savings. There are now reports that the costs of the BRAC Commission's recommendations were grossly underestimated. The original 2005 cost was expected to be $22.3 Billion; now the Defense Department is asking for over $33 Billion, about a 50% increase. The BRAC costs are skyrocketing to a point where what was originally supposed to be a savings to the DoD may likely turn into a loss. In addition, it has been documented that fewer than 20% of government employees actually relocate, so many will have to seek employment during these very difficult times. Of course, the DoD position is that these transitions can be accomplished seamlessly. However, the reality is that it is very difficult to replace an experienced workforce with similarly qualified workers.

As a result of the BRAC, our two Divisions of the Air Force Research Laboratory/Hanscom Research Site are slated to be reassigned to Wright-Patterson AFB, Ohio and Kirtland AFB, New Mexico. Our laboratory evolved from the MIT Radiation Laboratory and the Harvard Radio Research Laboratory after World War II and is one of the premier research laboratories in the world. We have many unique facilities and equipment that enable us to do cutting-edge research. We have a dedicated workforce of over 200 scientists and engineers, about half of who hold Doctorates. We receive additional support from close to 200 on-base contractors who work side by side with us. If the BRAC is allowed to proceed, all of these assets will be lost.

Our country is fighting wars in Afghanistan and Iraq that are costing hundreds of billions of dollars, and the global economy is spiraling downward. I respectfully submit that the DoD should not now be spending billions of dollars of up-front money to implement the BRAC when there is a strong possibility that we will never, even in the long term, realize a savings! In view of the fact that Massachusetts is slated to lose over 400 high-tech jobs and the millions of dollars that the Hanscom Research Site provides to Massachusetts businesses and universities, we ask your support in appealing to Congress to either rescind the BRAC or, at the very least, to delay its implementation.

Sincerely,

Ed

Dr. Edward E. Altshuler
NFFE Local 1384 Liaison to Congress
Air Force Research Laboratory
Electromagnetics Technology Division
80 Scott Drive
Hanscom AFB, MA 01731-2909
(781)377-4662
(781)377-1074 Fax

As expected, no response.

6.5.10 New Transfer of Function Date – 10 January 2011

After a long battle to delay the Transfer of Function date we learned that the Air Force was not authorized to move the date ahead. We did receive a follow up letter to the notification on 10 January 2011. It stated "all employees at the AFRL Hanscom Research Site included in the BRAC, were given an official notice of Management Directed Reassignment (MDR). They were given 11 calendar days to accept or decline reassignment. Those that accept had to report to their new location on or before 4 August 2011. Those that declined would be separated from the Air Force on 30 July 2011." Thus, our work force was at least given a reprieve on the move date. We do appreciate the effort of the Massachusetts Congressional Delegation regarding this issue.

6.6 Reports and Letters on the DoD Deception of BRAC 2005

Shortly after the BRAC 2005 was announced, there were reports being issued that questioned the expected cost savings. Some of these reports stated that the Pentagon had deliberately omitted important information and had deceived the BRAC Commission. I am amazed that the DoD officials who were responsible for this deception never faced charges.

There are two sets of key reports and letters. The first set of reports is from various sources including the Government Accountability Office (GAO) and reports on GAO reports. The second set of reports are related to the closure of Fort Monmouth including two scathing letters from members of the New Jersey Congressional Delegation to the House Armed Services Committee and to the Attorney General. The letter to the House Armed Services Committee accused the DoD of deception and asked that they take appropriate action via the authorization and appropriations process to withhold any funding for the consolidation or closure of Army RDT&E facilities under BRAC until the Congress has conducted a comprehensive review of the issues and allegations that have been raised.

The letter to the Attorney General accuses specific individuals in the DoD of deception and requests that the Department of Justice undertake a criminal investigation into this matter.

I am surprised that with all the evidence that was presented, Fort Monmouth could not be saved. Unfortunately, by the time that these reports surfaced, the BRAC was probably beyond the point of no return.

6.6.1 <u>Military seeks extra funding to cover shortages for base closures</u>

January 4 2007
By Megan Scully, CongressDaily

Senior military officials are pressuring lawmakers to add billions of dollars to a long-term continuing resolution to cover necessary base-closure costs and pay for military construction and quality of life projects in fiscal 2007, warning that failure to do so would have dire consequences for the services.

funding shortfall for a spate of base closures and realignments approved by the White House in 2005. The military must complete all personnel and equipment moves mandated during that base-closure round by September 2011, a tight deadline even without these budget constraints.

Army, Navy and Marine Corps leaders sent two strongly worded letters to House and Senate leaders and key members of the Armed Services and Appropriations committees late last month, after it became apparent that Congress would not pass most of the fiscal 2007 spending bills and instead hold funding for military construction at fiscal 2006 levels for the rest of the current fiscal year under a CR.

"Military construction and quality of life initiatives constitute large, crucial portions of [the Army's national-security] plan," Army Secretary Francis Harvey and Chief of Staff Peter Schoomaker wrote congressional leaders on December. 18. "Yet, the limitations imposed by the continuing resolution (CR) are already causing our plan to fray, and it is likely to unravel completely should we go through the entire fiscal year under a CR."

Schoomaker and Harvey warned that efforts to shut down and realign bases are "quickly coming apart at the seams," with the Army limited to spending less than one-quarter of the amount needed to keep base realignment and closure moves on schedule.

Navy Secretary Donald Winter, Chief Naval Officer Michael Mullen and Marine Corps Commandant James Conway warned of similar consequences in a letter delivered to Capitol Hill December. 22.

"The CR could stymie our efforts to construct facilities and move equipment and people to receiver locations, and impede our ability to harvest savings and organizational efficiencies already accounted for in the budget," they wrote.

Lawmakers have not yet determined whether to add money or otherwise alter the continuing resolution to pay for base closures, although Democratic leaders have indicated they would consider limited spending increases in certain areas.

But several House and Senate members -- including those who would gain personnel and military missions at their local bases -- would support fully funding BRAC at the $5.8 billion level requested by President Bush and authorized in the fiscal 2007 defense authorization bill, which Bush signed into law, several congressional aides said.

Many communities affected by base closures already are writing their lawmakers to press the issue.

"Everybody was very concerned there wasn't enough money to get [BRAC] done by [2]011 before this," said Paul Hirsch, president of Madison Government Affairs, which does base-closure consulting work, and a senior staffer on the 1991 base-closure commission. "Now everybody is going to be behind the power curve and both losing and gaining communities will be adversely impacted."

But the losers in the 2005 BRAC round, who comprise a formidable force of their own, could just as likely back decreased funding in the hopes of buying their communities time and the economic benefits from prolonged military spending.

"It's a ying and a yang," a BRAC lobbyist said. "I think they're going to have a hard row to hoe to get more funding for BRAC" in the CR.

But the Defense Department does not have to rely solely on Congress for adequate funding of base closures this year. Defense officials could opt to reprogram money, or add money to base-closure accounts in the fiscal 2007 supplemental spending bill due to Capitol Hill in the next several weeks.

"The secretary of Defense has wide latitude to reprogram funds, which he may decide to do given the statutory requirement placed upon him," said Daniel Else, a defense analyst at the Congressional Research Service.

By choosing not to pass fiscal 2007 military construction funding, Congress also would shortchange Army efforts to create a more modular and easily deployable force by $400 million -- a move that could affect operations abroad, officials said.

"Our force rotation plan to Iraq and Afghanistan, as well as our overall readiness posture, relies on completing these conversions to the Army modular force on time," Harvey and Schoomaker wrote. "We have recruited and retained the soldiers, purchased individual protection equipment, and established a training plan, but now we are faced with the real possibility of not having facilities ready for training, maintenance, communications and command activities."

*This next report indicates the impact that insufficient funds would have on BRAC 2005.

6.6.2 Pentagon Is Stunned By $3 Billion Cut

January 31, 2007
The Hill
By Roxana Tiron

A continuing resolution released Monday night axes more than half of the money the Pentagon needs to meet its base realignment and closure (BRAC) commitments, potentially preventing the military services from completing the process by 2011 as required by law.

The Army, which has 61 percent of the total BRAC budget, is preparing for the consequences of appropriators' decision to deny the Pentagon more than $3 billion out of the $5.8 billion authorized last year for BRAC. That decision could have widespread knock-on effects on the rotation of troops in and out of Iraq and Afghanistan, the building of new brigades and the Army's plan to bring troops back from Germany. Senior military officials had been pressuring lawmakers to add billions of dollars for necessary base closures as well as military construction and quality-of-life projects to the continuing resolution that would fund the government until the end of fiscal year 2007. A failure to do so could have a grim impact on the services, military officials warned. But appropriators did not heed the services' call and allotted $2.5 billion for BRAC costs for the military to begin work on the highest-priority programs. The money represents an increase of $1 billion over the 2006 budget level. "It is pretty devastating for us," said an Army official who asked not to be quoted by name. The service has put together a complex plan that links its military construction and troop movement plan with BRAC implementation. Faced with the loss of billions of dollars this year, the Army is considering how to bring in additional funding for its projects. The delay of those projects ultimately will have an impact on the service's tactical and operational units, according to the official.

The Army and the rest of the military services could get more money in the upcoming emergency supplemental, but several sources pointed out that it is unlikely the military would get the entire $ 3.3 billion, if much of it at all, in the 2007 war supplemental.

Currently, there is no request of such nature in the supplemental, according to the Army official. The Pentagon is submitting its supplemental request for the rest of 2007 together with its 2008 budget next week. The service would depend on Congress's "generosity" to get more money, the official added. Moreover, the service may be forced to readjust its 2008 budget submission because several requests for military construction are predicated on the completion of projects in 2007, the Army official said. "There is a trail of things predicated on getting BRAC money in a timely fashion," the official said. The Army is standing up new brigades as part of its so-called modularity effort. A lack of funds could shortchange the Army's plan to create a more easily deployable force and affect overseas operations. The Army's force-rotation plan and overall readiness rely on completing its "modularity" plan on time. The Army now faces the possibility of lacking adequate facilities to train new forces and maintain equipment. For soldiers rotating in and out of Iraq and Afghanistan, the Army also is building facilities; some of that construction is in part linked to BRAC. In addition, without full BRAC funding, the Army may delay bringing back forces from Germany and keep units returning from conflicts inactivated for a longer period than desired, the official said. A lack of funding may force the Army to resort to temporary housing — a practice that has long been criticized by Congress.

While it saves money in the short term, it becomes a "colossal waste of money," according to an industry source. The Army already was criticized for the use of temporary facilities to implement its modularity plans. "Congress does not consider BRAC as an emergency that they have to do," the Army official said.

"They seem to think that they can extend BRAC." Such decisions could have wider implications, the official added. The Army may look for authority to transfer, or reprogram money from its basic military construction accounts into BRAC accounts, said the industry source. Ultimately, the services and Congress may have to look at the possibility of delaying the implementation of BRAC, but that won't be able to happen without a change in the law. Currently, the Pentagon has six years after the approval of a BRAC round (in this case, 2005) to finish the process. In order to increase money for BRAC 2008 and 2009 to catch up, the Army may have to trade money from its regular military-construction accounts, the official said, and that does not come without consequences. The House is taking up the continuing resolution today and strong debate over the bill is expected.

6.6.3 Pentagon Officials Withheld Brac Data To Protect Proposals That Failed Legal Requirement

18 December 2007

SUMMARY

Enclosed documents show that high level Pentagon officials withheld data in order to protect proposals that had failed a mandatory requirement of the 1990 Base Realignment and Closure (BRAC) law (i.e., that all proposals support the Force Structure Plan). This action misled the independent BRAC Commissioners, the U.S. Congress, the President, the rest of the Department of Defense (DoD), and the American public about the legitimacy of BRAC actions involving the Department's laboratories. Internal DoD documents reveal that security concerns were used as a pretext to halt the scheduled release of the data to the BRAC Commission. Thereafter, officials within the Office of the Secretary of Defense (OSD) acted to ensure that the data remained suppressed during the Commission's hearings from May to August 2005. How did the data stay suppressed throughout the BRAC hearings? Internal emails show that the interests of the Pentagon and of a staffer in a powerful U.S. Senator's office converged in a way that kept the data from becoming public knowledge. Documents also reveal that prior to the Commission hearings, a DoD analyst informed the Government Accountability Office (GAO) that the laboratory proposals failed to meet the legal prerequisite. GAO failed to act. Internal DoD documents show that three OSD officials had central roles in suppressing the data. They are: Michael Wynne, former Acting Under Secretary for Acquisition, Technology & Logistics (USD AT&L), and now Secretary of the

Air Force; Ronald Sega, former Director for Defense Research and Engineering (DDR&E), and now Under Secretary of the Air Force; and Alan Shaffer, the DDR&E's Director of Plans & Programs. Why did OSD take the risk of illegally suppressing BRAC data? This aspect is speculative, but two official DoD documents disclose one compelling motive. Prior to BRAC's start, both Wynne and Gordon England, DoD's top BRAC policymakers (and both former General Dynamics executives), called in writing for closing DoD laboratories and outsourcing their workload to the private sector. If it were not withheld, the data would have derailed that political objective. What follows below is a timeline of events, with documents to substantiate each claim. This is an important story, and one that needs to be told for two reasons. First, the schedule and success of many DoD technical programs are being jeopardized at a time when our country is at war. Second, integrity in Government decision-making is fundamental and essential to democracy.

CONCLUSION

High-level OSD officials violated the law by withholding, and then suppressing, critical BRAC data. Sec. 2903 of the 1990 BRAC law (as amended through FY05 Authorization Act) is explicit:

In addition to making all information used by the Secretary to prepare the recommendations under this subsection available to Congress (including any committee or member of Congress) the Secretary shall also make such information available to the Commission …

Any information provided to the Commission by a person described in paragraph (5)(B) shall also be submitted to the Senate and the House of Representatives to be made available to the Members of the House…

Unfortunately, the suppression of vital BRAC data proved effective during the Commission's hearings. In the end, the illegitimacy of the TJCSG proposals did not become an issue. Of the TJCSG's 13 proposals, 9 were approved. In addition, the Army/TJCSG's co-proposed closure of Fort Monmouth was approved. To ensure success it was also necessary that the U.S. Congress believe in the integrity of the laboratory closure process. The following statements about TJCSG proposals show the degree to which the data's suppression was successful:

"Maryland was chosen to receive these new jobs from Fort Monmouth fair and square in a process insulated from everyday politics." Rep. C.A. Ruppersberger (Press Release, 2 August 2007)

"We fought to win BRAC as Team Maryland, and we will fight to make sure Maryland communities have what they need in the federal checkbook to 7implement the BRAC decisions." "We won this based on mission and merit." Sen. Barbara A. Mikulski

(Press Releases, 2 February and 2 August 2007)

"I am pleased that the Office of the Secretary of Defense is diligently protecting the integrity of the BRAC process." Rep. Kevin McCarthy (The Daily Independent, 23 May 2007)

These legislators could not have known the truth. Their characterizations of the BRAC process are unsupportable in light of extensive and irrefutable evidence in the form of official DoD documents and records, internal TJCSG email and analyses, Congressional correspondence, and 254 pages of unreported TJCSG data exposing the illegitimate nature of the approved BRAC actions.

SOLUTION

The only way to rectify the situation is to enact special legislation that annuls the closure of Fort Monmouth, along with all other BRAC laboratory actions proposed and/or supported by the Technical Joint Cross-Service Group. This is a justifiable solution given that the BRAC Commissioners, the Congress, the President, the rest of the DoD, and the American public were misled by the actions of DoD officials who suppressed data in order to protect proposals that had failed a mandatory requirement of BRAC law. This next document provides detailed references concerning the deliberate exclusion of information by the DoD that should have been given to the BRAC Commission and Congress.

6.6.4 Military Base Realignments and Closures

United States Government Accountability Office
Washington, DC 20548
December 11, 2007
Congressional Addressees

The Department of Defense (DOD) is currently implementing recommendations resulting from the 2005 Base Realignment and Closure (BRAC) round. BRAC 2005 is the fifth round undertaken by DOD since 1988 and, by our assessment, is the biggest, most complex, and costliest BRAC round ever. With this BRAC round, DOD plans to execute over 800 BRAC actions, relocate over 123,000 personnel, and spend over $31 billion—an unprecedented amount, given that DOD has spent about $24 billion to date to implement the four previous BRAC rounds combined. DOD viewed the BRAC 2005 round as not only an opportunity to achieve savings but also as a unique opportunity to reshape its installations and realign its forces to meet its needs for the next 20 years. The Secretary of Defense made clear at the outset that his primary goal for the 2005 BRAC round was military transformation. As such, many of the BRAC 2005 recommendations involve complex realignments such as designating where forces returning to the United States from overseas bases would be located; establishing joint medical centers; creating joint bases; and reconfiguring the defense supply, storage, and distribution network. However, anticipated savings resulting from BRAC implementation remained an important consideration and was a factor in justifying the need for the 2005 BRAC round.1

Unlike prior BRAC rounds, which were implemented during times of declining defense budgets and where the focus was on eliminating excess capacity and realizing cost savings, the 2005 BRAC round is being implemented during a time of conflict when many military capabilities are surging and DOD is also implementing or planning to implement other extensive worldwide transformation initiatives. For example, at the same time DOD is to implement the most recent round of BRAC, it is relocating about 50,000 soldiers from primarily Europe and Korea to the United States transforming the Army's force structure from an organization based on divisions to more rapidly deployable brigade-based units and seeks to increase its active end strength by

92,000, all of which will affect DOD. Two years after BRAC 2005 was approved it is becoming obvious that cost estimates were not accurate.

6.6.5 GAO: Base closings to cost more, save less

Associated Press
12/13/2007

The Pentagon plans to spend about $10 billion more than originally estimated on base closings and realignments and expects about $200 million less in savings, the Government Accountability Office said in a report Tuesday. The GAO said the Defense Department expects to spend $31 billion to implement the Base Closure and Realignment Commission's recommendations and predicted net annual savings of $4 billion. Also, it will take until 2017 for the Defense Department to recover upfront costs, four years longer than the base-closing commission predicted. The base-closing commission conducted its latest round of decision-making affecting U.S. military bases in the country and abroad in 2005. The GAO said the 2005 round was the biggest, most complex and costliest ever.

Rep. Solomon Ortiz, chairman of the House Armed Services Committee panel on readiness, plans a hearing Wednesday on implementation of the commission's recommendations. "This illustrates what we in Congress worried about from the beginning: that the process was flawed and would not achieve the savings DoD boasted it would," said Ortiz, D-Texas. The 2005 base-closing commission estimated the Defense Department would save $36 billion over the 20 years ending in 2025 from its recommendations, but the department now expects to save $15 billion, a 58 percent decrease.

Cost estimates are likely to change, too, because of uncertainties associated with some of the closings and realignments and increases in construction and other costs. Some of the one-time cost increases include:

- $970 million more for consolidating leased locations and closing other locations of the National Geospatial Intelligence Agency to Fort Belvoir, Va.

- $700 million more to realign Walter Reed Army Medical Center in Washington, D.C., and relocate medical care functions.

- $550 million more for establishing the San Antonio Regional Medical Center and realigning enlisted medical training to Fort Sam Houston, Texas.

Also, the GAO said the Pentagon will have trouble meeting a mandated September 2011 deadline for implementing the recommendations. The Defense Department said despite higher costs and reduced savings, the commission recommendations should improve defense capabilities. The Defense Department agreed with most of the report and said some of the construction increases, beyond inflation, include decisions to build new facilities rather than renovate existing space, enhance quality of life for military personnel with such things as child care and improve training ranges and other training infrastructure.

6.6.6 <u>Military Base Realignments And Closures</u>

This next report accuses Pentagon officials of deliberately withholding information that may have resulted in the cancelation of the BRAC.

Cost Estimates Have Increased and Are Likely to Continue to Evolve
Highlights of GAO-08-159, a report to congressional addressees
December 2007

The 2005 Base Realignment and Closure (BRAC) round is the biggest, most complex, and costliest ever. DOD viewed this round as a unique opportunity to reshape its installations, realign forces to meet its needs for the next 20 years, and achieve savings. To realize savings, DOD must first invest billions of dollars in facility construction, renovation, and other up-front expenses to implement the BRAC recommendations. However, recent increases in estimated cost have become a concern to some members of Congress. Under the Comptroller General's authority to conduct evaluations on his own initiative, GAO (1) compared the BRAC Commission's cost and savings estimates to DOD's current estimates, (2) assessed potential for change in DOD's current estimates, and (3) identified broad implementation challenges. GAO compared the BRAC Commission's estimates, which were the closest estimates available associated with final BRAC recommendations, to DOD's current estimates. GAO also visited 25 installations and major commands, and interviewed DOD officials.

What GAO Recommends

GAO recommends that DOD explain its estimated BRAC savings from personnel reductions as compared to other savings to provide more transparency to Congress. DOD concurred with our recommendation and agreed to explain savings estimates in its BRAC budget material to Congress.

Since the BRAC Commission issued its cost and savings estimates in 2005, DOD plans to spend more and save less, and it will take longer than expected to recoup up-front costs. Compared to the BRAC Commission's estimates, DOD's cost estimates to implement BRAC recommendations increased from $21 billion to $31 billion (48 percent), and net annual recurring savings estimates decreased from $4.2 billion to $4 billion (5 percent). DOD's one-time cost estimates to implement over 30 of the 182 recommendations have increased more than $50 million each over the BRAC Commission's estimates, and DOD's cost estimates to complete 6 of these recommendations have increased by more than $500 million each. Moreover, GAO's analysis of DOD's current estimates shows that it will take until 2017 for DOD to recoup up-front costs to implement BRAC 2005—4 years longer than the BRAC Commission's estimates show. Similarly, the BRAC Commission estimated that BRAC 2005 implementation would save DOD about $36 billion over a 20-year period ending in 2025, whereas our analysis shows that BRAC implementation is now expected to save about 58 percent less, or about $15 billion.

DOD's estimates to implement BRAC recommendations are likely to change further due to uncertainties surrounding implementation details and potential increases in military construction and environmental cleanup costs. Moreover, DOD may have overestimated annual recurring savings by about 46 percent or $1.85 billion. DOD's estimated annual recurring savings of about $4 billion includes $2.17 billion in eliminated overhead expenses, which will free up funds that DOD can then use for other priorities, but it also includes $1.85 billion in military personnel entitlements, such as salaries, for personnel DOD plans to transfer to other locations. While DOD disagrees, GAO does not believe transferring personnel produces tangible dollar savings since these personnel will continue to receive salaries and benefits. Because DOD's BRAC budget does not explain the difference between savings attributable to military personnel entitlements and savings that will make funds available for other uses, DOD is generating a false sense that all of its reported savings could be used to fund other defense priorities.

DOD has made progress in planning for BRAC 2005 implementation, but several complex challenges to the implementation of those plans increase the risk that DOD might not meet the statutory September 2011 deadline. DOD faces a number of challenges to synchronize the realignment of over 123,000 personnel with the completion of over $21 billion in new construction or renovation projects by 2011. For example, the time frames for completing many BRAC recommendations are so closely sequenced and scheduled to be completed in 2011 that any significant changes in personnel movement schedules or construction delays could jeopardize DOD's ability to meet the statutory 2011 deadline. Additionally, BRAC 2005, unlike prior BRAC rounds, included more joint recommendations involving more than one military component, thus creating challenges in achieving unity of effort among the services and defense agencies.

6.6.7 BRAC: Suppressed Internal Papers Disclosed

Project on Government Secrecy
Federation of American Scientists
January 2008

The decision of the Base Realignment and Closure (BRAC) Commission to shut down certain Department of Defense laboratory facilities was allegedly based on a record that was selectively altered to exclude certain relevant information. Some of the suppressed data have been recovered.

In January 2008, Members of Congress asked the Attorney General to Investigate the BRAC Recommendation to Close Fort Monmouth.

A December 2007 document collection presents an overview of the allegations. See Pentagon Officials Withheld BRAC Data to Protect Proposals That Failed Legal

Requirement. (The Federation of American Scientists does not specifically endorse the conclusions of this document.)

An unofficial Synopsis summarizes the argument that crucial data were suppressed and introduces several of the key official documents:

The final report of the Technical Joint Cross Service Group on DoD laboratories, dated May 10, 2005, with the complete text of Appendix A (267 pages) on current and future excess capacity at the labs.

The official version of the TJCSG Report, dated May 20, 2005, as it was presented to the BRAC Commission -- with 254 pages missing from Appendix A.

A "lessons learned" analysis by Don J. DeYoung, a TJCSG member, dated November 29, 2005.

An email message from the Office of Secretary of Defense describing the removal of most of Appendix A of the TJCSG Report on asserted security grounds.

On July 21, 2005, Senate Armed Services Committee Chairman John Warner wrote to the Department of Defense to request a copy of all papers written by defense analyst Don J. DeYoung concerning the Base Realignment and Closure (BRAC) process.

In a July 25, 2005 response, acting Deputy Secretary of Defense Gordon England forwarded six papers by Mr. DeYoung.

But two other sharply critical internal papers by DeYoung were not released to the Senate Armed Services Committee. They were obtained by the Federation of American Scientists and are provided here.

An explanatory introduction -- which is not an official document -- puts the two DeYoung papers in context.

"Shadows on the Wall: The Problem with Military Value Metrics" is a critique of the bias in military metrics that favors the largest DoD laboratories and centers in the realignment process. (1.5 MB PDF file).

"Defending the Technical Infrastructure Proposals of the 2005 Base Realignment and Closure Round" finds significant methodological flaws in the proposed consolidation of DoD technical facilities that "if implemented, will contribute toward a degradation of national defense capabilities."

See also the Technical Joint Cross Service Group, Analyses and Recommendations, Volume XII, 19 May 2005.

6.6.8 Moran wins reprieve for DoD agencies; no BRAC move until 2014 at earliest

September 23, 2009

By Max Cacas
Reporter
and
Dorothy Ramienski
Internet Editor
FederalNewsRadio

The Pentagon is backing away from a deadline mandating that agencies affected by the BRAC process meet a looming 2011 deadline to move agencies to new secure facilities.

The decision was announced by Rep. Jim Moran (D.-Va), who said the decision now allows most DoD agencies to extend their leases for existing facilities to 2014.

The ruling also gives agencies more time to move to facilities that meet DoD security requirements set by former Defense Secretary Donald Rumsfeld.

On In Depth with Francis Rose, the Congressman explained that not only does he think federal buildings should get a reprieve, but that the DoD standards need to be overhauled altogether.

I don't think they're possible to meet and I don't think they should be met. I think we need to revise these. There are any number of ways that you can make a building secure. You can have a lobby go around the perimeter of the building where people can still work and where functions can be carried out, but in the offices where people are housed -- you can put those offices above the ground floor, you can put them behind secure walls . . . there are a number of things that have been done throughout the country in major cities that have provided security without wasting an enormous amount of valuable land for these setback requirements.

Moran added that he doesn't think the requirements make sense in an urban area.

No one can possibly afford the cost of a 148-foot setback. It just doesn't make sense. We have worked with GSA [and they] have suggested any number of prescriptive remedies that are not as expensive and yet would be compliant with [their] standards. In other words, [GSA] says, "This is what we want you to achieve, you figure out how to achieve it," and then that has been done. DoD, on the other hand, told them exactly how to do it without any deviation for the circumstances and that just is impossible. We need to change the standards so that they are more like GSA's and less like DoD's because people do need to work in metropolitan areas, where land is valuable, and they also should have access to public transit.

During a news conference at the Arlington County Courthouse in Clarendon, Moran announced that the reprieve arrived early Tuesday morning in the form of a memo from Ashton Carter, the Pentagon's Undersecretary of Defense for Acquisition, Technology and Logistics, and overturns one provision of the original 2005 BRAC decision. That provision mandated beefed up security measures to protect DoD facilities away from the Pentagon from carbombers and other terrorist attackers.

Moran stressed over and over that although many local jurisdictions nationwide are impacted by BRAC, none are impacted with the same breadth and depth as Northern Virginia, which is why he and former Congressman Tom Davis (R.Va.) pressed so hard for an exemption, or at least a delay to the BRAC moves.

One of the agencies on the list of three dozen slated to move as part of BRAC and the Pentagon's security concerns is the Defense Advanced Research Projects Agency. Over the summer, DARPA signed an agreement to move its headquarters about a half mile from their Fairfax Drive location to a new building across the street from the Ballston Common Mall, on the site of a former Metrobus garage. Groundbreaking for the DARPA headquarters is slated to take place in October or November of this year.

Federal News Radio asked Arlington County Board Chairwoman Barbara Favola whether the new time extension will affect the scheduled 2012 opening date for the DARPA project.

"It is my expectation," she replied, "that that project will move forward on the timeline that was originally developed."

She adds that the extension negotiated by Moran gives local jurisdictions time to work with the Pentagon on meeting the BRAC security requirements.

Still uncertain is what the new time extension will mean for the other DoD agencies slated to move as part of the BRAC process.

On the Web:

Northern Virginia BRAC Working Group - Final Report (December. 2005 pdf)

6.6.9 Audit reviews BRAC savings

By MARC HELLER
TIMES WASHINGTON CORRESPONDENT
SUNDAY, NOVEMBER 15, 2009

WASHINGTON — The 2005 round of military base closures that spared Fort Drum will cost billions of dollars more, and save tens of millions less, than officials originally predicted, a federal audit indicates.

Researchers at the U.S. Government Accountability Office reported Friday that the 2005 round will cost $34.9 billion, up from the $21 billion that the Base Realignment and Closure Commission told Congress in September 2005.

On top of that 67 percent increase, the recurring savings from the round are now estimated at $3.9 billion a year, or $94 million less than the commission told lawmakers.

That means the Pentagon will not break even on the 2005 round until 2018, five years later than originally promised, the GAO reported.

The findings appear to validate arguments by congressional critics of base realignment, including former Rep. John M. McHugh, R-Pierrepont Manor, that estimated costs and savings are open to doubt. Mr. McHugh, now secretary of the Army, reluctantly supported the Bush administration's proposal.

The Defense Department agreed with the GAO's findings.

"Even though the BRAC 2005 round is costing more and savings are less than originally estimated in 2005, implementation of these recommendations is an important element of the Defense Department's ongoing effort to reshape our infrastructure to respond to global challenges," said Dorothy Robyn, deputy undersecretary of defense for installations and environment, in a letter responding to the GAO.

GAO investigators found that most of the cost increases are tied to construction, the largest being the closure of Walter Reed Army Medical Center and related expansion of the Bethesda National Naval Medical Center.

The Army, which faces the greatest BRAC-related costs, saw its estimated implementation expense climb from $17.3 billion last year to $18.2 billion this year, a 5 percent increase.

Defense officials and the GAO disagree about the estimates of savings. While the GAO repeated in its report a long-standing assertion that the Pentagon overstates savings, the sides disagree about savings from eliminating military personnel positions — a major source of the savings the Defense Department predicts.

In addition, the GAO estimated that 76 of the 182 recommendations in the base realignment plan will achieve no net savings.

6.6.10 <u>United States Government Accountability Office</u>

Washington, DC 2054
Congressional Committees
Subject: Military Base Realignments and Closures: DOD Is Taking Steps to Mitigate Challenges but Is Not Fully Reporting Some Additional Costs
July 21, 2010

Summary

DOD is implementing 182 BRAC recommendations for this BRAC round, but several logistical, human capital and other implementation challenges remain. First, many locations are scheduled to complete the construction, relocation, personnel, and other actions needed to implement the recommendations within months of and, in some cases, on the deadline leaving little or no margin for slippage to finish constructing buildings and to move or hire the needed personnel. As of March 2010, DOD had 57 construction projects scheduled to be completed within 3 months of the statutory deadline, representing about 30 recommendations. Second, some DOD locations that involve the most costly and complex recommendations have encountered delays in awarding some construction contracts as well as experienced additional delays in the expected completion of construction. Third, DOD must synchronize the relocation of approximately 123,000 personnel with the availability of about $25 billion in new construction or renovation of facilities. Fourth, delays in interdependent recommendations are likely to have a cascading effect on the timely completion of related recommendations. These challenges have continued since our last report on BRAC implementation challenges,1 especially contracting and construction delays, which have further squeezed an already tight time line. Furthermore, some DOD organizations that are realigning their missions to other installations face human capital challenges, such as the potential loss of intellectual capital if civilian personnel with unique skills or abilities choose not to relocate and DOD is unable to replace enough of their critical skills to avoid an adverse impact on mission performance or capabilities. This challenge is further complicated by various community effects of BRAC implementation growth, such as transportation, housing, schooling, and availability of medical care.

DOD is mitigating some BRAC implementation challenges, which is adding to implementation costs; however, DOD is not reporting all of these additional costs. To enhance its role in managing logistical challenges that could affect DOD's ability to achieve BRAC implementation by the statutory deadline, the military services are working with their leadership to develop solutions. For example, the Army has briefed its Vice Chief of Staff at least four times since 2008 on BRAC implementation challenges. Further, the military services and defense agencies are providing periodic briefings for BRAC recommendations exceeding $100 million in implementation costs, or that have significant concerns such as cost overruns or construction delays to the OSD Basing Directorate. For other BRAC recommendations, DOD is still weighing options, such as moving temporarily into different buildings while construction and renovations are completed, referred to as swing space, or accelerating the pace of construction to complete permanent facilities by the deadline, potentially incurring additional expenses. In addition, Army officials are mitigating some human-capital-related challenges by recruiting new personnel and offering financial incentives to civilian employees to relocate, again potentially incurring additional expenses. Swing space facilities, hiring or relocation financial incentives, and other mitigation actions may lead to additional costs, although some of these costs are not being reported in the services' BRAC budget materials provided to Congress. The DOD Financial Management Regulation requires the services and defense agencies to accurately capture BRAC-related costs in the annual BRAC budget justification materials submitted to Congress.12 Since DOD's recent fiscal year 2011 BRAC budget request—which was the final annual request for funds for the BRAC account before the statutory deadline for completion of closures and realignments—has already been submitted to Congress, such additional costs in our view may have to be funded from outside the BRAC account. However, we found that DOD's reported costs funded outside the BRAC account are not complete because the Army has not reported to Congress some of these costs as BRAC costs. Thus, OSD officials do not have full visibility over the extent of these costs funded from outside the BRAC account, given that the services prepare their own BRAC budget justification material. Until the Secretary of Defense ensures that all BRAC-related costs are captured and reported to Congress, neither congressional decision makers nor those within OSD who are charged with overseeing BRAC implementation will have a complete picture of the cost of implementing the 2005 BRAC round.

6.7 Letters from the New Jersey Congressional Delegation

The New Jersey Congressional Delegation made a concerted effort to prevent the relocation of Fort Monmouth to Maryland. Below are some of the many letters that were written along with newspaper articles.

6.7.1 <u>Letter to House Armed Services Committee</u>

Congress of the United States
House of Representatives
Washington, DC 20515
March 20, 2007

Rep. Ike Skelton Rep. Duncan Hunter Chairman Ranking Member

House Armed Services Committee House Armed Services Committee 2120 Rayburn House Office Building 2120 Rayburn House Office Building Washington, DC 20515 Washington, DC 20515

Rep. John P. Murtha Rep. C. W. "Bill" Young Chairman Ranking Member Subcommittee on Defense Appropriations Subcommittee on Defense Appropriations Committee on Appropriations Committee on Appropriations Room H-149, The Capitol 1016 Longworth House Office Building Washington, DC 20515 Washington, DC 20515

Dear Chairman Skelton, Ranking Member Hunter, Chairman Murtha, and Ranking Member Young,

Recently, our offices were made aware of previously undisclosed internal Defense Department memoranda that raise serious questions about whether the department was forthcoming in its declarations to the Base Realignment and Closure (BRAC) Commission and the Congress on the need to close or consolidate research, development, testing and evaluation (RDT&E) facilities in the 2005 BRAC round. We want to share that information with you, and request that you take action via the authorization and appropriations process to address the national security implications of these revelations.

In October 2006, the Federation of American Scientists published on their website a series of internal DoD documents from the Pentagon's Technical Joint Cross-Services Group (TJCSG), the joint DoD entity responsible for evaluating the military value of the various RDT&E facilities under consideration for consolidation or closure. Those documents can be found at the following URL:

http://www.fas.org/sgp/othergov/dodlbraclindex.html

Among these documents is a series of critiques of the TJCSG's methodology. The critique was prepared by Mr. Don DeYoung of the Naval Research Laboratory, a BRAC alternate representative. Mr. DeYoung served on previous BRAC commissions and is clearly an expert in the field of RDT&E infrastructure. Among Mr. DeYoung's central allegations are the following:

The methodology used by DoD and the TJCSG to determine which facilities to consolidate or close was fundamentally flawed, and that in fact the entire process was driven by a predetermined outcome (the desire to show facility closures) rather than by the data and facts.

For example, among all DoD sites performing work in Information Systems(IS), Fort Monmouth was ranked #3 in Research and #2 in D&A. Simarily, for the Sensors technology area, it ranked #9 and #4, respectively. The site's scores for the four "bins" show a multidisciplinary and multifunctional center. No other Army site appeared within the Top 10 for more than one of the four bins. Therefore, the Army already had an existing multidisciplinary and multifunctional center at Fort Monmouth. By the TJCSG's stated strategy, it would have seemed a logical "gainer" for workload. But that did not happen. Fort Monmouth was proposed for closure. Regarding the process that produced this illogical result, DeYoung stated that the above evidence shows two things about the co-sponsored closure: (a) military value was not "the primary consideration in the making of recommendations, " as the law requires; and (b) the exercise of expert judgment was not "reproducible, " a more stringent standard that could have minimized the negative effects of a judgment-driven process. As shown above the expert judgment at the basis of the TJCSG proposal failed to be reproduced in the Army proposal where each differed as to what skills at APG would enable the transformation. This disconnect does not inspire confidence in the asserted merits of the idea. We have also learned that DoD's cost estimate for moving Fort Monmouth's activities and people to Aberdeen Proving Ground will almost certainly be higher than the Department told the BRAC Commission and Congress. In 2005, DoD told the Commission that the Fort Monmouth Aberdeen move would result in a one-time cost of $780,400,000. However, at a February 13, 2007 town hall with Fort Monmouth employees, Army officials indicated that $744,800,000 had been allocated for construction alone at Aberdeen. Clearly, the cost estimates provided to the Commission and the Congress were not accurate, further undermining DoD's claims about the benefits of closing Fort Monmouth.

Finally, the President's announcement earlier this year of his intent to increase the Army's force structure by 65,000 personnel and the Marine Corps's force structure by 27,000 personnel has clear implications for the validity of the conclusions reached by both GAO and the BRAC Commission. This new 92,000 personnel increase was not part of the 2005 Defense Planning Guidance, nor was such an increase contemplated by DoD or the BRAC Commission during the last BRAC round.

All of these facts and developments raise troubling questions about how DoD and the TJCSG process dealt with our nation's unique yet fragile military RDT&E capabilities. In light of these developments, we ask that you take appropriate action via the authorization and appropriations process to withhold any funding for the consolidation or closure of Army RDT&E facilities under BRAC until the Congress has conducted a comprehensive review of the issues and allegations raised both by Mr. DeYoung's correspondence and the ability of our projected RDT&E infrastructure to support the

President's requested force structure increase. We appreciate your personal attention to this matter.

Sincerely,

Rush Holt, Frank Pallone, Jim Saxton, Chris Smith, Members of Congress

6.7.2 <u>GAO debunks BRAC logic Base-closing figures called way off-base</u>

Asbury Park Press
Sep. 14, 2007

The Army may have to choose between fully funding the wars in Iraq and Afghanistan or paying for all construction projects called for by the 2005 Base Realignment and Closure decisions, according to two federal reports released Thursday. The Government Accountability Office issued the latest in a string of reports critical of the Pentagon's 2005 military base consolidation effort, prompting incredulity from New Jersey's congressional delegation. In the two separate reports, the GAO examined portions of the 2005 BRAC decisions to shutter Fort Monmouth and other installations in a nationwide effort to streamline the military and save money. The GAO — Congress' investigative arm — took a look at 44 BRAC recommendations that call for the consolidation of Army National Guard and Reserve centers in 38 states. The office found that the Department of Defense overestimated the amount it would save from the moves and underestimated the costs. The report high-lighted other potential pitfalls, and questioned the method used by the Pentagon to calculate some savings, concluding that its numbers are bloated by as much as 92 percent.

In a separate report, the GAO found "implementation challenges" in the Army's plan to incorporate 154,000 personnel at domestic bases as a result of BRAC decisions and other restructuring. Among those challenges: discrepancies in the estimates of new personnel at various expanding installations and the affected installations; problems in synchronizing military construction with those personnel movements; and competing priorities that may force the Army to choose whether to fully fund the global war on terrorism or pay for BRAC-related construction.

"Full of flaws"

The reports released Thursday are the third and fourth studies by the GAO of the 2005 BRAC decisions. Two previous reports, also highly critical, were issued in May and June. "This is just another example how the DOD blew the cost and savings estimates and it just raises more questions about the whole process," said Rep. Rush D. Holt, D-N.J. "Whenever anybody looks closely at the BRAC process, it seems to be full of flaws." Holt and others in New Jersey's congressional delegation have resumed an effort to remove Fort Monmouth from the Pentagon's chopping block, following an Asbury Park Press investigation that found cost estimates to close the 90-year-old post have risen to $1.5 billion from $780 million since 2005. "The case of

Fort Monmouth epitomizes the Army's flawed process and it is exactly why we need congressional hearings," Rep. Christopher H. Smith, R-N.J., said in a statement. Reps. Smith, Holt and Frank J. Pallone Jr., D-N.J., have called on the House Armed Services Committee to conduct hearings on the BRAC process, which is costing $10 billion more than estimated two years ago, according to the investigation. "It certainly helps to make our case that there were a lot of mistakes made," Pallone said. "I think Fort Monmouth is the worst example of the themes the GAO is pointing out." The Defense Department estimated in 2005 that the consolidation of more than 100 Army Reserve centers across the country would generate $323 million annually, but the Pentagon's latest budget documents show a savings of $288 million, an 11 percent decrease, the GAO report says. But as much as 92 percent of that annual savings is dubious, the report says, because the Pentagon based that number on job cuts at sites it plans to close. Those jobs, however, are not going to be cut entirely, but moved to new locations. The savings may never be realized, the report says. Without counting the job cuts at closed locations, the GAO estimates the Pentagon will save just $23 million annually. "Military personnel position eliminations are not a true source of savings because DOD does not expect to reduce end strength," the report says. "DOD's treatment of military personnel saving represents a long-standing difference of opinion between DOD and us."

Other findings

The GAO's study on the impact of the BRAC decisions on those installations that will gain personnel or missions was conducted from March 2006 through July 2007.

It found that:

Army headquarters and the bases that were gaining personnel had different numbers of just how many people are involved. For example, the Army said that new personnel at Fort Benning, Ga., would bring with them about 600 school-aged children. Fort Benning officials estimated about 10,000. Vast discrepancies make it difficult for affected communities to properly plan for impacts to schools, transportation systems and local housing markets. Some of the moves require complex synchronization, which, if not done correctly, "could place the Army at risk of not meeting the statutory deadline for completing BRAC actions" of Sept. 15, 2011. Underestimated increases in construction costs are leading to some changes in construction schedules at bases that are gaining personnel. For example, the Army is not building any so-called quality-of-life construction — day care centers, athletic fields, post exchanges — at Forts Belvoir and Lee in Virginia, even though they were requested. "Military family advocates believe that not funding quality-of-life facilities could jeopardize military readiness by distracting deployed soldiers who may be concerned that their families are not being taken care of," the report says.

6.7.3 <u>Last-Ditch Plea From N.J.</u>

Congress is told BRAC move would mean loss of expertise

December 2007
By Matthew Hay Brown, Sun Reporter

Staging a last-ditch effort to hold off the impending closure of Fort Monmouth, New Jersey lawmakers told a congressional panel yesterday that plans to move operations to Aberdeen Proving Ground would endanger the lives of U.S. soldiers overseas.

Researchers at Fort Monmouth developed the signal jammers used to thwart the improvised explosive devices that have claimed the lives of more than 1,500 troops in Iraq. With 70 percent of Monmouth workers saying they would quit before moving to Aberdeen, the base's advocates warned of a devastating loss of knowledge and experience.

"It will take several years to replicate in Aberdeen what is currently a world-class facility," Rep. Christopher H. Smith, a New Jersey Republican, told the House Armed Services subcommittee on readiness. "We're at war. We don't have years."

Philip W. Grone, deputy undersecretary of defense for installations and environment, disagreed: "The needs of the technical community, the needs of the war fighter are all going to be met," he said. "The notion that somehow senior military leadership ... would put lives at risk on the battlefield is simply wrong."

New Jersey lawmakers sought the hearing yesterday to learn how the Pentagon is implementing the Base Realignment and Closure plan approved by Congress and President Bush in 2005. Maryland is preparing to receive some 15,000 direct jobs and up to 45,000 indirect jobs with the expansion of Aberdeen Proving Ground, Fort Meade and other facilities in the state. Fort Monmouth is one of 24 installations slated to close.

The hearing came a day after the General Accountability Office reported that the estimated cost of the realignment had climbed nearly 50 percent to $31 billion nationwide, while projected savings have dipped to $4 billion per year. The Pentagon says the move from Fort Monmouth to Aberdeen will cost $1.45 billion, nearly twice its initial estimate.

Unlike previous rounds of BRAC, the 2005 plan was aimed at maximizing war fighting power, not cost savings. Grone said the cost estimates were used to help planners choose among options, not gauge actual expenses.

Still, Maryland Rep. Elijah E. Cummings asked GAO official Brian Lepore to confirm that the realignment would help the Pentagon save money. Lepore, director of defense capabilities assessment at the congressional watchdog agency, said savings would be realized through both the move from Fort Monmouth to Aberdeen and the realignment nationwide.

The New Jersey delegation is given little chance of keeping Fort Monmouth open. Congress has not reversed a BRAC decision since it set up the independent process nearly 20 years ago, and readiness subcommittee Chairman Solomon P. Ortiz, a Texas Democrat, suggested it wasn't likely to start now.

"This committee is not here today to overturn any decision already made," Ortiz said. "Communities with bases closing should continue planning. Communities with new assets coming should continue to prepare for that eventuality."

The New Jersey lawmakers argue that Fort Monmouth is a special case. They say the BRAC commission made its closure contingent on certification by the Pentagon that the move would not disrupt support for the war on terror.

"With all due respect to our good friends in Maryland, they will find very quickly that they don't have the personnel" to continue operations without disruption, Smith said.

Lt. Gov. Anthony G. Brown, chairman of the "BRAC Cabinet" set up by Gov. Martin O'Malley, acknowledged "work-force challenges," but said a work force that leads the nation in advanced degrees and institutions such as the Johns Hopkins University and the University of Maryland made the state capable of rising to the challenge.

"Maryland understands its expanding responsibility to the country," said Brown, a lieutenant colonel in the Army Reserve who was awarded a Bronze Star in Iraq. "We embrace that responsibility."

Grone said the Pentagon would issue its certification by the end of the month. But he said the closure of Fort Monmouth "is not, as some may contend, a conditional closure."

"The BRAC Act requires the department to close and realign all installations so recommended by the commission," he said.

The Department of Defense, Grone said, "has already determined that Fort Monmouth can be closed and its functions relocated without jeopardizing its support for war fighters in the field, and the BRAC commission agreed with that conclusion. "

6.7.4 A letter from the New Jersey Congressional Delegation to the Attorney General

Congress of the United States

Washington DC 20315

January 16, 2008

Attorney General Michael B. Mukasey United States Department of Justice 950 Pennsylvania Avenue, NW Washington, DC 20530-0001

Dear Attorney General Mukasey,

We are writing today to request that you investigate whether officials within the Department of Defense and the Department of the Army deliberately and in violation of federal law withheld or otherwise sought to skew data presented to the 2005 Base Realignment and Closure (BRAC) Commission in support of DoD's recommendation to the BRAC Commission that Fort Monmouth, New Jersey be closed.

Just this week, we became aware of the egregious actions of a Department of the Army official, Deputy Assistant Chief of Staff for Installation Management Craig College. It has recently been brought to our attention that in 2005, Mr. College blocked the Army Audit Agency (AAA) from scrutinizing the Army's cost estimates for the closure of Fort Monmouth.

Recent press accounts have carried excerpts of an email sent by College to Dave Branham, a program director for the AAA. Branham had emailed College to notify him that he had "received a call from Fort Monmouth personnel today requesting that we validate some revised data (something to do with reimbursables that shouldn't have been included in earlier data calls, and it's considered significant.)" College subsequently responded to Branham, stating "This strikes me as something AAA should not participate in. Your work would become part of the community argument against the Army!"

Section 2903(c)(5) of the 1990 Base Realignment and Closure Act (P.L. 101-510) requires the Secretaries of the military departments, the heads of Defense Agencies, and "each person who is in a position the duties of which include personal and substantial involvement in the preparation and submission of information and recommendations concerning the closure or realignment of military installations" to certify that the information submitted is accurate and complete to the best of that person's knowledge. The email exchange cited above provides documentary evidence that suggests that College knowingly encouraged the distribution of false cost estimates to the BRAC Commission. Additionally, we call your attention to the sworn testimony of Mr. Victor Ferlise, formerly the senior civilian official at Fort Monmouth during the 2005 BRAC round. On December 12, 2007, Mr. Ferlise testified before the Readiness subcommittee of the House Armed Services Committee regarding the issue of the certification of the cost data. Mr. Ferlise told the subcommittee "On July 14th I personally certified all of that data, and that data was for $1.44 billion, not $700 million, and that data was transmitted to the Department of the Army, and I'm sure it went to DOD ultimately."

A separate but related issue is evidence that some officials in the Department of Defense sought to withhold information from the BRAC Commission.

In January 2007, we became aware of an email from an official in the office of Dr. Ronald Sega, then Director of Defense Research and Engineering (DDR&E) at the Department of Defense, that appears to direct subordinates working on a report due to be submitted to the BRAC Commission to withhold data from the Commission.

The email reads in part:

"Dr. Sega has concerns that the aggregated list of 282 locations should be FOUO. He has concerns that the aggregation of work years, test hours and building information should be classified. The mention of technologies which may be important in the future might be controlled information too. He solicits the advice of the Principals concerning the specific classification of each section of Appendix A being withheld. The remainder of Appendix A will be offered to the Commission with the appropriate classification markings."

The BRAC statute states that "Each meeting of the Commission, other than meetings in which classified information is to be discussed, shall be open to the public." Previous BRAC Commissions reviewed classified information in making their realignment and closure recommendations, as you will find if you examine previous BRAC Commission reports. Dr. Sega's contention that any material be withheld from the Commission appears to us to be a violation of the BRAC statute, including his attempted assertion of the non-statutory dissemination restriction "For Official Use Only" and other assertions that the material in question was classified.

The fraudulent costs estimates offered to the Commission and the Congress, along with the effort to withhold relevant data from the Commission, call into question the entire BRAC process as it pertained to the Fort Monmouth closure decision. Those deceitful actions have resulted in massively increased costs for taxpayers (more than double the fraudulent $780 million estimate offered by DoD to the Commission in 2005), and could place in jeopardy the continuity of Army communications and intelligence support to our troops in Iraq and Afghanistan. In light of the aforementioned documentary evidence and testimony, we request that the Department of Justice undertake a criminal investigation into this matter.

Sincerely,

FRANK LAUTENBERG, ROBERT MENENDEZ

United States Senator, United States Senator

CHRISTOPHER SMITH, RUSH HOLT, FRANK PALLONE

Member of Congress, Member of Congress, Member of Congress

6.7.5 Judge tosses Fort Monmouth suit

The following report was in response to an effort by the American Federation of Government Employees Local 1904 to block the move of Fort Monmouth to Maryland. It should be noted that our Hanscom Union was in touch with Atty Eugene LaVergne, who had represented the Fort Monmouth Union. Had he been successful, we would have hired him to represent the AFRL Hanscom Research Site.

By Keith Brown, COASTAL MONMOUTH BUREAU
July 25, 2008

TRENTON — A lawsuit seeking to block the closure of Fort Monmouth has been dismissed by a federal judge, officials said Thursday.

Federal District Court Judge Mary L. Cooper, sitting in Trenton, dismissed the suit brought by a Fort Monmouth employees union, saying, in part, the union had no standing to bring some of the charges and that Cooper lacked jurisdiction to hear other portions, a union official said.

The American Federation of Government Employees Local 1904 — which represents about 5,000 civilian fort employees — brought the suit. It claims the Defense Department "committed intentional and knowing acts of criminal fraud, intentional misrepresentation, and deception" in recommending closing the 90-year-old Army post.

But while Cooper's dismissal had more to do with the technical elements of legal procedure and precedent than the merits of the union's arguments, union officials were still decidedly downbeat about the outcome.

"It's a sad day for the soldier, for the taxpayer and for Fort Monmouth," said John Poitras, AFGE Local 1904 president. "The soldiers are unfortunately going to be affected, the economy is going to suffer because of the jobs lost and we're going to end up paying for the enhancement of Aberdeen (Proving Ground) so they can receive Fort Monmouth in the appropriate manner."

Fort Monmouth was one of dozens of military installations closed or consolidated during the Pentagon's 2005 Base Realignment and Closure round — a nationwide shuffling of installations aimed at streamlining the military and saving money.

Under the BRAC decisions, Fort Monmouth, which employs more than 5,000, supports another 22,000 and pumps about $3.2 billion into the state's economy, is to be closed by 2011. Much of its research and development mission is to be transferred to Aberdeen Proving Ground in Maryland.

Eugene LaVergne, the West Long Branch attorney representing the union, said he was unfazed by the decision.

"No one ever thought Judge Mary L. Cooper was going to have the final say," LaVergne said. "The final say will be the 3rd Circuit or possibly the U.S. Supreme Court."

LaVergne said there was little doubt that the case would be appealed to the 3rd Circuit Court of Appeals. The union has a 30-day window to decide whether to continue.

Keith Brown: (732) 643-4076 or kbrown@app.com

6.8 A Plan for Saving the Hanscom Research Site

Sen. Kennedy's office had asked whether we had any ideas as to how we may propose an alternative use of the Hanscom Research Site. I sent his office the following letter suggesting three options
- a UMass Hanscom Research Laboratory
- a DoD "purple" laboratory
- a Department of Homeland Security Research Laboratory.

We sent the following letter to his office.

We have been asked to propose creative ideas as to how we may save the Hanscom Research Site; we are proposing several options, which we wish you to consider. The first option is to transfer the assets of the Hanscom Research Site to the University of Massachusetts so that a new research establishment, the UMASS Hanscom Research Laboratory, could be created. This new laboratory could be administered in a way similar to that which MIT uses to administer Lincoln Laboratory. We believe that this plan would result in a win-win outcome for both the Air Force and Massachusetts. The Air Force will benefit since they will finally have achieved their goal of eliminating the Hanscom Research Site and they will not have to go through the expense of building new facilities at WPAFB and KAFB. Also the expertise that has been available to conduct research on important Air Force programs would not be lost. Massachusetts will benefit since this plan would provide UMASS with a laboratory of world-renowned scientists and engineers who have worked closely with both UMASS-Amherst and UMASS-Lowell for many years. Hanscom AFB will benefit since it would retain the research capability that is needed to expand future research and development. Although the initial programs would probably be DoD oriented, so that important Air Force programs could be completed, the laboratory could eventually branch out into new areas of research, such as biotech, wireless communications, photonics, the environment and homeland security.

Another option would be to establish a tri-service (purple) laboratory at Hanscom AFB. The DoD has been considering "purple" laboratories for many years and it would seem that this would be an excellent opportunity to use the Hanscom Research Site as their first laboratory. In this scenario, it could easily be envisioned that the laboratory could, for the first time in a long time, actually grow in size and in mission.

The final option would be to establish a Federal Laboratory at Hanscom AFB such as those that fall under the Department of Commerce; the National Oceanic and Atmospheric Administration (NOAA) or the National Institute of Standards and Technology NIST). For example, the Department of Homeland Security does not currently have a federal research laboratory. The expertise that currently exists at the Hanscom Field Site, in the areas of sensors and environment, is exactly what is needed to establish this new laboratory.

There are obviously many details that will have to be worked out before a transfer and reestablishment of the Hanscom Research Site assets can take place. However I cannot presently think of any problems that appear to be insurmountable. It is imperative that we do everything within our power to prevent the closure of the Hanscom Research Site, since the loss of this site will leave Hanscom AFB completely devoid of any research activity; we must not allow this to happen!

Sincerely,

Ed
Dr. Edward E. Altshuler
NFFE Local 1384 Liaison to Congress
Air Force Research Laboratory
Electromagnetics Technology Division
80 Scott Drive
Hanscom AFB, MA 01731-2909
(781) 377-4662
(781) 377-1074 Fax

Unfortunately, I received no response.

6.8.1 UMass Contingency Plan

As a contingency plan, in the event that the BRAC could not be rescinded, I thought that it may be possible to interest UMASS into taking over the AFRL Hanscom Research Site and establish a University Affiliated Research Center. Scientists from the Battlespace Environment Division had collaborated with their colleagues at UMass-Lowell for many years in the area of geophysics while scientists from the Electromagnetics Technology Division had collaborated with colleagues from both UMass- Lowell and UMass-Amherst for many years in the area of electromagnetics.

6.8.2 Letter to UMass President – 19 October – 2005

At this point in time, having not received a response from my letter to Sen. Kennedy, I decided to write directly to President Wilson of UMass along with copies to Chancellors Lombardi and Hogan of UMass-Amherst and UMass Lowell respectively. I also coordinated this letter through my focal points, Prof. Dan Schaubert of UMass–Amherst and Prof. Bodo Reinisch of UMass-Lowell.

NATIONAL FEDERATION
OF
FEDERAL EMPLOYEES
PROFESSIONAL LOCAL 1384
HANSCOM AFB MA 01731

19 October 2005

Dear President Wilson

The purpose of this letter is to explore the possibility for the University of Massachusetts to establish a research laboratory at Hanscom Air Force Base. The Base Realignment and Closure (BRAC) Commission has recommended that the Air Force Research Laboratory (AFRL) Electromagnetics Division of the Sensors Directorate and the Battlespace Environment Division of the Space Vehicles Directorate be relocated to Wright-Patterson AFB in Ohio and Kirtland AFB in New Mexico, respectively. As a result, these divisions, which make up the Hanscom Research Site will be closed.

The Hanscom Research Site, which evolved from the MIT Radiation Laboratory and the Harvard Radio Research Laboratory after World War II, has had a long and rich history and is considered one of the premier research laboratories in the world. Based on a recent survey, we expect that close to 200 scientists and engineers, about half of whom hold doctorates, would be interested in continuing to work at the Hanscom site; less than 10% are planning to relocate. We have many unique facilities and equipment that enable us to conduct cutting-edge research. We have collaborated with scientists and engineers from UMASS-Amherst and UMASS-Lowell for many years. Our Electromagnetics Technology Division and UMASS-Amherst has established the Center for Advanced Sensor and Communications Antennas; this Center has received $6 million from the DoD during these past two years. The UMASS-Amherst focal point for this Center is Prof. Daniel Schaubert of ECE. In addition, for decades our Battlespace Environment Division has maintained strong interactions with UMASS-Lowell to study ionospheric effects on radiowave propagation and electrical coupling between the ionosphere and the magnetosphere with funding of about $1 million per year. Key UMASS-Lowell researchers in these studies have been Professors Bodo Reinisch, Gary Sales, and Paul Song.

As you know, it is not uncommon for universities to have off-site research laboratories. For example, MIT is associated with Lincoln Lab, Stanford with the Stanford Research Institute, Georgia Tech with the Georgia Tech Research Institute, Ohio State with the Electroscience Lab, Univ. of Michigan with the Radiation Lab, Cal Tech with the Jet Propulsion Lab, and the list goes on and on. Would it not make sense for UMASS to establish a research laboratory at facilities to be vacated at Hanscom AFB?

Our Hanscom Research Site has a current budget of about $30 million. A large part of this funding comes from the Defense Advanced Research Projects Agency (DARPA) and we believe that this support would continue. Since our Divisions are currently involved in many on-going Air Force programs, we expect that Air Force funding would still be available in the near term. We may, however, need additional near term support but this amount remains to be determined; for the long term, there are many new and exciting areas of research such as the environment, biotechnology, photonics, nanotechnology, and wireless communications that the new laboratory could enter. Both Governor Romney and Senator Kennedy have emphasized the importance of the research that is conducted at Hanscom AFB and the need to expand it. We expect that they would help to find ways to get us through the transition period.

There are obviously many details that will have to be worked out before a transfer and reestablishment of the Hanscom Research Site as a UMASS Hanscom Research Laboratory can take place. However, I cannot presently think of any problems that appear to be insurmountable. We believe that this is an excellent opportunity for the University of Massachusetts to take over an established research laboratory, which currently has a dedicated workforce of scientists and engineers along with excellent facilities. Please give this proposal your consideration. If you need any additional information, we will be happy to make this available. I will be attending the URSI General Assembly in Delhi, India but should be back in my office on Wednesday, 2 November.

Sincerely,

Ed
Dr. Edward E. Altshuler
National Federation of Federal Employees
Local 1384 Liaison to Congress
Air Force Research Laboratory
Electromagnetics Technology Division
80 Scott Drive
Hanscom AFB, MA 01731-2909
(781)377-4662
(781)377-1074 Fax

Unfortunately, I received no response from this letter.

6.8.3 <u>Letter to Senator Hart – 26 November 2005</u>

I noticed an article entitled "UMass seeks $120M boost for facilities", that was published in the 26 November 2005 issue of the Boston Globe. It stated that Senator Hart would be the focal point on the Joint Committee on Economic Development and Emerging Technologies that would consider the $120M request. I wrote a letter to Senator Hart suggesting that a UMass takeover of our Hanscom Research Site might be a cost savings means of acquiring an established research laboratory. I further suggested that with Congressional support, UMass could probably obtain buildings and equipment along with an experienced workforce at a very low cost. I also mentioned that scientists and engineers at AFRL were already collaborating with researchers at both UMass-Lowell and UMass Amherst.

NATIONAL FEDERATION
OF
FEDERAL EMPLOYEES
PROFESSIONAL LOCAL 1384
HANSCOM AFB MA 01731

Dear Senator Hart,

I read with interest the article entitled "UMass seeks $120m boost for facilities" in the Saturday, 26 November edition of the Boston Globe. The purpose of this letter is to explore the possibility for the University of Massachusetts to establish a research laboratory at Hanscom Air Force Base (AFB). The Base Realignment and Closure (BRAC) Commission has recommended, and the President and Congress have approved, that the missions of the Air Force Research Laboratory (AFRL) Divisions at Hanscom AFB be relocated to Wright-Patterson AFB in Ohio and Kirtland AFB in New Mexico. We anticipate that many of the AFRL scientists and engineers will choose to remain in the Boston area, because of family, professional and cultural ties. This creates an important opportunity for UMASS to exploit.

The AFRL Hanscom Research Site is considered one of the premier research laboratories in the world. It evolved from the MIT Radiation Laboratory and the Harvard Radio Research Laboratory after World War II and has a long and rich history of important technical contributions to the Defense Department. We also have the good fortune to be located in the Boston area, which has one of the greatest concentrations of high tech workers in the country. Based on a recent survey, we

217

expect that close to 200 of our scientists and engineers, about half of whom hold doctorates, would be interested in continuing to work in the Hanscom area for a new establishment; less than 10% are planning to relocate with the Air Force. We have unique facilities and equipment that enable us to conduct cutting-edge research in many areas that are of mutual interest to both UMASS and our scientists and engineers. In fact, we have collaborated with both UMASS-Amherst and UMASS-Lowell for many years.

The Globe article states that the Joint Committee on Economic Development and Emerging Technologies will be considering the $120M funding request. We believe that it would be in the best interest of our Commonwealth for your committee to consider the option of the UMASS establishment of a research laboratory in the vicinity of Hanscom AFB. It could prove to be an excellent low cost opportunity to build on. Please review the attached letter which was previously sent to President Wilson with copies to Chancellors Hogan and Lombardi and my colleagues at UMASS-Lowell and UMASS-Amherst. Also, we would like to extend an invitation to your committee to visit the AFRL Hanscom Research Site so that you may view first hand our excellent establishment.

Sincerely,

Ed
Dr. Edward E. Altshuler
National Federation of Federal Employees
Local 1384 Liaison to Congress
Air Force Research Laboratory
Electromagnetics Technology Division
80 Scott Drive
Hanscom AFB, MA 01731-2909
(781)377-4662
(781)377-1074 Fax

Unfortunately, I did not receive a reply to my letter.

6.8.4 Letter to UMass Lowell Chancellor Meehan

I continued to keep in touch with Profs. Schaubert and Reinisch to see if there was any feedback from my letters but there wasn't any. In the interim Rep. Marty Meehan had resigned from Congress to become the new Chancellor of UMass-Lowell. I had met Rep. Meehan on previous occasions and it seemed to me if I could interest him in having UMass take over our site, with his connections in Congress, he could probably arrange to have the buildings and left over equipment transferred to UMass. I sent him the following e-mail.

From: Altshuler, Edward E Civ USAF AFMC AFRL/RYHA
[mailto:Edward.Altshuler@hanscom.af.mil]

Sent: Fri 9/11/2009 4:47 PM
To: Meehan, Marty
Subject: UMASS Hanscom Research Laboratory

Dear Chancellor Meehan,

The purpose of this letter is to explore the possibility for the University of Massachusetts to establish a research laboratory at Hanscom Air Force Base. The Base Realignment and Closure (BRAC) Commission has recommended that the Air Force Research Laboratory (AFRL) Electromagnetics Division of the Sensors Directorate and the Battlespace Environment Division of the Space Vehicles Directorate be relocated to Wright-Patterson AFB in Ohio and Kirtland AFB in New Mexico, respectively. As a result, these divisions, which make up the AFRL Hanscom Research Site, are scheduled to be closed on or before 15 September 2011.

The Hanscom Research Site, which evolved from the MIT Radiation Laboratory and the Harvard Radio Research Laboratory after World War II as Air Force Cambridge Research Laboratories, has had a long and rich history and is considered one of the premier research laboratories in the world. We have many unique facilities and equipment that enable us to do cutting-edge research. We have a dedicated workforce of over 200 scientists and engineers, about half of whom hold Doctorates. We receive additional support from close to 200 on-base contractors who work side by side with us. As a result of this closure, Massachusetts is slated to lose over 400 jobs. We expect that many of our government scientists and engineers would be interested in continuing to work at the Hanscom site; less than 15% are planning to relocate. As far as we know, the Air Force does not have plans as to how they will use the vacated buildings and equipment that are left behind.

Over the years our Electromagnetics Technology Division has collaborated with scientists and engineers from UMASS-Amherst and UMASS-Lowell in the area of antenna technology. Our Battlespace Environment Division has maintained strong interactions with UMASS-Lowell to study ionospheric effects on radiowave propagation and electrical coupling between the ionosphere and the magnetosphere. One of the regrets that the UMASS scientists have had is the difficulty of conducting classified research. A Hanscom laboratory would make this possible.

As you know, it is not uncommon for universities to have off-site research laboratories. For example, MIT is associated with Lincoln Laboratory, Stanford with the Stanford Research Institute, Georgia Tech with the Georgia Tech Research Institute, Ohio State with the Electroscience Lab, Univ. of Michigan with the Radiation Lab, Cal Tech with the Jet Propulsion Lab, and the list goes on and on. Would it not make sense for UMASS to establish a research laboratory at research facilities to be vacated at Hanscom AFB?

In addition to Air Force support, our Hanscom Research Site receives funding from the Defense Advanced Research Projects Agency (DARPA) and other government agencies. We believe that this support could continue. Since our Divisions are currently involved in many on-going Air Force programs, we expect that Air Force funding would still be available in the near term. For the long term, there are many new and exciting areas of research such as the environment, biotechnology, photonics, nanotechnology, and wireless communications that the new laboratory could enter. Both Governor Patrick and our Congressional Delegation have emphasized the importance of the research that is conducted at Hanscom AFB and the need to expand it. We expect that with your encouragement, they could find a way that would make it possible for UMASS to take over the abandoned facilities and equipment.

There are obviously many details that will have to be worked out before a transfer and reestablishment of the Hanscom Research Site as a UMASS Hanscom Research Laboratory can take place. However, I cannot presently think of any problems that appear to be insurmountable. We believe that this is an golden opportunity for the University of Massachusetts to take over an established research laboratory. It is ironic that after World War II, the employees at the MIT Rad Lab and Harvard Radio Research Lab faced the loss of their jobs. They were rescued by the establishment of the Air Force Cambridge Research Laboratories. Can a university such as UMASS now reciprocate? "What goes around comes around!"

I have had the pleasure of interacting with you when you were a Congressman. I would truly appreciate your giving this proposal your consideration. If possible, I would be pleased to meet with you and provide any additional information that you request.

Best regards,

Ed
Dr. Edward E. Altshuler
Air Force Research Laboratory
Electromagnetics Technology Division
80 Scott Drive
Hanscom AFB, MA 01731-2909
(781)377-4662
(781)377-1074 Fax

I was pleasantly surprised to receive the following e-mail from Chancellor Meehan.

6.8.5 Reply from Chancellor Meehan – 14 September 2009

Dear Dr. Altshuler,

Thank you for your email regarding this potential opportunity for collaboration. I would like to recommend that you discuss this proposal with our Vice Provost for Research,

Dr. Julie Chen, who oversees all such matters. She can be reached at Julie_Chen@uml.edu

Please let me know if I can be of additional assistance.

Regards,

Martin T. Meehan
Chancellor

6.8.6 Exchange of Letters with Julie Chen

For the first time, I was cautiously optimistic that maybe something may come out of my plan. I promptly sent the following e-mail to Julie Chen and we continued to exchange further e-mails to arrange a meeting.

14 September 2009

Dear Dr. Chen,

As suggested by Chancellor Meehan, I would appreciate being able to meet with you to discuss the possible establishment of a UMASS Hanscom Research Laboratory. As mentioned in my letter below, I think this would be an excellent opportunity for UMASS to expand its research program at a very low investment.

It is interesting to note that Dr. Nicholaos Limberopoulos, a student of Prof. Alkim Akyurtulu, has recently joined our laboratory to conduct nanotechnology research.

I would be pleased to meet with you at UMASS-Lowell, or if you wish to visit our laboratory, we could meet at Hanscom AFB. Please let me know your preference and a convenient time.

Best regards,

Ed

14 September 2009

Dear Ed,

Thank you for your email. As you mentioned, there are several UMass Lowell faculty that have had long-term relationships with Hanscom. We are always interested in opportunities to expand and enhance these types of productive partnerships.

If you would like to meet next week, it would be best if we can meet here at UML. Otherwise, I can visit Hanscom the following week.

Let me know what you would prefer.

Julie

221

Julie Chen
Interim Vice Provost for Research
Professor, Mechanical Engineering
Co-Director, Nanomanufacturing Center of Excellence
(part of the CHN/NCOE Nanomanufacturing Center at UML)
co-Director, Advanced Composite Materials and Textile Research Lab
University of Massachusetts Lowell
1 University Avenue
Lowell, MA 01854
(978) 934-2992
Julie_Chen@uml.edu

15 September 2009

Dear Julie,

I would be pleased to meet with you any day of next week, preferably early morning, if possible. I will get directions from Nick regarding the location of your office.

Best regards,

Ed

Dear Ed,

Next Tues or Wed would be the best for morning...does 8:30am work for you?

Julie

I met with Dr. Julie Chen and Prof. Alkim Akyurtlu, who is under contract to Dr. John Derov, on 22 September. We reviewed the letter that I had sent to Marty Meehan. They were both enthusiastic about the possibility of establishing a UMASS Research Laboratory at Hanscom AFB. They were concerned that Marty Meehan would want to know how the new laboratory could be supported. I agreed to find out how much money we currently receive from AFOSR, DARPA and other agencies. We also agreed to investigate how other university-affiliated research laboratories received startup money. We agreed to keep in touch by e-mail as new information became available.

24 September 2009

Dear Julie,

I have done some research on University Affiliated Research Centers (UARC) and Federally Funded Research and Development Centers (FFRDC). I have attached the UARC document which lists some of these centers. Of particular interest is the last

222

paragraph which refers to Univ. of Hawaii at Manoa as another UARC. There is a lot of relevant information regarding the establishment of their UARC. I have attached some of these documents for your review.

I think that we should form an Adhoc Committee to explore the establishment of a UMASS Hanscom Research Laboratory which could initially focus on e.g. "Electromagnetic Sensors and the Environment." Our first goal would be to develop a plan that would address the areas of research and a procedure for obtaining grants.

Please let me know if you agree with this approach.

Best regards,

Ed

Since I did not receive a response to this e-mail, I sent Julie a follow up e-mail.

Dear Julie,

I am somewhat disappointed that our plan to explore the possibility of establishing a UMass Hanscom Research Laboratory has not moved forward. A prompt response from Chancellor Meehan to my e-mail of 11 September followed by our meeting on 22 September was a very encouraging start. Since that meeting, I have obtained background information regarding University Affiliated Research Centers in general and have passed along the procedure that was used to set up the University of Hawaii at Manoa UARC and the Penn State University UARC at Warminster. Admittedly, there is a lot of work required to set up a UARC, however, I believe that the establishment of a UMass Research Laboratory at Hanscom AFB would make this effort worthwhile.

I have suggested that our next move should be to form an ad hoc committee to further investigate our endeavor. I believe that since time is of the essence, we must act now. If for some reason, UMass does not have a genuine interest in having their own research laboratory at Hanscom AFB, we would appreciate being informed of such, so that we may pursue other options.

Best regards,

Ed
Dr. Edward E. Altshuler
Air Force Research Laboratory
Electromagnetics Technology Division
80 Scott Drive
Hanscom AFB, MA 01731-2909
(781)377-4662
(781)377-1074

I did receive the following prompt response to my e-mail so once again I was hopeful that the plan would move forward.

16 October 2009

Hi Ed,

Thank you for the information you had forwarded earlier. My apologies for not keeping you updated on the progress on our end.

In fact, there has been ongoing activity here at UMass Lowell with respect to your inquiry. Since we last met, Prof Alkim Akyurtlu has kindly agreed to chair a small committee to discuss this opportunity. The committee is comprised of some people who are familiar with and have collaborated with Hanscom in the past (Bill Goodhue, Paul Song, Craig Armiento, Xue June Lu).

They have had some email exchanges already and are having a meeting soon for more detailed discussions. If you have any questions or additional information to provide, please feel free to contact Alkim and cc: me.

Thanks.

Julie

16 October 2009

Hi Julie,

Thank you for your prompt response to my e-mail. I am pleased to hear that there is some activity regarding a UMass lab at Hanscom going on. Alkim, I would appreciate if I could be kept abreast and possibly participate in future discussions.

Best regards,

Ed

I then sent the following e-mail to Bodo Reinisch.

28 October 2009

Hi Bodo

I am pleased that there seems to be an interest in further exploring the possibility of a UMass Hanscom Research Laboratory. Personnel from our Electromagnetics Technology Division have been collaborating with Prof. Alkim Akyurtlu and she has proposed that we meet. I would appreciate it if you and someone from the Battle Space Environment Division could also join us. Please let me know if you are able to meet with us and also who you have been collaborating with at Hanscom, so that that person could also join us.

Best regards,

Ed

His reply.

28 October 2009

Hi Ed,

I am leaving town on Friday morning and will be on travel until 11/8. Good people from the Battle Space Environment Division would be Todd Pedersen and Keith Groves. Unfortunately, Todd will be on a campaign in Alaska from 11/8 to 11/20. I am cc-ing both Todd and Keith so that they are informed.

Best regards,

Bodo

We next arranged a meeting on 12 November to plan our next move. They asked me for detailed information regarding the costs that would be incurred, if UMass were able to take over our lab. This information could be used to apply for a UARC. I sent the following e-mail.

Original Message -----
From: Altshuler, Edward E Civ USAF AFMC AFRL/RYHA
To: Akyurtlu, Alkim
Cc: Derov, John S Civ USAF AFMC AFRL/RYHA ; Song, Paul ; Armiento, Craig ; Goodhue, William ; Morris, Adrianna ; Lu, Xue June ; Reinisch, Bodo ; Chen, Julie ; schaubert@ecs.umass.edu
Sent: Friday, December 11, 2009 8:22 AM
Subject: UMass Hanscom Research Laboratory

Dear Alkim,

Per our discussion at the meeting on 12 November, I would like to provide you with some organizational information regarding our Hanscom Research Site. This includes the names of the Divisions/ Branches/Sections along with the approximate number of government civilians in each. The total number of S&E's is about 140. Come September, 2011, some will relocate to Ohio and New Mexico, some will retire and some will seek employment. We estimate that approximately half of the employees, about 70 S&E's, would consider UMass employment. In addition, there are about 40 support personnel. We assume that about 10, would consider UMass employment.

The Battlespace Environment Division, which is part of the Space Vehicles Directorate at Kirtland AFB, NM has two Branches. Each Branch has five Sections. (attached)

The Electromagnetics Technology Division, which is part of the Sensors Directorate at Wright Patterson AFB, OH is the smaller Division and has four Branches, but no Sections (attached).

As a starting point, if we assume that each S&E, including overhead, would cost about $200K/year, then the total salaries for 70 S&E's would be about $14M. The cost of 10 support personnel at $100K/year would cost another $1M. Finally, the cost to maintain the facility would be about $1M. As a ballpark estimate we are at about $16M/year. These numbers could be incorporated into a spread sheet similar to that which was prepared by the University of Hawaii for their UARC. The bottom line would be to ask our Congressional Delegation to find approximately $50M of "seed money" to establish either a UARC or an FFRDC for a period of three years. The UMass Hanscom Research Laboratory should be self sustainable within that three year period.

The personnel of the Battlespace Environment Division(RVB) are primarily located in four buildings. We have been told that the Electronic Systems Center (ESC) is interested in utilizing these buildings when RVB departs.

Personnel of the Electromagnetics Technology Division are located in about six smaller buildings. We have been told that ESC does not have plans to utilize these buildings, which can accommodate about 200 personnel. Thus, new construction should not be necessary.

Although, this information is very preliminary, I believe that it is something for you to think about. Please let me know whether you need any additional information at this time. I hope that you will have a chance to review this and possibly bring it to the attention of Chancellor Meehan. As I have stated many times, if UMass truly wants to establish their own Research Laboratory, this is a golden opportunity.

Wishing you a happy holiday season,

Ed

Dr. Edward E. Altshuler
Air Force Research Laboratory
Electromagnetics Technology Division
80 Scott Drive
Hanscom AFB, MA 01731-2909
(781)377-4662
(781)377-1074

Unfortunately, this was the last correspondence that we would have. I was naturally very disappointed that UMass did not have an interest in establishing a UMass Research Laboratory at Hanscom AFB since I thought that they could hit the ground running considering all the resources that could have been made available at little or no cost.

6.9 Examples of Air Force Mismanagement and Waste

During my career I experienced many issues of Air Force mismanagement and waste. The Lab Demo was certainly one of the most unfortunate examples of mismanagement. The Unit Compliance Inspection was the most wasteful use of manpower and funds that I witnessed. The Screen Saver was one of my "pet peeves" that resulted mostly in a loss of employee time, but also caused unnecessary aggravation.

6.9.1 Lab Demo - 1997

For many years, government salaries were based on a Government Schedule (GS) system. The grades went from GS-1 to GS-15 and each grade had 10 steps. Higher-level employees were originally in a category called PL-313 and was later changed to Senior Executive Service (SES); they had their own pay system. Employees under the GS system would generally receive a salary increase each year for the first three steps; every two years for the next three steps and finally every three years for the remaining steps. Since employees received, for all practical purposes, these automatic pay increases, there was concern, and rightfully so, that outstanding employees could not be promoted more quickly than average employees. Thus a new pay system called Lab Demo was implemented. It only had 4 levels; DR-1 thru DR-4. Each level had a wide range of salaries, so it was possible to increase the salaries of outstanding employees more quickly.
- The employee performance was based on the following six factors.
- Technical Problem Solving
- Communications and Reporting
- Corporate Research Management
- Technology Transition & Transfer
- R & D Business Development
- Cooperation and Supervision

Each factor could have a weighting from 0 to 1. Unfortunately, Management decided that all engineers and scientists should have the same weightings, regardless of whether they were experimental, computational, theoretical or primarily contract monitors.

To digress, it reminded me of the Officer Effectiveness Reports (OER) that I use to submit for each officer as his or her Supervisor. These factors were also the same for all officers, regardless of the organization for which they worked or the kind of work they did. Each factor had five ratings from poor to excellent. On my very first report, I rated an officer excellent for most factors, good for two and average for one. After submitting the OER, I received a call from the Vice Commander asking me if I wanted to get rid of this officer; I said absolutely not, he's an excellent engineer who had a

Ph.D. from Syracuse. I was told that if he were planning to have a career in the Air Force I would have to straight line his ratings as excellent. Unfortunately, each factor required a justification, so I had to fabricate a justification. The Lab Demo plan was very similar; a supervisor would have to fabricate a justification for each rating.

I decided to submit the following letter to the Commander of AFRL in an attempt to have a more appropriate rating system for the employees.

RL/ERCP
Hanscom AFB, MA 01731-3010
14 February 1997

Maj Gen Richard R. Paul
HQ AFMC/ST
4375 Chidlaw Road, Suite 6
Wright-Patterson AFB OH 45433-5006

Dear Gen Paul,

I have reviewed the Air Force Laboratory Personnel Demonstration booklet. First, let me congratulate the committee that formulated this program; it is obvious that many months of effort went into its preparation. In general, I support this program, however as with most new programs, there are always some elements that should be reconsidered. I would like to share my thoughts with you regarding the weighting system that is planned for the rating of bench level S & E's.

I understand that all bench level S & E's will be assigned the weights listed below for each of the six factors:

- Technical Problem Solving
- Communications and Reporting
- Corporate Research Management
- Technology Transition & Transfer
- R & D Business Development
- Cooperation and Supervision

- 1.0
- 1.0
- 0.7
- 0.6
- 0.5
- 1.0

Let me preface my remarks by stating that I have had many years of laboratory experience; I have worked at AFCRL/RADC/RL since 1960 as both a scientist and a supervisor with the exception of two years that I spent in industry as Director of Engineering of an electronics company. I have also taught courses in the Graduate

228

School of Engineering at Northeastern University for 27 years, 20 years of which were in the Department of Engineering Management. My concern is that this plan fosters conformity and as a result penalizes some of our most productive S & E's. I agree that it is essential that a Laboratory have personnel who have expertise in all these factors, however, is it logical to expect that all S & E's, individually, have this expertise and be rated on the same six factors; I think not and let me explain why. Most companies have Marketing and Sales Departments that are responsible for Technology Transition and Business Development. As Director of Engineering, I used to work with the marketing and sales people and occasionally travel with them, but in general the S & E's did not participate. Not only is it very rare for S & E's to become directly involved in these areas, it is unwise, since most have had neither the training nor the experience. The S &E's who are responsible for R & D Business Development and Technology Transfer should be encouraged to pursue training in these areas; however, this training should not be forced on all S&E's.

During my years of experience as a Bench Level Scientist, as a Supervisor and as a Professor, I have observed that not all S & E's are alike. Some are gifted theoreticians who are most productive working somewhat independently; some are superb experimentalists who work most effectively as a team leader; some have the insight to plan the R&D program; some are best qualified to monitor contracts; some like to present papers while others prefer to simply publish papers; some have the ability and personality to deal with customers, others would prefer not; rarely does one have all the attributes or the interest to participate in all six factors. Fortunately, it is not necessary for each of the employees to have skills in all of these factors for an organization to be successful. What is more important is that the organization has balance and utilizes the skills of the various types of employees in a productive way. With this approach, all of the employees will play a very important role in the Laboratory mission and in a capacity in which they can best contribute.

A creative scientist should not have to fear that he will be penalized if he is lacking in R & D Business Development, nor should an engineer who has done and outstanding job in monitoring some very complex contracts, but who has not been able to contribute to Technical Problem Solving feel that he will be penalized. Some S & E's can be represented as round pegs, others as square pegs. They should not be forced into both round and square holes; it is very unfair to the employee and very unproductive for the Laboratory.

May I suggest that the following procedure be used to evaluate the performance of each employee. The supervisor and the employee should review the needs of the Directorate and determine how he can best contribute towards these needs; then he should be rated on those factors that most closely represent his goals. In this way the employee can concentrate on those tasks for which he is best qualified to work and not have to worry about those factors in which he would probably not have an opportunity to participate. I believe that this would result in both a fairer and more meaningful rating system and also provide the employee with the motivation that he needs to advance his career.

I wish you success in implementing this new program and look forward to participating in it. It is certainly very innovative and with some changes could evolve into a program that will be fair and beneficial for all of the employees.

Sincerely,
EDWARD E. ALTSHULER
GS-15, Physicist (E&M)

I did receive the following reply from Dr. Daniels, Deputy Director of AFRL. He politely told me that the Lab Demo with its fixed weightings for all scientists and engineers would not be changed.

DEPARTMENT OF THE AIR FORCE
AIR FORCE RESEARCH LABORATORY
WRIGHT-PATTERSON AIR FORCE BASE OHIO 45433

10 June 1997

AFRL/CD
4375 Chidlaw Road, Suite 6
Wright-Patterson AFB OH 45433-5006

Mr. Edward E. Altshuler
RL/ERCP
31 Grenier Street
Hanscom AFB MA 01731-3010

Dear Mr. Altshuler

I would like to thank you for taking the time to make such thoughtful inputs concerning the laboratory demonstration project. In addressing your concerns, I would like to make several points.

While the demonstration project was designed and implemented using processes and procedures which are believed to be in the best interest of the laboratories, we recognize the need to keep a constant eye on the effects our initiatives are having. This will be done through a project evaluation approach that I guarantee is both detailed and very broad. Should we find that an initiative is producing an undesirable outcome, action will be taken to modify the demonstration.

The Contribution-based Compensation System (CCS) process, and specifically the six assessment factors, were also designed in what we believe to be in the best interest of the laboratories. These six factors are viewed by the laboratory management as being critical to the success of our laboratory system. They help us combine the need for specialized skills with a need to focus on overall mission accomplishment. Our intention is not to make every scientist and engineer (S&E) a specialist in every area, but to influence behavior in such a way that the S&E work force develops an understanding and appreciation for the criticality of each of these factors and incorporates them to some measure in their work. Our focus must now be on the outcomes and the products that we produce; and to accomplish this, we need to do the right things well. Activities such as R&D business development, corporate resource management, and technology transition/transfer are believed to be the right things for our laboratories. This philosophy was the basis for developing the factor weights; the factor most prevalent in an S&E's work can be given full weight, while contributions in the other areas will still have an influence in an employee's final CCS assessment rating.

I understand that this approach to the design of CCS may cause some concern to the individual S&E. Let me point out several features which may alleviate some of these concerns.

First, the CCS factor descriptors were written in such a manner that supervisors have a fair amount of latitude in each of the six areas. Each pay pool, with its unique culture, will interpret the factors in a manner relevant to their organization. I fully expect every S&E to contribute, at least to some extent, in each of the six factors. In fact, we want accountability from each employee in each area. It is important to remember, however, that your contribution will be measured only within the context of your immediate peer group or pay pool. Secondly, in response to your inputs and other inputs from the field, we have instituted CCS Process Workshops to be conducted by each organization. These 1 1/2-day facilitated sessions will furnish our supervisors with a firm understanding of the CCS system and afford them the opportunity to discuss and decide how they will interpret the broadband level descriptors within the context of their organizational environment and culture. During these sessions it will be stressed to the supervisors that they must consider each employee and ensure everyone is given the opportunity to contribute in each of the six areas.

I hope this has helped to alleviate some of your concerns with the CCS system. Again, I appreciate your inputs on the subject. Please keep in mind that we will be open to making changes if the project evaluation effort indicates they are needed. Should you have any questions or require additional information, please contact Mr. Chris Remillard, AFRL/DSD, DSN 787-9594.

Sincerely

DONALD C. DANIEL, PhD
Executive Director and Chief Scientist

6.9.2 Unit Compliance Inspection (UCI) - 2006

The Commander of AFMC felt that the scientists and engineers of the Air Force Research Laboratory were too lax in their control of equipment, components and tools so he decided to teach them a lesson. He mandated that all tools, components and equipment had to be subjected to the same controls as those of a flight line. Now, it is certainly very appropriate for safety reasons for a flight line to have strict regulations regarding the storage of tools and equipment – but a research laboratory! That would mean that every tool, component and piece of equipment had to have a "home," which meant that every tool and component had to be placed in a "cut out" of its proper shape in a foam pad in a draw of a tool chest. The chests would be locked when not in use and there would be a sign out sheet that had to be filled out each time a tool, component or each piece of equipment was removed. As a result, experimental engineers and scientists were forced to spend months of valuable time that would ordinarily be used for research, to cut foam pads for their tools and components. Ordinary small tool boxes, which many engineers had previously used, would need a foam pad cutout for the shape of each tool, thus one could only store maybe a half dozen tools in a tool box that also needed a sign out sheet; thus, it was no longer practical for an engineer to have his own tool box. Also, it was no longer allowed to stack pieces of equipment on either open shelves or cabinet shelves. There were taped areas for each piece of equipment. Thus, available storage space became a problem under this regulation. As a result, truckloads of perfectly good equipment and tools had to be turned in, for lack of a "home". The end result was that thousands of hours were wasted on this regulation and millions of dollars of equipment were turned in (probably to be sold by the pound). In addition, it was not uncommon to see engineers arguing about how the UCI guidelines should be followed, a further waste of time.

Before the UCI, there were places, such as the Ipswich Field Site, where one could obtain certain equipments, tools and components that were essentially in storage, but always readily available. This was a great convenience. It reminded me of the days when I was a coop student working at MIT. It seemed that whenever someone needed a piece of equipment or a tool, they would go to Building 20 and more often than not, they would find what they needed. Unfortunately, Ipswich could not find "homes" for the excess equipment, so they had to turn them in; what a waste!

A final example of how idiotic this regulation became is the following. A network analyzer, a piece of equipment, which is used to measure parameters of microwave and antenna components, came with a calibration kit. This kit had connectors that were inserted into the feed lines, to perform the calibration. There was also a torque wrench in the calibration kit that was used to properly tighten the connectors. The connectors and torque wrench were neatly stored in a box with a foam pad cutout for each component. But the UCI regulation stated that the torque wrench, which was a "tool", could not be stored with calibration components, so it had to be removed from the kit, and stored with tools. This was obviously an asinine regulation and anyone with an ounce of common sense would question it. Yet our managers, determined to follow the UCI regulations to the letter of the law, stated that this flight line regulation had to be enforced.

At an out briefing, I brought a calibration kit with me. I proceeded to explain to the UCI personnel that the torque wrench is an integral part of the calibration kit and belongs in the kit. Yet my appeal fell on "deaf ears" and I was told that if I could not comply with the regulation, perhaps it was time for me to retire. I must confess that I lost my "cool" and politely stated that I would determine when I planned to retire and that it would not be because I refused to comply with a stupid regulation.

The pity of the UCI, which many of us referred to as the "Useless Compliance Inspection" was that all of the managers knew that it was a waste of time and that it should at the very least be modified. I suggested that we should propose a more applicable UCI for a research laboratory rather than one for a flight line. Yet not one manager had the "testicular fortitude" to discuss this with his superior and bring it to the attention of the 4-star General who had mandated it; he obviously had no understanding as to how laboratory research is conducted.

I personally could not bring myself to waste many hours of my time to comply with this regulation. I had about 40 small genetic antennas, with unusual shapes, that they wanted me to label and place in cut outs in a foam pad; totally ridiculous. In order to avert a confrontation with management, whenever there was an inspection, I simply placed all of my antennas, and other items that were not "UCI legal", in a box and put them in the trunk of my car. I believe that I was not the only one to do this. Even though I was not pleased in having to resort to this maneuver, I considered it "the path of least resistance." I also sent the following letter to the Director of the Sensors Directorate, Joe Sciabica, who I knew reasonably well.

4 October 2006

Dear Joe,

I have tried very hard to restrain myself from speaking out against the UCI, but I can no longer in good conscience continue to do so. Very briefly, to comment on one of the issues that was raised in your recent Q&A, there is no doubt in my mind that all of our managers are followers. If there were one leader among the managers, he would question the value of this UCI for a research laboratory.

I have been conducting research for more than 50 years. In all my years I have never experienced a directive that has resulted in more waste of manpower and funds. It wouldn't be too bad if the time required to comply with the UCI were hours, but we are spending days, weeks and even months. It is unfortunate that the hours being spent to implement the UCI are not being tracked because I suspect that the costs would be exceedingly high. I do not know who was responsible for forcing our lab to comply with the UCI, but I am thoroughly convinced that that manager has had absolutely no experience in a research lab environment, since he obviously does not know the difference between a flight line and a research laboratory. I question whether you could find one unbiased bonafide researcher who would support the UCI. A good researcher thrives on being creative. He works under very dynamic conditions, always prepared to try new directions that may lead to a discovery. He does not always know in advance exactly what equipment will be required for his next experiment. He is least concerned that every tool and piece of equipment has a "home."

Our lab has evolved into a classic example of a derivative of "Parkinson's Law." We are spending so much time on our internal problems, that we no longer have the time to spend on the problems that should be our output. Subjecting our scientists to the UCI is a sin, since they are being forced to waste their time doing chores that are totally counter productive and as a result, many of the creative scientists are totally demoralized.

Please Joe, use your ingenuity to try to figure out a way of minimizing these disastrous effects.

Ed Altshuler

As expected, no response.

6.9.3 Screen Saver - 2008

Another "pet peeve" that I had was the screen saver. Our government computers were controlled by a central office. For security reasons, in order for an employee to log on to his computer, he had to insert a Common Access Card (CAC) into the computer slot and type in a password. If he left his computer unattended, he was to remove his CAC. This was not a problem. Initially, personnel set the time limit for their screen saver for about one hour. However, for what was considered to be additional security, Hanscom AFB mandated that all computers have a screen saver that would kick in after 5 minutes. This would not ordinarily have been a problem for someone who works with the computer for long periods of time, however a scientist, in the course of his research, often refers to other documents and has other diversions, such that he does not use the keyboard continually. Having to log on every time the computer was unused for 5 minutes was really not necessary since if I left the computer unattended and took my CAC, it would not be possible for an unauthorized person to log on. This unnecessary regulation was forcing me to log on 25 or 30 times a day and was driving me out of my mind so I decided that I had to come up with a countermeasure. Some of our talented programmers tried writing programs to overcome the 5-minute screen saver, but without success. Thus, I had to figure out a way to move the mouse within a 5-minute period so the computer would appear to be in use. I was not able to come up with a convenient method to accomplish this. There is the saying" "If the mountain won't come to Muhammad, Muhammad must go to the mountain." I thought about this and I came up with a clever idea that worked perfectly. I placed a watch with a sweep second hand under the mouse, which had a motion detector, and each time the second hand passed under the detector the computer was activated. The final configuration consisted of the watch imbedded in a mouse pad with a cutout for the mouse to be properly positioned. Before long, many of my colleagues resorted to this countermeasure. I must confess that I got a lot of satisfaction using this method. It was suggested that I apply for a patent, however, this would have been pushing things too far.

Finally, the CAC served two purposes. The first was to log on to the computer, the other was to gain entry to the base. If one accidently left his CAC in the computer when departing, he would have to go to the Visitor's Center, wait in line and show a photo ID to get on to the base. Since there was often a wait, one could waste as long as 30 minutes of time. It would have been convenient if the Guards at each gate, had access to an employee listing, which I believe would have been possible. However, this was the government's way of disciplining an employee.

6.10 Research Accomplishments

In spite of all of these unnecessary regulations, most S&E's still managed to be productive.

6.10.1 The Digital Ionospheric Sounding System (DISS) - 2005

DISS is a network operated by the Air Force Weather Agency (AFWA) and the Air Force Research Laboratory (AFRL) to observe and specify the global ionosphere in real time. Eighteen digital ionosondes were deployed worldwide by the Air Force to provide data for many atmospheric weather products. DISS was originally built using an off-the-shelf TCI model 613F communications antenna. This antenna transmitted radio signals of different frequencies across a specified sweep (2-30 MHz) in a vertical direction; these signals were then reflected, absorbed, or distorted by the ionosphere. Colocated receive antennas intercepted the returning signals for algorithmic processing. The current transmit antenna did not exhibit a consistent gain in the vertical direction for all desired frequencies. The goal was to use a genetic algorithm to obtain a new configuration that would perform better than the current design and one that could also be retrofitted at a low cost. The genetic optimization revealed the strong and weak points in the model and led to changes that optimized both the gain and VSWR of the DISS antenna. One of the changes was to insert 600-ohm resistors in the antenna elements. The final configuration performed significantly better than the original design and also proved to be an easy retrofit.

6.10.2 Mapping Near-Equatorial Particle Distributions to Higher Latitudes: Estimates of Accuracy and Sensitivity -2005

Particle distributions measured near the magnetic equator were often mapped to higher latitudes to obtain estimates of global distributions. There were at least four sources of error in this mapping process: 1) neglect of the electric field term in the equation of motion, 2) the adiabatic invariant approximation to the equation of motion solution, 3) the inaccuracies of magnetic field models used to map from a near-equatorial position to a lower altitude position along a magnetic field line, and, 4) the uncertainties generated by mapping measurements from an imperfect instrument. Upon examining these errors it was found that in the heart of the inner proton belt, the error was less than 10% for energies up to 10MeV, 15% for 100MeV, and 50% for 1 GeV. The error for electrons was less than 10% for energies from 10 keV to 100MeV for radial positions less than 2.5 Re, and less than ~6% at the heart of the inner belt. These results indicated that in-situ flux measurements made by a near-equatorial satellite with arbitrarily high accuracy in energy and pitch angle could be used to create particle distribution functions at higher latitudes using standard mapping techniques.

6.10.3 AFRL Instruments Enhanced Space Weather Forecasting - 2006

Ionospheric-created disturbances disrupt radar and global positioning systems as well as satellite and high frequency communications. The Battlespace Environment Division received approval from the Danish government to install equipment measuring the different properties of the ionosphere at Station Nord, a military outpost located in the far northeast portion of Greenland. In the polar region, located above the Arctic Circle, instabilities in the ionosphere created structuring of sunlight-produced plasma, which caused significant effects on radio wave transmissions. For the many years, the Air Force conducted ionospheric research at Danish Meteorological Institute sites in western Greenland, and also since the mid-1990s at a civilian facility at Svalbard, a group of islands belonging to the Kingdom of Norway, situated between the Scandinavian nation and the North Pole. Both stations provided real-time data to the Air Force Weather Agency at Offutt AFB, Neb., but the bulk of the information was returned months later to the Battlespace Environment Division for further analysis. With the new instruments, it was possible to observe the forces that created the disturbances, as well as how they evolved and their impact on systems such as GPS and radar, They were able to use these data to forecast the creation of ionospheric disturbances.

AFRL scientists also installed five instruments aboard a Danish Air Force C-130 aircraft capable of determining ionospheric density profiles; an all-sky imager for viewing aurora and ionospheric plasma clouds; and three other systems employed to identify ionospheric scintillation through fluctuations in the strength of radio signals transmitted by various satellites such as GPS.

6.10.4 Cirrus Cloud Analysis for Airborne Laser Terminal - 2006

An analysis of cirrus cloud coverage was conducted in preparation for a field experiment that would prototype laser communication links from satellite to high-altitude aircraft. The High-Altitude Pseudo-Satellite (HAPS) experiment required an estimate of the probability of cloud-free line of sight (PCFLOS) between the proxy satellite (aircraft at 65 K feet) and the receiving aircraft. Hourly satellite imagery grids were combined with daily numerical weather prediction model forecasts executed on the MHPCC supercomputer for February 2003 as a trial month. Analyses yielded retrievals of cirrus top and base height and optical depth for the relevant wavelength in 5 km X 5 km picture elements for circular areas of radius 200 km centered on locations of interest. These data sets were used to determine the PCFLOS between HAPS aircraft for typical months at the locations. This in turn gave guidance on the likelihood of communications outages in the experiment.

6.10.5 New Camera Enhanced Forecasting Of Sun-Generated Storms - 2006

Every 100-plus minutes, while orbiting approximately 50 miles above the earth onboard the Coriolis satellite, the Solar Mass Ejection Imager experiment, managed by the AFRL Battlespace Environment Division, scanned the darkness of space-seeking, sun-generated magnetic clouds of particles intent on striking the planet. The imager's three cameras photographed more than 200 coronal mass ejections. Approximately 30 reached Earth, causing a variety of problems including disruption of communication to the war fighter and damaging spacecraft components. It generated a data set never seen before. Lots of space weather forecasts had been previously made, but the track record was not that good. The Solar Mass Ejection Imager demonstrated a 30-percent improvement in the accuracy of forecasts.

During the early 1990s, with an increasing reliance on satellites, the Department of Defense initiated space weather forecasts to protect its critical assets in the cosmos. The sun periodically discharged large blobs of plasma and embedded electromagnetic fields, known as coronal mass ejections, traveling at speeds approaching 4 million miles per hour. The fast and furious solar material can impact the Earth within one to three days after departure. They also trigger geomagnetic storms, which disrupt electric power and communication systems on Earth, as well as damage spacecraft circuitry and degrade performance. In addition to monitoring solar storms, the Solar Mass Ejection Imager observed high-altitude auroras, asteroids, debris, stellar variability and some unique comet tail disconnections and definitely aided the warfighter by providing improved space weather forecasts.

6.10.6 Analysis of the Electrospray Plume from the EMI-Im Propellant Externally Wetted on a Tungsten Needle - 2006

The room temperature ionic liquid propellant, 1-ethyl-3-methylimidazolium bis(trifluoromethylsulfonyl)imide (EMI-Im) was being tested for the NASA DRS-ST7 mission. A capillary thruster configuration is planned for ST7, and time-of-flight experiments had shown that the spray of EMI-Im produced a mixture of primarily droplets and low levels of ions, resulting in a low specific impulse. Recently, pure ion emission was achieved for EMI-Im in a wetted needle thruster, suggesting that this propellant, which has passed all space environmental exposure tests, may also be a candidate for high specific impulse missions. The use of wetted tips raises the question whether electrochemistry at the liquid-metal interface causes significant propellant fouling that -will ultimately result in performance degradation due to the significantly longer propellant metal interaction times in comparison with the capillary design and-the higher flow rates. Electrochemical fouling can be mitigated through a polarity alternation approach, which adds complexity to the power-processing unit.

6.10.7 Enhancing GMTI Performance in Non-Stationary Clutter Using 3D STAP -2007

In side-looking ground moving target indication (GMTI) radar, the 2-dimensional (2D) space-time (azimuth-Doppler) domain could adequately define a clutter spectrum, which was accurate for all range gates. However, in applications where the array boresight was not perpendicular to the velocity vector (e.g. forward-looking radar), the azimuth-Doppler clutter spectrum exhibited a dependence on elevation angle-of-arrival, creating range-varying (but elevation-dependent) clutter statistics, or non-stationary clutter. Classical space time adaptive processing (STAP) algorithms suffered substantial performance losses in non-stationary clutter since classical STAP assumed clutter stationary along the range (training) dimension. Planar arrays were inherently able to observe the azimuth-Doppler clutter spectrum as a function of the elevation angle, a capability which linear arrays lacked. The incorporation of the planar array's vertical dimension into the joint azimuth-Doppler (2D) STAP domain had previously resulted in 3D STAP. This investigation demonstrated the ability of 3D STAP to solve the non-stationary clutter problem by accounting for the elevation-dependent clutter statistics in a 3D covariance matrix. A forward-looking array was used to provide non-stationary clutter, and the performance of 2D and 3D versions of the adaptive matched filter (AMF) and joint domain localized (JDL) were used in a close-in sensing paradigm. The results showed a > 55 dB improvement in output SINR near the clutter null using 3D STAP algorithms in lieu of 2D STAP algorithms applied to the same (subarrayed) data.

6.10.8 Orientation Patterned Gallium Arsenide Structures for Laser Applications -2008

Orientation-patterned GaAs (OPGaAs) showed great promise as a nonlinear optical material for frequency conversion in the 2-5 µm and 8-12 µm regions. Progress was made in each of the three main areas of OPGaAs development: fabrication of patterned templates using a combination of wafer bonding and MBE techniques; thick-layer HVPE growth; and material and OPO device characterization. This work led to significant improvements in material quality, specifically reduced optical loss, increased sample thickness, improved patterned domain fidelity, and greater material uniformity. Advances in material quality have in turn enabled demonstration of OPO devices operating in the 3-5 µm spectral region. Optical loss and OPO performance measurements on a series of OPGaAs samples showed how the properties were influenced by growth conditions, and how OPO performance could be improved.

6.10.9 Infrared Sky Surveys - 2008

A survey was conducted with the Infrared Astronomical Satellite (IRAS), the first sensitive mid-to-far infrared all-sky survey. The emerging technology for space-based surveys was highlighted as was the prominent role of the DoD, particularly the Air Force which developed and applied detector and cryogenic sensor advances to early mid infrared probe-rocket and satellite based surveys. This technology was transitioned to the infrared astronomical community in relatively short order and was essential to the success of IRAS, Cosmic Background Explorer (COBE) and Infrared Space Observatory (ISO).

6.10.10 Satellite's Instrumentation Provided Scintillation Forecast Data - 2008

Whether it's static interrupting a radio station, or crackling noises interfering with a theater commander's attempt to contact a deployed unit, scintillation can cause communication chaos. Within the Air Force, a six-instrument payload onboard the Communication/Navigation Outage Forecasting System spacecraft helped researchers forecast when and where this natural phenomenon would occur. This was the first mission by any organization dedicated to ionospheric scintillation. The six sensors installed on the satellite to monitor scintillation, along with their function, were:

- Planar Langmuir probe: calculated the amount of charged particles in the satellite's course. When the material impacted the metal plate on the front of the device, it generated an electric signal, which if fluctuating, could indicate scintillation.
- Ion velocity meter: measured charged particles' speed and direction, perpendicular to and in the same path, of the satellite's orbital movement in a particular region of the ionosphere.
- Neutral wind meter: computed the pace and track of the gas (uncharged particles) travelling in the spacecraft's route and in a vertical course to C/NOFS' movement in the ionosphere.
- Vector electric field instrument: gauged the existing force in a region between opposite-charged particles. This amount was referred to as the electric field and the instrument's payload computes the power and direction of it.
- Coherent electromagnetic radio tomography: evaluated the signals calculated by ground receivers to verify the quantity of scintillation along the course between the C/NOFS spacecraft and the planet's surface. If the signals displayed distortion, scintillation was evident and vice versa.
- C/NOFS occultation receiver for ionospheric sensing and specification: measured signals originating from numerous global positioning system satellites orbiting the globe. The system examined these signals to

determine the extent of charged matter between the GPS spacecraft and C/NOFS.

Data collected by the six instruments were sent to a processing center at the Battlespace Environment Division where project staff ran forecasting models and created forecast products. The analysis done on the information compiled by the six instruments paved the way for the next generation of scintillation forecasting models, thus improving upon the accuracy of forecasting and extending the forecasting time period further into the future.

6.10.11 Electrically Small Supergain Arrays - 2008

In principle, two quarter-wavelength monopoles over a ground plane can achieve an endfire gain of about 10.5 dB by decreasing their separation distance to a value of about 0.15 wavelength or less. However, the amplitude and phase of the currents that drive the antennas have to be precisely controlled in order to realize this supergain. This is extremely difficult to accomplish in practice because of the strong coupling that occurs as the antennas become very close to each other. Also, as the monopoles are brought closer together, ohmic losses increase, thus decreasing the gain.

Scientists at the AFRL Electromagnetics Technology Division designed and tested a two-element supergain endfire array, first using a pair of quarter-wave monopoles and then using electrically small [less than $1/(2\pi)$ wavelengths] resonant antennas that were designed using a genetic algorithm. At frequencies on the order of 400 MHz, they showed that it was indeed possible to achieve a supergain for two, 0.1 wavelength separated, driven elements of about 9.5 dB, which is about one dB below the theoretical limit.

They further showed that using a single driven resonant element along with a similar short-circuited parasitic element, they could approach almost the same supergain that was achieved using two driven elements and without the need to precisely control the amplitude and phase of the driven elements. A patent was obtained for this method of achieving supergain using a parasitic element in place of a second driven element.

6.10.12 A Characterization of Cirrus Cloud Properties That Affect Laser Propagation - 2008

Laser transmission models were applied to measured and retrieved cirrus properties to determine cirrus impact on power incident on a target or receiver. A major goal was to see how well radiosondes and geostationary satellite imagery could specify the required properties. Based on the use of ground-based radar and lidar measurements as a reference, errors in cirrus-top and cirrus-base height estimates from radiosonde observations were 20%-25% of geostationary satellite retrieval errors. Radiosondes had a perfect cirrus detection rate as compared with 80% for satellite detection. Ice water path and effective particle size were obtained with a published radar-lidar retrieval algorithm and a documented satellite algorithm. Measured radar-lidar cirrus thickness was consistently greater than satellite-retrieved thickness, but radar-lidar microphysical retrieval required detection by both sensors at each range gate, which limited the retrievals' vertical extent. Greater radar-lidar extinction and greater satellite-based cirrus thickness yielded comparable optical depths for the two independent retrievals. Laser extinction-transmission models applied to radiosonde-retrieved cirrus heights and satellite-retrieved microphysical properties revealed a significant power loss by all models as the laser beam transited the cirrus layer. This suggested that cirrus location was more important than microphysics in high-altitude laser test support.

6.10.13 Spacecraft Charging and Mitigation - 2010

Satellites and spacecraft materials can become charged to tens or even thousands of volts when ions in the space environment collide with spacecraft. This can sometimes cause electrical discharge of differentially or internally charged spacecraft materials, which can adversely affect satellite operations. Additionally, high-energy ions can penetrate spacecraft materials and deposit their energy within sensitive electronics, causing component damage or failure. To consider various approaches for spacecraft charge mitigation, Battlespace Environment scientists met with 150 technologists from around the world representing government, academia, and industry at the 11th Spacecraft Charging Technology Conference (SCTC) in Albuquerque, N. M., on 20–24 September 2010. The conference was held against the backdrop of the apparent charging event of the Galaxy 15 satellite, which some speculated triggered this geosynchronous communications satellite to cease operations, thereby adversely affecting related satellite-reliant communities.

6.10.14 Demonstrations and Science Experiment (DSX) Space Weather Experiment (SWx) -2011

The AFRL Battlespace Environment Division developed the Demonstration and Science Experiments (DSX) to research technologies needed to significantly advance the capability to operate spacecraft in the harsh radiation environment of medium-earth orbits (MEO). The ability to operate effectively in the MEO environment significantly increased the capability to field space systems that provide high-speed satellite-based communication, lower-cost GPS navigation, and protection for satellites from space weather effects. One of DSX's physics based research areas was the Space Weather Experiment (SWx), characterizing and modeling the space radiation environment in MEO, an orbital regime attractive for future space missions.

Chapter 7: Conclusions

AFCRL certainly had its "rise and fall." Its rise was phenomenal; its fall was regrettable. It is hard to believe that even though the Air Force and DoD systems benefited from the technical breakthroughs that evolved from the basic and applied research at AFCRL, they did not have the foresight to appreciate its importance. One of the things that is difficult to understand is that on the one hand, the Air Force felt that basic research could be conducted by the Universities, which is a viable option. However, on the other hand, they emphasized the need to couple basic research to systems. Research being conducted at the Universities is much further removed from system applications than research conducted at in-house government laboratories. Thus the coupling would be much weaker. There just doesn't seem to be any logic in the way that decision was made, however, since the decision was political, so be it.

Another issue that was difficult to fathom was the logic in spending millions of dollars to relocate a productive laboratory to other locations. For the case of the Hanscom Research Site, the Air Force spent well over $100M to move about 50, mostly junior employees, to the new locations in Ohio and New Mexico. They said that moving the employees would bring more synergy to the laboratory. The end result was that they lost their expertise in the areas of sensors and geophysics since most of the senior people did not relocate. Finally, in this age of e-mail and video teleconferenceing, synergy has lost its importance, since S&E's can now communicate with one another very easily, without being collocated.

After reading through the documentation regarding the BRAC, I am truly amazed that it was not rescinded. If one can believe the many news reports regarding the fraud that took place, particularly, that stated in the GAO reports, it seems impossible that Fort Monmouth would be closed. This is a good example of how our political system can be manipulated.

I believe that the S&E"s who worked at the Hanscom Research Site should feel very proud of their legacy, since it was truly extraordinary. They were probably one of the most productive research laboratories in the history of our country. I experienced both dedication and teamwork from my colleagues, something I will always treasure. When our laboratory was threatened for closure or a move, the SAVE Committee always rose to the occasion and with the help of members of the Massachusetts Congressional Delegation always managed to have our Laboratory remain at Hanscom AFB. Regrettably, BRAC 2005 was our downfall. Our SAVE Committee worked extremely hard and exhausted all efforts to try and rescind this action. We wrote letters to anyone and everyone who we thought could help our cause. Even though we gave it our "best shot", we failed to get the same kind of support from our Congressional Delegation that we had received on previous occasions. Unfortunately, all good things come to an end.

As I write this book, I read that Hanscom AFB is once again under attack. It has been reported that Hanscom's Electronic Systems Center (ESC) could lose three-quarters of its funding for contract workers over the next four years and an additional 380 government jobs due to a reduction in military spending. Cuts to ESC, which employs 1250 contractors, are supposed to begin shortly. The Center may see a 10% to15% budget reduction in the first year. This is not a good omen, since this will be followed by a planned BRAC in 2014. If our Massachusetts Congressional Delegation is not able to avert these cuts, then all of Hanscom AFB may be lost, as was the AFRL Hanscom Research Site.

Epilogue

In summary, I felt that the Hanscom Research Site and its predecessor organizations, most notably AFCRL, had a very fascinating history that should be documented. I have tried to include as much of the information that was available to make this history possible. Sixty-six years is a long period of time so obviously, I have missed many events that would have been of interest to the reader. Although our downfall was unfortunate, we are grateful for the many good years of research that we had in the laboratory. Since I chose not to relocate to Dayton, Ohio, I had to retire. Having worked at the Lab for 49 years I was probably one of the longest serving members at the Hanscom Research Site and I am very thankful for that. I had a very memorable retirement party with about 150 attendees of my family, relatives and friends. I decided to retire in May 2011, in advance of the mandatory retirement date of August, since we had recently bought a summer cottage on Cape Cod and were looking forward to spending a relaxing summer. C'est la vie.